THEN, NOW AN~

british
beat
1960-1969

TERRY RAWLINGS

EDITED BY ANDY NEILL
& CHRIS CHARLESWORTH

ISBN: 0.7119.9094.8   ORDER NO: OP 48620

Copyright © 2002 Omnibus Press
(A Division of Book Sales Limited)

Cover & Book designed by:
Paul McEvoy & Julien Potter at **BOLD** Graphic Design, London.
Picture research by: Terry Rawlings
with additional research by: Alec Palao & Phil Smee at Strange Things Picture Library

The Author hereby asserts his/her right to be identified
as the author of this work in accordance with Sections 77 to 78
of the Copyright, Designs and Patents Act 1988.

EXCLUSIVE DISTRIBUTORS
Book Sales Limited, 8/9 Frith Street, London W1D 3JB, UK.

Music Sales Corporation, 257 Park Avenue South, New York, NY 10010, USA.

Macmillan Distribution Services, 53 Park West Drive, Derrimut, Vic 3030, Australia.

TO THE MUSIC TRADE ONLY:
Music Sales Limited, 8/9 Frith Street, London W1D 3JB, UK.

Photo credits:
The Not Fade Away Collection, Strange Things Picture Library.
Every effort has been made to trace the copyright holders of the photographs in this book
but one or two were unreachable.
We would be grateful if the photographers concerned would contact us.

Printed in Spain.

A catalogue record for this book is available from the British Library.

Visit Omnibus Press on the web at:
www.omnibuspress.com

OMNIBUS PRESS

FOREWORD

I have this enduring memory of the 'Blue Boar' motorway café in the early hours of the morning. Lines of musicians, from different bands, queuing up for their breakfasts of greasy food, before climbing back in to ailing vans full of guitars, amps and drum kits. This was where bands met on the journey back to London after playing gigs in the Midlands and the North. It was the feeding trough of the mid-'60's 'Beat Boom' which followed the Beatles' explosive expansion into the American markets. Here we met and discussed good and bad venues, the latest equipment and what recording deals were being done. This was the time when British 'rock' was born and I, as a member of The Zombies, was proud to be a part of it. We, the British, gave the world an injection of pure enthusiasm.

CHRIS WHITE – THE ZOMBIES

INTRODUCTION

This book, intended as a testimony to the durability of the music and imagery of the Sixties, was a true pleasure to assemble. After all, here in what is cringingly referred to as the 'noughties', The Beatles are the only band ever to become bigger than The Beatles.

Elsewhere, as I write, The Rolling Stones are gearing up for yet another sell-out world tour. The Who will take on America again this summer – and earn millions. Tom Jones has never been busier, nor David Bowie. Rod the Mod is still wearing it well and Eric Clapton is still good... if not quite God anymore. In fact the era's entire musical back catalogue is currently alive and well and available in a record shop near you, all of it faithfully reissued, repackaged, remixed and regurgitated, either on compilation CD, mini disc, video or DVD. We can't wait to get our hands on box sets that offer the opportunity to own albums that you've already bought at least twice over, in order to obtain the extra bonus discs with rare and alternative versions of all your old favourites.

There are also 'live' releases and special 'collector's edition' packages, crammed with material which when originally recorded 'to a track' was deemed too woeful for the public's ears. But we want it... and we want it all!

It's not just recordings by the obvious big hitters either, oh no, because now thanks to the heightened interest in all things 'groovy', 'fab' and 'swinging' we want the obscure, the forgotten and the downright unheard of. Bands that didn't quite get their full fifteen minutes of fame first time round... maybe not even ten or, alas, five.

No longer are the names of such fabled groups as The Attack, The Pudding, or even Pinkerton's Assorted Colours whispered solely by huddled cliques of earnest young men and nimble-fingered record collectors sitting in dark alcoves. They are enshrined in box sets of their own, and some are reforming too – Rupert's People, John's Children, The Zombies and The Action to name but a few – all playing to packed out clubs and theatres, with more of a platform than they ever had during their original existence.

Call me old-fashioned but will the boy bands, toy bands and teenage sensations of the Nineties, even with their tireless and tacky cover versions of recognised classics, be awarded such acclaim in thirty years time? OK, I know it's a cliché to relegate them to future obscurity, but I think not. Will we really care what happened to the punky one in Boyzone, or the beardy one, the nerdy one or for that matter the gay one? No. No. No. But we do want to know where Eddie Phillips from The Creation is now, or Reggie King from The Action or even Arthur Brown? You bet we do and, where possible, we have tried to find out – our unquenchable vampire-like thirst for all things Sixties positively craves it! Therefore, don't trawl through these pages with too retro an eye, or even a nostalgic one, because the past is now our present. So, grab yourself a beer and put your reading glasses on because here comes the Action!

Author's note

In painstakingly researching and assembling an encyclopaedia of this nature there will be inevitable inaccuracies or omissions. The basic premise was to assemble a guide to the sung and the unsung of the British Beat era, chronicling the bands and singers that operated within the Beat era of 1963 – 1968, and is by no means definitive (though it's as near as damn it!).

The early Sixties of Cliff Richard, Adam Faith and Helen Shapiro falls before the scope of this book, while similarly the post–'68 progressive era with the likes of King Crimson, Jethro Tull and Yes falls beyond it. Therefore, you won't find them among these pages.

Groups or artists that don't necessarily qualify as British – Jimi Hendrix, The Bee Gees, The Easybeats, Los Bravos – have been included on the premise that they achieved British chart success with records recorded in British studios during the era. Their success emanated from Britain and seemed somehow to be a part of all things British during the Swinging Sixties.

A Band Of Angels

Orchestras   Cabaret Artistes

DRINK UP THY ZYDER IT'S THE—
MPION DUNG SPREADER COLUMBIA DB 8145
By ADGE CUTLER & THE WURZELS
Personal Manager & Sole Representation—JOHN MILES.
81, Whiteladies Road, Bristol, 8. Telephone: 39696.

GALAXY ENTERTAINMENTS LTD.

The MOVE
ACTION! AMEN CORNER
Featuring ANDY FAIRWEATHER LOW
ASHVILLE TEENS ★ RICK 'N BECKERS
LONELY ONES
AT 7 DENMARK STREET, LONDON, W.C.2 01-240-1955

e GOOD TIME LOSERS
REPRESENTATION :
O BURNS — HAROLD DAVISON LTD.

HE TROGGS
E LOOT · BARRY BENSON
g Agents for Ballrooms in Association with Page One Records Ltd.
ARVEY BLOCK ASSOCIATES LTD. CHANDOS HOUSE.
6 CHANDOS PLACE, LONDON, W.C.2 01-240 2907/8

HE HERD
gents: KENNEDY STREET ENTERPRISES LTD.
DY HOUSE, 14 PICCADILLY, MANCHES

W YOU'RE BUYING THE RECORD GO OUT
ND BUY ANOTHER FOR YOUR GRANNY

It's THE ACTION
"LAND OF 1,000 DANCES"
b/w "IN MY LONELY ROOM"
on PARLOPHONE R5354
Recorded by: GEORGE MARTIN
Management: RIKKI FARR
DRUCE Management, PAD 0135

ACTION!
S ALAN KING/RHYTHM GUITAR VOCALS PETE WATSON/12 STRING LEAD GUITAR ROGER POWELL/DRUMS

The Action

A BAND OF ANGELS

A bunch of public schoolboys who dreamt of pop stardom and performed in straw boaters, blazers, and bow ties. Sounds an awful combination, but that's what happened. Singer Mike D' Abo, guitarists John Baker and Christian (John) Gaydon, bass player James Rugge-Price, and drummer David Wilkinson, formed while studying together at Harrow Public School. They actually got signed to United Artists in 1964 and released four singles for the label and Pye subsidiary Piccadilly between '64 and their break up in '66, the last of which, 'Invitation', is now regarded as a Mod soul classic.

D'Abo did indeed go on to fulfil his musical ambition when he took over from Paul Jones in Manfred Mann in 1966, while Gaydon became successful in artist management in partnership with ex-Band Of Angels manager, David Enthoven, forming EG Records.

(see also Manfred Mann)

THE ACCENT

Yorkshire lads The Accent, so named because they presumably had such a thing, were originally known as The Blue Blood Group before moving to London in 1966. They secured a residency at Billy Walker's Upper Cut Club and in 1967 recorded one Decca 45: the Mike Vernon-produced 'Red Sky At Night'; a true psychedelic classic with an inspired folk-freakbeat arrangement and dark, ethereal vocals. John Hebron was guitarist-singer, Rick Birkett (guitar), Alan Davies (bass), and with such a surname, Pete Beetham was inevitably the drummer. Birkett later released a rare solo album, credited to Rick Hayward, on the collectable British blues label, Blue Horizon, in 1971.

THE ACTION

History has unjustly downgraded The Action to mere runners-up in the mid-Sixties Mod league, forever tailing behind leading lights like The Who and The Small Faces. However, a three decade layoff has seen the group's popularity rise to a significant level, resulting in not only a complete reappraisal of their short, but solid career but also a reformation by all five original band members for sold-out club and festival dates in the UK and Europe.

The Action were formed in Kentish Town, North London in 1963 as The Boyfriends – a backing group for Decca recording artiste Sandra Barry – and comprised Reggie King (vocals), Alan King (rhythm guitar/vocals), Mike Evans (bass) and Roger Powell (drums). They shortened their name to The Boys and added a fifth member, lead guitarist Pete Watson, before eventually becoming The Action in 1965.

The newly-named band had an uninspiring start. According to Evans: 'We were turned down by every label going including Decca, who didn't turn down anyone after The Beatles fiasco!'

The groups' fortunes began to look assured when weeks of constant telephone calls to Beatles' producer George Martin paid off and they eventually drove him in person to an Action gig in Balham,

South London. Suitably impressed, Gentleman George signed on as their personal producer and was instrumental in getting them a deal with EMI and Parlophone.

Thereafter The Action built up a sizeable Mod following throughout the country, utilising a brilliant amalgamation of original pop, R&B and obscure soul covers. They released five quality singles for the label between '65 and '67, all of which bizarrely failed to catch the nation's ear. These included superlative covers of Chris Kenner's 'Land Of 1000 Dances', The Marvelettes' 'I'll Keep On Holding On', The Temptations' 'Since I Lost My Baby', and inventive originals like 'Never Ever' and 'Shadows And Reflections' – both a nod to the US West Coast harmony groups. Consequently, plans to release their own self-penned début album, *Rolled Gold*, in 1967 were aborted. 'In the Sixties you only got to do an album if you'd had a hit single, and we hadn't had one,' says Mike. 'We should have asked The Beatles to write us one. They wrote them for everyone else and they were always hits! People they'd never even met before – and here we were, seeing them almost every single day and using their studio and even their producer!'

It was probably The Action's lack of a particular cohesive sound that led to their commercial failure. 'We didn't know if we wanted to be a pop band, a soul band, or a show band,' says Mike. 'It was lack of proper management, lack of direction and possibly a lack of really trying.'

Watson left in late-1966 and after a period as a four-piece, the group were supplemented by multi-instrumentalist Ian Whiteman, and ex-Savoy Brown guitarist Martin Stone. A frustrated Reggie King jumped ship in early 1968 after a disastrous Cornish gig. The 'well read' remnants of the band temporarily renamed themselves Azoth, in reference to the Philosopher's Stone, before another name change in 1968. Mighty Baby was born.

The Action

The Action

Amen Corner

Evans sums up The Action's demise. 'The industry had changed. Singles were no longer the barometer to measure success by. We found you could now make albums and be judged on their merits, which is what I think we'd wanted all along. We finally realised we could be an albums band and the pressure was off, but alas it was too late.'

In 1998, the original five-man line-up reformed for a series of successful gigs, culminating with a show at London's 100 Club in 2000, featuring original fan and drummer, Phil Collins sitting in. *(see also The Boys)*

ADAM, MIKE, & TIM

You could never accuse Decca Records, or Dick Rowe in particular, of not learning a lesson or two following his infamous, and quite possibly apocryphal, 'Groups with guitars are on the way out' Beatles rejection. Of course they redeemed themselves with The Rolling Stones, Small Faces, John Mayall, etc, but you can't help but wonder at how far this once mighty British establishment had sunk by the mid-Seventies.

Where did it all start to go wrong? Well, it could have something to do with the fact that following their catastrophic Beatle blunder in 1962, Decca signed just about anything and anyone, from all points of the compass. It's only a theory but here's a few A&R puzzlers to mull over. Adam, Mike, and Tim, were a Liverpool trio, two brothers Peter 'Adam' and Mike Sedgewick, and pal Tim Saunders, a sort of beat-style Bachelors who managed three non-charting 45s, 'Little Baby', 'That's How I Feel' and 'Little Pictures' before Decca took the cheque book else where. In 1965 they moved to Columbia releasing covers of the Statler Brothers' 'Flowers On The Wall' and Paul Simon's 'A Most Peculiar Man', featuring a then-voguish sitar arrangement, but still to no commercial avail.

AMEN CORNER

Cardiff 'boyos' Amen Corner featured vocalist Andy Fairweather-Low, Derek 'Blue' Weaver (Hammond organ), Neil Jones (guitar), Clive Taylor (bass), Alan Jones (baritone sax), Mike Smith (tenor sax), and Dennis Byron (drums).

The septet first entered the British charts in August 1967 with their classic début single, the slow 'Gin House Blues' – a record that belied their true leanings as a show band – which reached number 12. However pop became the name of the game with 'World Of Broken Hearts' (number 24; Oct '67), 'Bend Me, Shape Me' (a rearranged cover of the American Breed's US hit – number three; Feb '68), and 'High In The Sky' (number six; Aug '68).

An album, *Round Amen Corner*, followed before the group switched labels, leaving Deram for Immediate Records in 1968. The group's first release for the label became the timeless number one '(If Paradise Is) Half As Nice' in Feb '69. A further two singles (the Roy Wood-composed 'Hello Susie' and an ill-advised cover of the

Beatles' 'Get Back') and albums (*The National West Coast Explosion Company*, *Farewell To The Real Magnificent Seven*) fared less successfully, being cut short at the end of '69 when Immediate fell into disarray and finally collapsed, splitting the band into two factions. The brass section became Judas Jump while the remainder rechristened themselves simply Fairweather.

Aside from Andy Fairweather-Low, who has pursued a successful career as a solo artist and guitarist sideman, most notably for Eric Clapton, the only other member to carve out a modest living was organist Blue Weaver, with keyboard stints in Mott The Hoople, The Strawbs and in the Bee Gees' touring band.

Amen Corner

TIM ANDREWS

Chris Andrews changed his first name to Tim to avoid confusion with the 'Yesterday Man' hitmaker and in 1965, on the advice of friend Davy Jones, reputedly auditioned in Los Angeles (along with over 400 other young hopefuls) for a part in *The Monkees* TV and group phenomenon, but was supposedly turned down by producers Bob Rafelson and Bert Schneider because one Englishman was enough. Unfortunately that's also about as good as it got for the singer-guitar player.

Unless you count him being called Tiny Tim before Tiny Tim was? Either way there's very little else to report outside the fact, that he was fleetingly in the concocted Rupert's People in 1967 before leaving to record three non-charting singles for Parlophone between '67 and '70 and also teamed up with the equally unknown singer-songwriter Paul Korda for three which made it all doubly disappointing. *(see also Rupert's People)*

THE ANIMALS

Newcastle's favourite sons, The Animals were formed in 1963 after vocalist Eric Burdon joined the long standing Alan Price Combo, which since 1959 comprised of Price, drummer John Steel, bass player Bryan 'Chas' Chandler and Hilton Valentine on guitar.

The introduction of Burdon to the band by John Steel – the two had been in a college jazz band – was the vital ingredient that set the previously organ-led outfit on the road to stardom. It also saw the band move from their near-residency status at the slightly discouragingly named Down Beat Club to the more positive, upbeat Club-A-Go-Go, run by future manager, Mike Jeffrey.

Their new, improved, wild stage act of raucous R&B covers, discerningly plucked from the repertoires of the usual suspects – Jimmy Reed, Chuck Berry, Bo Diddley – led to them being dubbed The Animals in December 1963 by their loyal Geordie following. The local excitement surrounding the group quickly brought them to the attention of several predatory music business entrepreneurs, including pirate radio founder and London's Scene Club manager, Ronan O' Rahilly. His suggestion was for the band to take the next inevitable step and move to London. As soon as they did so, there followed the predictable switch in allegiance. Within months of arriving in 'the smoke' the group came under the persuasive spell of record producer Mickie Most.

The Animals quickly established themselves as an integral, and indeed vital part of the London R&B club scene and, with Most at the helm, a record deal with Columbia and a début single, cribbed from Bob Dylan's first album, was in the bag. 'Baby Let Me Take You Home', a take on Eric Von Schmidt's blues ditty 'Baby Let Me Follow You Down' (and not, as has been previously stated in some quarters, 'Momma Don't You Tear My Clothes') was a respectable hit, reaching number 21 in April 1964 and paving the way for a hasty follow-up single that almost didn't happen.

Once again Most and the band looked to Dylan's début album and chose a rare cover of Josh White's 'House Of The Rising Sun', a four-and-a-half-minute ode to a New Orleans brothel or burlesque house. Columbia originally refused to release it, claiming that it wasn't so much the song's content that they objected to but its length, arguing that pop hits lasted no longer than three minutes. However the battle was won on the group's behalf and in an instant a million bedroom guitarists were born, all of them picking out Valentine's now legendary and evocative guitar intro (which has proved a bone of contention to this day as Price continues to claim he came up with the distinctive arrangement).

'The House Of The Rising Sun' sold a quarter of a million copies within three days in the UK alone and rose to the coveted top spot in June. The US version was abridged to two minutes, editing Price's organ solo, in order to comply with juke-box restrictions, yet this too hit the number one spot. It was arguably The Animals' finest moment.

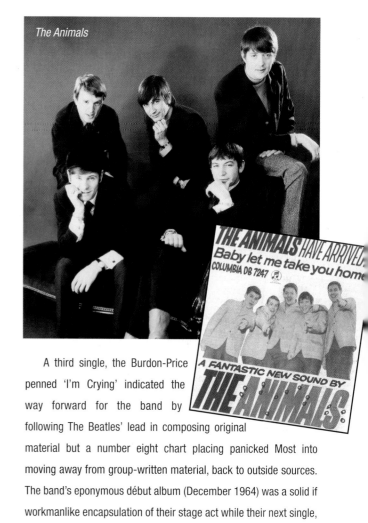

The Animals

A third single, the Burdon-Price penned 'I'm Crying' indicated the way forward for the band by following The Beatles' lead in composing original material but a number eight chart placing panicked Most into moving away from group-written material, back to outside sources. The band's eponymous début album (December 1964) was a solid if workmanlike encapsulation of their stage act while their next single, 'Don't Let Me Be Misunderstood' (February 1965), was an inventive interpretation of a Nina Simone song which nudged into the number three slot, despite a severe slating from Ms. Simone herself, who described it as the worst version she'd ever heard, no doubt feeling it had been 'stolen' and reappropriated for a white pop audience.

After a reworking of Sam Cooke's 'Bring It On Home To Me', (number seven in April '65) and the group's second album Animal Tracks, Price didn't so much leave as to totally disappear, claiming to be suffering from 'aerophobia', although a week later it emerged that the organist had in fact taken ownership of 'The House Of The Rising Sun's' lucrative publishing rights. Unsurprisingly this act of betrayal sat uneasily with the rest of the group. Price's boots were filled temporarily by fellow Geordie (and future Blockhead), Mickey Gallagher before the gig was given to Londoner, Dave Rowberry, the keyboardist with The Mike Cotton Sound. However, this first crack in the group's solidarity set off a self destructive trend within the ranks, prophetically summed up by their next release, the Barry Mann/Cynthia Weil composition, 'We've Gotta Get Out Of This Place' (number two – August '65). A similar cry of indignity – the Atkins/Carl D'Errico song 'It's My Life' – provided a further Top 10 hit in October 1965, but Burdon was publicly disparaging about the song, which suggested a division between group and producer.

When the Animals recording contract came up for renewal, Burdon refused point blank to re-sign with either Most or Columbia. The group were snapped up by Decca, but in February 1966 the dependable Steel quit to be replaced by Nashville Teens drummer Barry Jenkins. The group's first Decca single was the self-composed 'Inside Looking Out' (number twelve – March '66), a forceful prison song adapted from an old blues tune, 'Rosie', followed by their last major hit, Goffin-King's 'Don't Bring Me Down' – reaching number six in June – and album *Animalisms*. By now divisions had opened up within the group. Burdon and Valentine were consuming LSD for breakfast, effectively alienating them from the other members and thus triggering the band's final disintegration in September 1966.

Chandler went on to discover and manage Jimi Hendrix and Slade, while Burdon retained the group's name in part and, together with Jenkins, formed The New Animals. Valentine's drug descent saw a failed folk singing career stall at the blocks and he fled to a Buddhist monastery in Scotland. Steel, who foolishly sold his share of The Animals royalties for £4,000, went on to work for Chandler and twice reformed the band, in 1977 and 1983 respectively. On both occasions new albums were recorded but appeared to deaf ears and after an American tour, once again, the group fell apart in acrimony. Burdon continues to record and gig around the globe, and has published two autobiographies. Price found chart success with the Alan Price Set, before heading into the world of cabaret with another Sixties veteran, Georgie Fame. To this day Steel, Valentine and Rowberry continue to tour as The Animals. In later years, Chandler became the leading figure behind the construction of the Newcastle Arena, now the biggest rock venue on Tyneside. Sadly he died of a heart attack in 1996.

(see also Eric Burdon & The Animals, Alan Price Set, Nashville Teens)

APOSTOLIC INTERVENTION

The Apostolic Intervention are best known, not so much for their music (because there wasn't much), but for their strong ties to The Small Faces. This connection stemmed from their original incarnation as The Little People (spot the name similarity) supporting their heroes at a Hertfordshire gig, resulting in the Faces enthusiastic patronage. Originally called RAF, the group signed to Immediate Records in 1967 at the insistence of the diminutive ones. Steve Marriott suggested to manager Andrew 'Loog' Oldham that they should be renamed The Nice – a nod to his constant catchphrase 'nice' when getting high. However Oldham gave Marriott's suggestion to another four-piece he'd signed, preferring the portentious Apostolic Intervention.

This roughly translates as the interruption of the transmission of spiritual authority from the Apostles through the succession of popes and bishops which was absurd for a band of unholy mods who wanted to be The Small Faces, but it was the Summer of Love, and those wags at Immediate just loved a bit of controversy! It's a shame they didn't spend as much time nurturing the group as after one Marriott-Lane produced single, a cover of The Small Faces '(Tell Me)

Have You Ever Seen Me' (on which Marriott played bass), with a Booker. T-style instrumental, 'Madame Garcia' (a codename for hash) on the flip, they were gone. Shirley was later drafted into Marriott's post-Faces outfit, Humble Pie. *(see also Small Faces)*

THE APPLEJACKS

This Solihull beat group set out their stall as The Crestas, then The Jaguars, before agreeing on the innocuous Applejacks. The group featured guitarists Martin Baggott and Philip Cash, singer Al Jackson, bassist Gerry Freeman, and keyboard player Don Gould. They had a certain novelty angle for the time in the fact that their bass player was a girl, one Megan Davies. This helped them no end when it came to securing maximum TV and radio coverage for their début Decca single 'Tell Me When', a number seven hit in April 1964. A second single 'Like Dreamers Do', a Lennon-McCartney song taken from the legendary Beatles Decca audition tape, reached number 20 in July, and their third 'Three Little Words' managed to climb to number 23 in November. From then on in it was a steady slide into the abyss as the group's lightweight pop (they even covered the *Mary Poppins* song 'Chim Chim Chiree'!) and rather dated image began to look and sound contrived. Their eponymous 1964 début album also sold poorly and is now a collector's item. A well-chosen cover of a Ray Davies song, 'I Go To Sleep' (commercially unrecorded by The Kinks) should have restored a smidgen of credibility in 1965 but when it missed by a mile it was clear that these Apples had gone decidedly bad.

Arrival

The Applejacks

The Applejacks

AQUARIAN AGE

This one off psychedelic free-for-all was the idea of ex-Tomorrow members, 'Twink' (aka John Alder), and John 'Junior' Woods, who brought together the pedigree-perfect studio expertise of ex-Tornado Clem Cattini, and piano wizard Nicky Hopkins, on a 1968 Parlophone 45, laboriously titled '100,000 Words In A Cardboard Box'. Continuing the Tomorrow connection, this now-collectable single was produced by Mark 'Excerpt From a Teenage Opera' Wirtz. Alder replaced Skip Alan in the Pretty Things shortly thereafter, while Woods, after a short stint with the Jeff Beck Group the following year, drifted into obscurity as a croupier.

(see also Jeff Beck, The Fairies, The In Crowd, The Pretty Things, Tomorrow)

PP ARNOLD

Born Patricia Arnold, this gospel-trained vocalist came to Britain with Ike and Tina Turner's Ikettes in September 1966 as part of a Rolling Stones package tour. Being spotted by Andrew Oldham she was persuaded to stay in the UK and was signed to Oldham's Immediate label. Her first release 'Everything's Gonna Be Alright' flopped at the end of '66 but her exceptional version of Cat Stevens' 'The First Cut Is The Deepest' entered the Top 20 reaching 18 in May '67. On stage, Pat was backed by The Nice who began their own career with Immediate the same year. A follow-up to 'The First Cut…' 'The Time Has Come' was less successful, as was her Mick Jagger-produced début album *The First Lady Of Immediate*.

Pat's strong vocals were appreciated by her peers and an association with Immediate labelmates The Small Faces almost resulted in her recording their classic 'Tin Soldier' first. However, her distinctive backing vocals ended up on the disc while Steve Marriott and Ronnie Lane offered her '(If You Think You're) Groovy' as a compromise, which reached 41 in Feb '68. (She also sang back-up vocals on several of their album tracks). Her final Immediate single 'Angel Of the Morning', arranged by John Paul Jones, saw off competition from Billie Davis and the Merrilee Rush US original to reach the UK Top 30 in August '68. A second album *Kafunta* appeared (produced in parts by Jagger and Marriott) which again sold poorly.

As the Sixties closed, Pat became an in-demand session vocalist and appeared in such musicals as Jack Good's *Catch My Soul*, and Tim Rice and Andrew Lloyd Webber's *Jesus Christ Superstar*. Relocating back to her native Los Angeles Pat appeared on sessions for Nils Lofgren and Dr. John amongst many others. After the tragic loss of her daughter in a car accident, Pat returned to London and graced the charts again in a 1988 collaboration with The Beatmasters, 'Burn It Up'. As interest in The Small Faces increased in the Nineties, the fawning likes of Paul Weller, Primal Scream and Ocean Colour Scene asked her to guest on their recordings. Now residing in Spain, Pat is currently employed as

The Artwoods

back-up vocalist on ex-Pink Floyd man Roger Waters' solo tours.

(see also The Nice, The Small Faces)

ART

Formed from Carlisle group The VIPs in 1967, Mike Harrison (vocals), and Greg Ridley (bass) joined forces with Midlanders Luther Grosvenor (ex-Deep Feeling, Hellions – guitar), and Mike Kellie (drums). Aided by legendary DJ and eccentric Guy Stevens, the group recorded for Island; releasing a cover of The Buffalo Springfield's 'For What It's Worth' as 'What's That Sound' and an album for Island, *Supernatural Fairy Tales*, an acknowledged and now-collectable piece of English psychedelia. The album's florid sleeve was created by Granny Takes a Trip boutique designers Michael English and Nigel Weymouth who, with Stevens, comprised the experimental outfit Haphash And The Coloured Coat. The accompaniment on the trio's self-titled début album was provided by Art who evolved into Spooky Tooth later in 1967.

(see also Spooky Tooth, The VIPs)

THE ARTWOODS

Some bands are destined to be remembered not so much for their recorded output but for the band members they harboured. The Artwoods were such a band.

Fronted by Ron Wood's elder brother Art, the group featured guitarist Derek Griffiths, bassist Malcolm Pool while the keyboard player was none other than Deep Purple maestro Jon Lord. Drummer Keef Hartley had replaced Ringo Starr in Rory Storm & The Hurricanes in August 1962 and had moved to London the following year.

An exciting first LP
THE ARTWOODS
ART GALLERY
LK 4830   12" mono LP record
The Decca Record Company Limited   Decca House   Albert Embankment   London   S E I

The Artwoods live at The 100 Club

The Artwoods

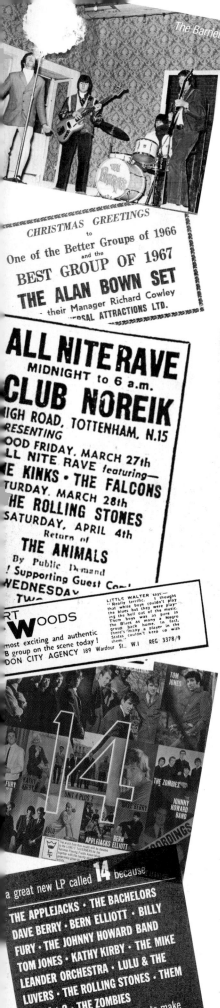

Formed in 1964 following the amalgamation of two short lived West Drayton, Middlesex bands – The Red Bloods Blucicians and The Art Wood Combo – the new group quickly earned themselves a thoroughly deserved reputation as one of the hardest working and best loved live outfits on the country's R&B circuit. Art had already gained a fair amount of notoriety and kudos for himself by helping to set up the legendary Ealing Blues Club (opposite Ealing Broadway station) whilst a founder member of Alexis Korner's Blues Incorporated.

Art Wood

The Artwoods belted out a live show that was a curious mix of Chicago blues, carefully crafted jazz-tinged originals and humourous oddity. It was a strange combination but it won the band the sort of accolades that many of their contemporaries could only dream of, and residencies at Eel Pie Island and the 100 Club at 100 Oxford Street.

Art remembers, 'The American blues giant to us was Little Walter, and he actually came along to see us. Afterwards he said in an interview that although he thought white boys couldn't play the blues, he thought we played the hell out of it. He said we were as pure in the blues as many a negro group from the US. He even said that there was many a blues player over there who wouldn't have been able to keep up with us. After that we were the band to catch live – it was such a boost!'

High praise indeed, but alas, not enough. The group signed with Decca in 1964, but despite releasing the near-miss 'Sweet Mary' (also recorded by the late Cyril Davies) and a trio of great 1966 singles – 'Goodbye Sisters', Sam and Dave's 'I Take What I Want' and Art Neville's 'I Feel Good' – plus a ridiculously collectable and valuable LP Art Gallery and EP Jazz In Jeans, chart success and ultimately, pop stardom eluded them.

The band didn't help matters by changing their name in 1967 to the ill-advised St. Valentine's Day Massacre and releasing a single, 'Brother Can You Spare A Dime?', in a lame attempt to cash in on that particular years' 'gangster' fashion craze. Art: 'We even did a promotion all dressed up as gangsters posing with Faye Dunaway who was in Bonnie And Clyde, which was the big film at the time. But people just asked 'why?''

Unsurprisingly the record failed to chart and Art wisely left the band. In 1969 Wood swept up his little brother Ron and his mate Rod Stewart from the ashes of The Jeff Beck Group, and Ronnie Lane, Ian

McLagan, and Kenny Jones from the recently defunct Small Faces. Together they played a handful of gigs throughout the summer, using Ron's old Birds and Creation chum Kim Gardner on bass. Several demos were recorded for Pye, who rejected the tapes on the basis of the group being a bunch of holdovers from other once successful outfits. Unfortunately this theory, shared by other record companies, brought the Melon to a premature expiry date. Art and Gardner bowed out, paving the way for The Faces.

Following a stint with John Mayall's Bluesbreakers, Keef Hartley went on to have a modicum of solo fame, dressing up like a Red Indian and a mountain man for The Keef Hartley Band. His greatest non-claim to fame, however, had to be his refusal to let the KHB's name, likeness or performance be used in the film or advertising for the massive Woodstock event. Nowadays Hartley can be found along the canals of middle England where he runs a studio equipment business.

Then, of course, there's Hammond supremo and Deep Purple sage Jon Lord, a musician long rumoured to be an inspiration for many of the comical situations in the hilarious rock spoof This Is Spinal Tap, plus other howlers too numerous to mention here.
(See also Alexis Korner's Blues Incorporated, Jeff Beck Group, Small Faces, The Flowerpot Men, John Mayall)

THE ATTACK

The small caché of singles The Attack recorded for Decca in 1967-68 are rightly regarded as the stuff of legend. The Attack's shifting personnel saw at least two future guitar heroes, Davey O'List and John DuCann, pass through their ranks.

In late-1966 the first line-up featured Richard Shirman (vocals), Gerry Henderson (bass), Bob Hodges (organ), Alan Whitehead (drums), and David John (aka O'List) on guitar. The group, formerly The Soul System, were signed and re-named by the notorious Don Arden who found them their début single, a forceful cover of The Ohio Express song, 'Try It' (also covered in the US by The Standells), released in January 1967.

Caught between mod-soul punch and psychedelic experimentation, the group were forced to record commercial novelties like 'Hi Ho Silver Lining' and 'Created By Clive' as their A-sides (both competing with versions by Jeff Beck and The Syn respectively), whilst showing their true inclination on B-sides such as 'Any More Than I Do' and 'Colour Of My Mind'.

By mid-67 personnel upheavals resulted in O'List leaving to join The Nice and Whitehead to Marmalade. Shirman assembled a new Attack featuring George Watt (organ), Chris Allen (drums), Geoff Richardson (guitar) Kenny Harold (bass) and guitarist John DuCann. The line-up continued to have a revolving door of personnel. Harold left to be replaced by bassist Jim Pitman-Avory (later with Thunderclap Newman and Third World War) and The Attack issued their final single 'Neville Thumbcatch' in January '68. DuCann went on to Andromeda (formed from the ashes of The Attack) and Atomic Rooster.

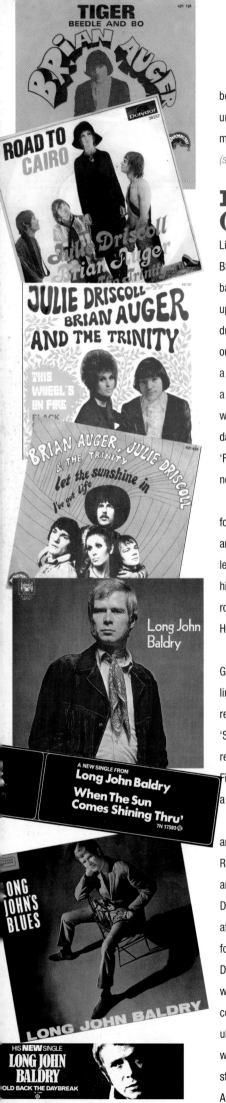

In 1990 a compilation, *Magic In The Air*, collected together the best of the group's output together with several previously unreleased recordings from the period that confirmed their magnificence.

(see also Marmalade, The Nice, Five Day Week Straw People)

BRIAN AUGER (& THE TRINITY)

Like most young classically trained musicians in the late Fifties, Brian Auger started his professional music career playing in a jazz band, switching to R&B with his first Trinity formed in 1962. The line-up consisted of guitarist John McLaughlin, bass player Rick Laird, drummer Phil Kinorra, and sax player Glen Hughes, but this turned out to be a short lived aggregation which broke up without recording a single note. Auger formed a second, scaled-down Trinity featuring a rhythm section of Micky Waller (drums) and Rickie Brown (bass), while Auger himself switched from piano to the hip instrument of the day, the Hammond organ. This line-up cut two singles for Columbia, 'Fool Killer' and 'Green Onions '65', both released in 1965, to little or no acclaim.

Auger promptly abandoned any immediate Trinity plans and opted for the role of bandleader behind singers Julie Driscoll, Rod Stewart and Long John Baldry, in Steam Packet. This rolling R&B revue lasted less than a year and following their demise in 1966, Auger resumed his Trinity work, cutting a third Columbia single, the wild Hammond roar of 'Tiger' with a B-side calling itself 'Oh Baby, Won't You Come Home To Croydon, Where Everybody Beedle's And Bo's'.

Auger retained 'Jools' from Steam Packet and recruited guitarist Gary Boyle, Dave Ambrose (bass), and Clive Thacker (drums). This line-up signed to Giorgio Gomelsky's Marmalade label in 1967, releasing an album *Open*, from which a cover of Aretha Franklin's 'Save Me' was extracted as a single. In June 1968 the group's recording of the Bob Dylan 'Basement Tapes' track 'This Wheel's On Fire', credited to Julie Driscoll, Brian Auger, and The Trinity became a deserved international hit, reaching number five in Britain.

All the signals pointed to the Trinity becoming huge third time around, but they mistakenly spread themselves far two thinly. Releasing a whole slew of albums and singles in quick succession and crediting them to both Brian Auger and The Trinity, and Julie Driscoll, Brian Auger, and The Trinity caused no end of confusion, and affected sales. With billing an issue, together with their inability to follow-through on that breakthrough hit, something had to give and Driscoll quit mid-way though an American tour, leaving the band without their charismatic vocalist. Auger struggled on but the collapse of the Marmalade label shortly after forced him to ultimately abandon the group. He fared a little better in the Seventies with the jazz-rock group Oblivion Express, who released a further string of records aimed solely at the US market. Today the US-based Auger enjoys a measure of credibility, especially among the acid jazz

fraternity where some apparently regard him as a bona fide genius.

(see also Long John Baldry, Jeff Beck, Julie Driscoll, Rod Stewart)

LONG JOHN BALDRY

Born in London Baldry started out singing in Soho's folk and coffee bars in the late Fifties. He acquired his 'Long John' prefix, not from any pirate fixation, but due to his 6 foot 7 inch height.

When the R&B boom hit the capital in the early Sixties Baldry began singing with the hugely influential Blues Incorporated, appearing on their 1962 album *R&B At The Marquee* before spending almost a year on the continent. He returned a year later, singing with Cyril Davies' All-Stars up until Davies' death in January 1964. Baldry took over the band and renamed them The Hoochie Coochie Men, recruiting Rod Stewart as second vocalist. This took Baldry though to 1965 and the formation of the Steam Packet project, while he also continued to record as a solo artist and issued a series

Long John Baldry

of singles and two albums, *Long John's Blues* and *Looking At Long John* for United Artists – none of which troubled the charts.

When Steam Packet folded Baldry hired another backing band Bluesology, which included a young Reginald Dwight (soon to be better known as Elton John) on piano. In 1967 he switched labels to Pye and embarked upon a change of musical direction that saw him ditch R&B in favour of big production ballads. Composer and producer Tony Macauley presented the perfect vehicle in the song 'Let The Heartaches Begin' which went to number one in November 1967. Baldry may have become the new Housewives Choice but his original audience deserted him in droves. He had three more Top 30 places over the next two years, including 'Mexico', the theme tune to the 1968 Olympic Games before the hits dried up.

ON THE STAGE

ODEON
HAMMERSMITH Tel: RIV 4081

BRIAN EPSTEIN Presents

ANOTHER 'BEATLES' CHRISTMAS SHOW

THE BEATLES

FREDDIE and the DREAMERS

JIMMY SAVILE · SOUNDS INCORPORATED

ELKIE BROOKS · THE YARDBIRDS · MICHAEL HASLAM
THE MIKE COTTON SOUND · RAY FELL

OPENS 24th DECEMBER to 16th JANUARY 1965
(EXCEPT SUNDAYS)

BOX OFFICE NOW OPEN
Performances at 6.15 pm & 8.45 pm
One performance Christmas Eve at 7.30 pm
One performance 29th Dec at 6.15

STALLS :	20/-	:	15/-	:	10/-	
CIRCLE :	20/-	:	15/-	:	10/-	:	7/6

SEND NOW TO THE ODEON THEATRE HAMMERSMITH Tel: RIV 4081
ENCLOSE A STAMPED/ADDRESSED ENVELOPE

Please send .... Stalls tickets @ .... each for 6.15 or 8.45
Circle
performance on alternative date(s) ....
Cheque/P.O. Number .... enclosed
Name ....
Address ....

Baldry pursued a career on the cabaret circuit and in 1971, called in a few production favours from old colleagues Rod Stewart and Elton John for a return-to-form album *It Ain't Easy*. When it bombed commercially Baldry vanished to Canada's club scene.

His vocal talents got a completely different outing in the early Nineties when his voice was used for the character Robotnik on the computer game Sonic The Hedgehog. An album, cryptically titled *It Still Ain't Easy*, appeared in 1993. Baldry can be currently found doing the nostalgia package tour circuit accompanied by the likes of The Manfreds.

(see also Brian Auger, Bluesology, Cyril Davies R&B All-Stars, Julie Driscoll, Alexis Korner's Blues Incorporated, Rod Stewart)

THE BANSHEES

Often cited as the musical birthplace of Brylcreem balladeer Brian Ferry, this Newcastle R&B band had a fluctuating line-up that saw at least three singers come and go. Ferry's involvement was brief and came at the end of the group's reign. Consequently he did not appear on any of their three 45s released on Columbia between 1964 and 1965.

THE BEATLES

On New Year's Eve, 1961, John Lennon, Paul McCartney, George Harrison and Pete Best loaded their equipment into a van and drove from Liverpool to London, where, the following morning, they auditioned for Decca Records. As is now famously known, the label turned them down. Within two years, The Beatles were to become the most popular recording artists on the planet...

The group's saga actually began on July 6, 1957, at St. Peter's Church in Liverpool. Sixteen-year-old John Lennon's skiffle group, The Quarry Men, was between sets at the church's annual Garden Fete when a mutual friend, Ivan Vaughn, introduced him to fifteen-year-old Paul McCartney. McCartney showed off by playing Eddie Cochran's 'Twenty Flight Rock' and a few weeks later Lennon invited him to join the band. The following year, McCartney brought in his friend George Harrison, and in 1960 John's art-school pal Stuart Sutcliffe became the group's bass player. Later that year, in honour of Buddy Holly's group, The Crickets and John's fondness for puns, the band's name was changed to The Beatles. In August of 1960, Pete Best joined them as drummer and they headed to Hamburg, West Germany, where they played all-night sets in seedy clubs, taking amphetamines for energy and honing their rough, driving covers of American rock-and-roll songs. They stayed in Hamburg for three months but Sutcliffe, who had fallen in love with German photographer Astrid Kirschherr, quit the band and didn't return to Liverpool. (He died of a brain haemorrhage in April of 1962.)

Back in England, club owners were amazed by how much progress The Beatles had made, fans went wild, and the press started writing about Liverpool's 'Beat' music scene. Another three-

The Beatles

month stint in Hamburg the following spring continued their development. In June of 1961, they served as the backing group for vocalist Tony Sheridan on six songs, including 'My Bonnie', which was a minor hit single in Germany. In November of 1961, Brian Epstein, who managed his family's local NEMS record shop, saw The Beatles at the Cavern Club, and offered to manage them, arranging their audition with Decca two months later. Despite their failure to win a contract, The Beatles signed a management contract with Epstein, and he set about refining their image, convincing them to give up their scruffy outfits and wear suits onstage. In June of 1962, they auditioned for George Martin, the head of A&R at the EMI subsidiary Parlophone Records, who offered them a contract the following month even though he was unimpressed with their original songs and thought Pete Best wasn't a good enough drummer. Best was promptly sacked from the group in August and replaced by Ringo Starr, a fellow Liverpudlian whom they'd met in Hamburg, where he had been playing drums with Rory Storm & The Hurricanes.

When he showed up with the other Beatles for their first official recording session at EMI

Studios on September 11, 1962, Martin had hired seasoned studio drummer Andy White for the session, and the humiliated Starr instead ended up playing tambourine on 'Love Me Do', the A-side of the first Beatles single. Legend has it that Brian Epstein ordered 10,000 copies of the single to ensure that it would be a Top 20 hit, and the song did peak at No. 17 on the English charts. Their second single, 'Please Please Me', went straight to No. 1 (in certain charts) in February of 1963, and The Beatles were on their way to superstardom. In March, their début album, also titled *Please Please Me*, was released, and it remained at the top of the charts for thirty weeks until it was dislodged by their follow-up, *With The Beatles*. As 1963 came to a close, on November 4, The Beatles played a Royal Command Performance attended by the Queen Mother and Princess Margaret, during which Lennon uttered the famous line, "The people in the cheaper seats clap your hands, and the rest of you if you'd just rattle your jewellery."

Despite their lightning ascent in England, where the press was now freely using the term 'Beatlemania' to describe the frenzy the band created, as 1963 came to a close The Beatles had yet to make any inroads into the American music scene. Neither the single 'Please Please Me' nor the album *Introducing The Beatles* (a shortened version of the British *Please Please Me* album) made the US charts. But in January of 1964, with the release of the single 'I Want To Hold Your Hand', 'Beatlemania' hit America. Two weeks after it landed in stores, the record had sold more than one million copies. On February 9, two days after their American arrival, The Beatles made their first, phenomenal live appearance in the US on *The Ed Sullivan Show*. The CBS TV show was seen by an estimated seventy-three million people or sixty percent of television viewers and by the end of the month, The Beatles practically owned the *Billboard* charts. In addition to having the No. 1 single, they had four other 45s on the singles chart and three LPs on the album chart, including *Meet The Beatles* in the No. 1 spot. Over the next two years, they had twenty-six singles in the *Billboard Top 40* (including ten number ones, which held the top spot for thirty-eight of 104 weeks), and seven No. 1 albums. In addition to this prolific recording pace, they were touring constantly, including Australia as well as Europe and North America (where they played before 56,000 fans at Shea Stadium in August of 1965), and they made two hit movies, *A Hard Day's Night* and *Help!*

Remarkably, the album they released in December of 1965, *Rubber Soul*, was their most vibrant and subtle work so far, betraying no signs of the exhaustion they no doubt felt. Reacting to the work of Bob Dylan and The Byrds and the advent of folk-rock, *Rubber Soul* featured more introspective lyrics and a greater reliance on acoustic instruments on such Lennon-McCartney classics as 'Drive My Car', 'Norwegian Wood', 'In My Life' and 'Michelle' as well as Harrison's 'If I Needed Someone'. The same day the album was released in England, The Beatles also released a single containing two non-LP tracks, Lennon's 'Day Tripper' and McCartney's 'We Can Work It Out', both of which became additional hits. Not surprisingly, given the artistry displayed on *Rubber Soul*,

they were tired of spending all their time on the road, and decided to stop performing in August following their summer tour of the US. Just before that tour was set to begin, the American teen magazine *Datebook* reprinted a British interview with Lennon in which he was quoted as saying, "We're more popular than Jesus now. I don't know which will go first, rock and roll or Christianity." These comments caused frenzy in the southern part of the US, where Beatles records were burned, numerous death threats were received, and fans were urged to boycott the band's concerts.

By the end of their final show, at San Francisco's Candlestick Park on August 29, 1966, they'd had enough. It was just as well. Their concerts had long since devolved into events where the fans' screaming was louder than the music, while their studio work was becoming more and more sophisticated. The same month they toured America for the last time, *Revolver* was released; an outstanding set of songs that increased the progress they'd made on *Rubber Soul* by leaps and bounds. Featuring backwards guitar loops and strange, hallucinogenic lyrics, it was a brilliant sonic collage unlike anything they'd previously committed to vinyl. Late in 1966 The Beatles reunited at EMI Studios to record their next album. Among the first songs they cut was Lennon's 'Strawberry Fields Forever', a haunting, acid-inspired masterpiece named for a Liverpool orphanage that he remembered from his childhood; the song eventually ended up not on the album, but on a single, paired with McCartney's cheerfully nostalgic 'Penny Lane'. The album that followed, *Sgt. Pepper's Lonely Hearts Club Band*, continued in the same vein, alternating between McCartney's chipper mid-tempo numbers and Lennon's psychedelic pieces. Their increasingly disparate approaches to songwriting came together on the album's last track, the superb 'A Day In The Life', which combined a not-quite-finished Lennon number with an embryonic McCartney bridge to create a stunning aural collage. While it didn't tell any kind of coherent story, critics took to referring to *Sgt. Pepper* as a concept album. Musically, it far surpassed anything anything else pop music had attempted to date, and it quickly became a huge critical and commercial success, holding the No. 1 spot on *Billboard's* album chart for a record-breaking fifteen weeks.

While *Sgt. Pepper* marked a new peak for The Beatles, it also hinted at the dissolution that was to follow. No longer a seamless unit, Lennon, McCartney, and Harrison were each heading in separate directions, and creative tensions were bound to follow. This situation was exacerbated in August of 1967, when manager Epstein died of a drug overdose. He had always handled The Beatles' business decisions, allowing the band members to focus on their work. Now, in the wake of Brian's death, they started branching out, starting their own record label and clothing boutique, both named Apple. They also began studying with Maharishi Mahesh Yogi, who taught Transcendental Meditation and other forms of Indian spirituality. These were confusing times for The Beatles, and that confusion showed in *Magical Mystery Tour*, a 50-minute television film that aired on BBC 1 on Boxing Day, 1967. It was regarded by many as the band's first critical failure, despite containing some great music, including Lennon's 'I Am The Walrus' and McCartney's 'The Fool On The Hill'. 'Lady Madonna' (March 1968) was followed in September with the classic 'Hey Jude', a hymn-like McCartney ballad that clocked in at more than seven minutes, making it far and away the longest No. 1 single of all time. A couple of months later, *The Beatles*, a two-record set in an all-white cover, which soon became known as *The White Album*, was released. Packed with great songs, the album spurned the conceptual pretensions of *Sgt. Pepper* in favour of straightforward rock- and acoustic-based material, but in reality The Beatles were now three solo artists using each other as session musicians. Starr, tired of the constant bickering, even quit the band for several days, Harrison brought in Eric Clapton to play lead guitar on 'While My Guitar Gently Weeps' and Lennon's new lover, Yoko Ono, was a constant presence in the studio, much to everyone's discomfort.

By the time The Beatles reconvened in Twickenham Film Studios on January 2, 1969, McCartney had a new companion of his own, Linda Eastman, a rock photographer and daughter of a prominent New York lawyer. The Twickenham sessions were set up to film The Beatles at work for a documentary tentatively titled *Get Back*, but the sessions were anything but harmonious, and this time, it was Harrison who threatened to quit. Despite a loose, joyful concert – the final time they played together as a unit – on the rooftop of their Apple Corps building in Savile Row on January 30, the tapes for the proposed album and film were temporarily shelved until May of 1970.

That summer, The Beatles reunited at EMI Studios to record *Abbey Road*, their final album of new material. The sessions proved remarkably productive and free of the dissension that had plagued *The White Album* and the *Get Back* sessions. The music, too, was (of course) magnificent. Side Two featured a (McCartney constructed) song suite that was the most musically inventive and melodically gorgeous music The Beatles ever created. Despite the success of the *Abbey Road* sessions, the group finally disintegrated. Business problems led Lennon to seek out Allen Klein, The Rolling Stones' adviser, to represent The Beatles, while McCartney wanted his father-in-law, attorney Lee Eastman, to manage the band. Harrison and Starr sided with Lennon, but the point was moot, as The Beatles had effectively split up anyway. Eventually, it was McCartney who announced the break-up of the group in a 'self interview' included with his first solo album, *McCartney*, which was released in April of 1970. A month later, the *Get Back* sessions, which had now been retitled *Let It Be*, were finally released, but McCartney denounced the results, which had been re-mixed and overdubbed by the legendary American producer, Phil Spector.

On December 8, 1980, just weeks after the release of his *Double*

The Beatstalkers

Fantasy album, Lennon was gunned down by a deranged ex-fan in front of his Central Park apartment building, and any chance of the Fab Four reuniting was lost. In 1995, the remaining Beatles got together to record new backing tracks to some Lennon demos which were included as part of The Beatles' *Anthology* albums and documentaries. That project earned the surviving Beatles three Grammys and introduced their music to a whole new generation of fans. But further bad luck befell the group when, on November 29, 2001, Harrison lost his battle against cancer. Now, 55 years after Lennon and McCartney's first fateful meeting, no one doubts their place in the history books. They are still the greatest band in rock'n'roll history, and the most important musicians and composers of the twentieth century.

(see also The Pete Best Four)

THE BEAT MERCHANTS

Along with The Primitives and The Fairies, The Beat Merchants have been credited with releasing the most primal, frenzied Brit R&B single with 'Pretty Face'. Formed in Horsham, Sussex in 1962, as Peter and The Hustlers, The Beat Merchants (Chris Boyle – vocals, Ralph Worman – guitar, Geoff Farndell-bass, Gavin Daneski – guitar, harmonica, Vic Sendall – drums) attracted a loyal South Coast following and were torn between signing for Decca or EMI. They chose the latter and the self-composed 'Pretty Face', a frenzied, Pretty Things-styled number was released on Columbia in September 1964. Despite television appearances on *Thank Your Lucky Stars* and *Scene At 6:30* the single only managed to crack the Top 50.

A follow up, 'So Fine', released February '65, failed to make amends and the group were dropped by Columbia and eventually disbanded.

THE BEATSTALKERS

This crew were a tough, concise and nattily-trousered Glasgow soul outfit, popular enough north of the border to be referred to as 'The Scottish Beatles'. Although years ahead in the wardrobe department –

The Beatstalkers

drawing complementary sartorial praise from The Kinks and Small Faces on a shared *Ready, Steady, Go!* appearance in November 1965 – the group failed in their bid to capitalise on their Caledonian following.

After three singles for Decca – including the mod-soul of 'Left Right Left' b/w 'You'd Better Get A Better Hold On' (1966) – The Beatstalkers were signed to CBS for an equally dismal run of four singles between '67 – '69. Three of these releases elicit interest for being early David Bowie compositions, as the two acts shared the same manager in Kenneth Pitt.

Unfortunately neither 'Silver Treetop School For Boys' (1967), 'Everything Is You' (1968) or 'When I'm Five' (1969) were the future Ziggy's more inspired moments. Bassist Alan Mair went on to play with The Only Ones in the late Seventies.

JEFF BECK

Jeff Beck needs little introduction as one of the era's or any era's leading and defining guitar virtuosos. Beck studied at Wimbledon Art School in 1964 where he joined his first band called The Tridents. They played their earliest live appearances supporting The Birds at Twickenham's Eel Pie Island where Beck quickly made a name for himself as an exceptionally gifted guitarist. By February 1965 he was auditioning to replace the considerable slot Eric Clapton had left vacant in The Yardbirds. Impressing singer Keith Relf with his playing and knowledge of American blues guitarists like Buddy Guy, Beck officially joined the group in March.

His turbulent two-year stint with The Yardbirds not only sealed his reputation as one of the country's finest lead guitarists but also one of the most paranoid and problematic. After walking out of a particularly gruelling Dick Clark 'Caravan Of Stars' package tour of America (by which time, his mate Jimmy Page had joined as auxiliary guitarist), suffering from nervous exhaustion, Beck was eventually sacked from The Yardbirds in December 1966 whilst topping the *Beat Instrumental* 'Best Guitarist' poll ahead of Hank Marvin, Eric Clapton, and George Harrison.

Beck signed a solo recording deal with producer Mickie Most in January '67 and took on Most's sidekick Peter Grant as manager. However Grant found he only had 50% control of his new charge due to a bizarre contractual set up which still tied Beck to his old Yardbirds manager Simon Napier-Bell. Grant eventually gained control of the remaining 50% and ended up managing both Beck and the last gasp Yardbirds, and – more importantly in the long term – the new band formed from their ashes, Led Zeppelin.

Beck went into rehearsals with an ever-fluid parade of musicians he admired, including ex-Shadows bassist Jet Harris and ex Pretty Things drummer, Viv Prince. In a London nightclub, Beck mentioned the band he was forming to out-of-work Shotgun Express vocalist Rod Stewart who became singer. When neither the notoriously unpredictable Harris nor Prince showed up to rehearsals,

Jeff Beck

OUT TODAY!
JEFF
BECK
GUITAR INSTRUMENTAL
"LOVE IS
BLUE"
Coupled with
"I'VE BEEN DRINKING"
MICKIE MOST PRODUCTION
ON COLUMBIA RECORDS

R VALEN... ...SEND
... STILL HAVE TIME ...AY
JEFF BECK
...OVE IS BLUE
INSTEAD OF A CARD

JEFF BECK

Beck-Ola

their roles were respectively offered to ex-Birds guitarist Ron Wood and Mojos-John Mayall drummer Aynsley Dunbar. Despite having a ready made outfit, Beck's first studio undertaking with Most featured session players John Paul Jones and Clem Cattini backing him on an uncharacteristic pop single, the party perennial 'Hi Ho Silver Lining', with Stewart on backing vocals, which made it to number 14 in March '67.

Both follow up singles, 'Tallyman' (a Graham Goldman composition featuring a fine Beck solo) and the popular Paul Mauriat instrumental 'Love Is Blue' made the Top 30, despite being totally unrepresentative. The real evidence of the Jeff Beck Group's prowess was to be found on stage, and on the odd radio session the group recorded. It was Beck's 1968 début album Truth that finally consolidated that promise with Stewart's vocals firmly in evidence, and Beck's inspired reworkings of such blues outings as Willie Dixon's 'I Ain't Superstitious' and Muddy Waters' 'You Shook Me'. The album was a major success in America, and the group's attendant tours, watched by an enterprising Page, laid the blueprint for Led Zeppelin.

The second album, the patchy *Beck-Ola*, featuring Waller's successor, ex-Sounds Incorporated drummer Tony Newman and pianist Nicky Hopkins, crept into the Top 40 at number 39 in September 1969. The combination of Beck and Stewart was formidable and the group carved out a reputation playing live, particularly in America where they spent most of their time. Unfortunately internal tensions began to undermine the group's

stability as Beck instigated an unpredictable hiring and firing policy throughout 1968. First to go was Aynsley Dunbar to be replaced by Mickey Waller. Then pianist Nicky Hopkins was brought in as Ron Wood was sacked. Wood was replaced by ex-Tomorrow bassist, 'Junior' Woods, only to be reinstated after a disastrous American show. This sort of erratic behaviour kept the band in a constant state of disarray, and Beck's self-destructive tendency to cancel gigs at a moment's notice eventually brought the group to breaking point.

There was, however, one last attempt at making a go of it. Following Ron Wood's return the group were invited to perform at the Woodstock Music and Arts Festival being held in upstate New York in August 1969. Unfortunately this last effort to keep the group afloat proved fruitless as Beck announced his intention to play the festival with Tim Bogert and Carmine Appice from US band Vanilla Fudge, which amounted to nothing.

Their potential unfulfilled, the group disintegrated, and in November 1969, Beck suffered a near-fatal auto accident in Maidstone, Kent requiring several months recuperation. He returned in 1971 with a new group, featuring singer Bobby Tench, bass player Clive Charman, pianist Max Middleton, and drummer Cozy Powell. His much-vaunted collaboration with Bogert and Appice eventually happened in 1972 and lasted until '74 when they too split up. Since then Beck has pursued a disjointed solo career which has seen him drift into experimental areas. He's toyed with just about every form of music from rock and jazz fusion through to dance and film scores. While being still regarded as one of the all-time greatest rock guitarists he has never really managed to recapture the public's interest in quite the same way he did in his Sixties heyday – which the media shy antihero is no doubt happy to maintain. Stewart and Wood's post-Beck careers are well documented. Newman returned to session work, as did Nicky Hopkins, after a brief period in Mill Valley, California, with Quicksilver Messenger Service. Waller went on to play a substantial role on Stewart's solo albums up until *Atlantic Crossing* before sustaining a career as a session drummer. He has since retired from the music scene and lives quietly in Barnes, London.

After leaving Beck Aynsley Dunbar formed Aynsley Dunbar's Retaliation, joined Frank Zappa's Mothers Of Invention in 1970, and established a reputation as a session drummer, including David Bowie's *Pin-Ups* album and an appearance in Bowie's rarely-seen *1980 Floor Show* NBC TV special in 1973. He joined AOR act Journey in 1974 and continued on this path with Jefferson Starship in 1978 until his departure in 1982, when he returned to occasional session work.

(see also The Yardbirds)

THE BEDROCKS

A group of British based West Indians who took their name from the band featured in the cartoon series *The Flintstones*. The Bedrocks lost out in a chart battle with Marmalade and couldn't survive the fall-out when both groups released simultaneous versions of The Beatles' *White Album* track 'Ob-La-Di, Ob-La-Da' in 1968. The Bedrocks' effort stalled at a respectable 20, while Marmalade's rendition went all the way to the top. Undaunted, the group released another three singles in quick succession, including a version of 'It's A Wonderful World' in 1969, none of which charted. One last effort was released in early 1970, the insightful title of 'Stone Cold Dead In The Market' which at least drew attention to their sense of humour. Stand up Messrs: Trevor Wisdom (vocals), William Hixon (organ), Owen Wisdom (guitar), Reg Challenger (bass), Paul Douglas (drums), and Leroy Mills (brass).

THE BEE GEES

Without doubt the most successful harmony trio in pop history, the English born but Australian reared Gibb brothers continue to add to their already impressive line of achievements. Born on the Isle of Man, eldest brother Barry and twins Robin and Maurice formed a vocal trio in Manchester in the Fifties that performed at Saturday morning picture shows. With Barry and Robin showing an unhealthy penchant for juvenile delinquency, the Gibb family emigrated to Australia in 1958.

The brothers continued to perform as a vocal trio, calling themselves The Bee Gees after the initials of eldest brother Barry, plus local champions DJ Bill Gates and Bill Goode. Over the years it became an acronym for 'Brothers Gibb'. The trio soon attracted local

attention and were signed to the Festival imprint where between 1960 and 1966, they released a string of unsuccessful singles and albums, most containing originals penned by Barry. Ironically, just as the group decided to broaden their horizons and return to England, they were rewarded with an Australian number one single, 'Spicks And Specks'.

In February '67 the Gibb family returned to England, where the group's demo tape had been rejected by almost everybody bar fellow Aussie Robert Stigwood, who signed them to NEMS Enterprises, The Beatles company. It was an ironic choice as the Gibb siblings idolised the Fab Four, so much so, that many untrained ears thought the Bee Gees first English-recorded Polydor single, 'New York Mining Disaster 1941' was the Fabs' in disguise. The record was an instant success – number 12 in the UK in May; 14 in the US – and the group had found acceptance within months of their return. The five-man Bee Gees line-up was completed by the Gibbs' Australian chums Colin Peterson (drums) and Vince Melouney (guitar). 'To Love Somebody' (originally written for Otis Redding) stiffed in Britain but rewarded the group with another US Top 20 hit in July. The group's début album *Bee Gees 1st* (released in August) featured many strong Beatle-esque tracks, particularly 'Holiday', 'In My Own Time', 'Please Read Me' and the psychedelic 'Red Chair Fadeaway'. The singles, 'Massachusetts (a number one in October) and 'World' (nine – December) completed a successful year. The group also produced and donated songs to other fellow Aussies domiciled in Blighty, most notably Johnnie Young ('Craise Finton Kirk') and The Tangerine Peel ('Every Christian Lion-Hearted Man Will Show You'), featuring future renowned record producer Mike Chapman.

The hits continued through 1968 into 1969, with 'Words', 'I've Gotta Get A Message To You' (another number one in August '68), 'I Started A Joke' and 'First Of May', but there was dissension in the ranks. Melouney left at the end of a German tour in November '68 and an ever-widening rift between Barry and Robin, resulted in the latter going solo in '69; scoring a number two hit with 'Saved By The Bell'. Peterson was unceremoniously fired in August '69 and Barry and Maurice entered the Seventies as a duo. Of course, all was forgiven when Robin's subsequent releases stiffed and he was readmitted back into the fold. After the hits dried up in the early Seventies and a perilous career in cabaret all but sunk them, The Bee Gees were given the Lazarus touch with the *Main Helping* album in 1975, featuring the US hit single 'Jive Talkin'. It was only a short step away from *Saturday Night Fever* and the mega-stardom that keeps them in Miami mansions to this day.

BELFAST GYPSIES

Formed in late 1965 by the McAuley Brothers – Jackie and Patrick – after their tempestuous tour of duty in Them, The Belfast Gypsies (also featuring guitarist Ken McLeod and bassist Mark Scott) came

to the attention of ex-Hollywood Argyles and all-round scenester, Kim Fowley, who got them signed to Island. The group's first 1966 single was a punkified re-make of 'Gloria', rewritten as 'Gloria's Dream', while its B-side was an equally punk piece of paranoia 'Secret Police.' Predictably the single failed to sell as did it's follow-up, 'People Let's Freak Out', (1967, credited to The Freaks Of Nature). A whole Fowley-produced self-titled album of similar madness was released only in Sweden in 1967 where the band had diverted their energies.

Following the Gypsies demise, Jackie returned to Dublin to pursue a solo career. His brother Pat withdrew from the music business and died in a boating accident in Donegal in 1984.

(see also Them)

CLIFF BENNETT & THE REBEL ROUSERS

One of the most versatile R&B vocalists from the British Beat era, Cliff Bennett put together The Rebel Rousers, named after Duane Eddy's 1958 hit, in early 1961, featuring Mick King (guitar), Frank Allen (bass), Ricky Winters (drums) and Sid Phillips (piano/sax). Contrary to what their name suggested the short-haired Rebel Rousers were quite tame – wearing matching stage outfits of tartan jackets, shirts and ties. The group's repertoire of rock 'n' roll and early R&B covers gained them a sizeable following, and in 1961, under the auspices of producer Joe Meek, they signed with Parlophone. Meek likened Bennett's voice to Elvis Presley's – a trait displayed on Bennett's self-penned début single, 'You Got What I Like'. Two more Meek-helmed singles followed before band and producer parted company.

In 1962, a residency at the Star Club in Hamburg, Germany, brought Bennett and the Rebel Rousers into contact with The Beatles, and manager Brian Epstein, who signed Bennett and the Rebel Rousers to his NEMS stable of acts . The group continued to release a series of competent if workmanlike R&B cover versions for Parlophone, while replacing King and Winters with Dave Wendells and Mick Burt respectively as well the addition of a second sax player in Moss Groves.

In May 1964, bass player Frank Allen replaced a departing Tony Jackson in the more successful Searchers, and was replaced by Bobby Thompson. Despite being a well respected and busy live act, chart success continued to elude Bennett & The Rebel Rousers until a classy cover of The Drifters' 'One Way Love' got to number nine in October 1964. Shortly after 'One Way Love' was recorded Roy Young – a friend from the group's Hamburg days joined the group as keyboard player and backing vocalist. The group's self-titled début album was a predictable selection of cover versions and failed to sell in great quantities. Neither did the group's latest single, another Drifters cover, 'I'll Take You Home', which could only reach number 42 in February 1965.

More line-up changes occurred towards the end of the year when Wendells was sacked for drunkenness (Bennett was a strict disciplinarian) and joined Lulu's Luvvers, while Thompson quit for a post in The Rockin' Berries. The replacement for both was one Chas Hodges, who had played with The Outlaws. He overdubbed his guitar in the studio but concentrated on bass for stage work. Bennett and his Rebel Rousers still couldn't kick their losing streak as far as finding that elusive hit single. By mid-1966 the group looked in serious danger of breaking up. Thankfully this was averted by the invaluable patronage of The Beatles. Bennett & The Rebel Rousers supported them on a German tour in June and Paul McCartney stepped in and produced a cover of the *Revolver* track 'Got To Get You Into My Life', which sailed up the charts to number six. Although the song's chances were undeniably helped by it being a Lennon-McCartney composition The Rebel Rousers performed it creditably.

Sadly it was only a short respite as the single proved to be their second and last Top 10 hit. A cover of Sam & Dave's 'Don't Help Me Out' and an album *Got To Get You Into Our Lives* both failed to alleviate the situation. In 1967 R&B and soul were out and hippies and psychedelia were in. Bennett was forced to concede the group had fallen victim to a changing musical climate and attempted to bring about a change of direction by renaming the group Cliff Bennett & His Band and suggesting a heavier, more progressive sound although not every one in the band agreed.

Bennett didn't know it but he was about to become a casualty of a rock and roll mutiny. While he was away doing promotional work in Germany in 1968, Young usurped him and renamed the band The Roy Young Band. Of the original Rebel Rousers, Phillips worked with Screaming Lord Sutch, while Young made solo albums with the help

Toe Fat

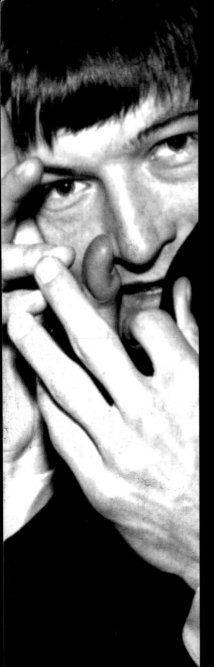

of Dave Wendells. Hodges had the most success with a stint in Heads, Hands & Feet and is now one half of the 'cor blimey' cockney duo, Chas & Dave.

Bennett gamely assembled a new backing band using The Pirates (Robin MacDonald – bass, Frank Farley – drums, and guitarist Mick Green) who were basically the discarded remnants of The Dakotas, and a brass section before he ditched the brass and reverted back to a four piece. The group tried to go The Beatles route again by releasing a cover of 'Back In The USSR' in December 1968 but the public literally didn't buy it. Green took a less artistically inclined but better-paid job in Englebert Humpedinck's cabaret big band, and was replaced by ex-Gods member Ken Hensley, but then Bennett finally called it a day in mid-1969.

Bennett grew his locks and a beard and took Hensley with him to form Toe Fat, most notable for having two of the grossest album sleeves in rock! When they disbanded a year later Hensley and drummer Lee Kerslake formed Uriah Heep. In 1971 Bennett formed the equally short-lived Cliff Bennett's Rebellion, and in 1974, Shanghai featuring the guitar expertise of Mick Green. Nowadays, Bennett keeps a low profile musically but continues to perform occasionally.

(see also The Searchers)

DAVE BERRY & THE CRUISERS

Berry (along with Joe Cocker) was Sheffield's premier R&B performer, beginning his journey to fame at 18, after quitting his job as a welder to sing professionally in northern working mens' clubs as one half of an Everly Brothers-styled duo.

He chose Berry as his stage name in homage to idol Chuck Berry after being asked to front a local band who'd just secured a residency at Sheffield's Esquire Club, but were in dire need of a singer who knew their repertoire of Chicago blues and soul covers. The group were originally The Chuck Fowler Group, but with Fowler now gone, they were calling themselves The Cruisers, whose line-up included bespectacled guitarist Dave Donovan – one of the first in England to own a double-necked 6 and 12-string Gibson guitar.

The successful Esquire Club residency led to more live work further afield and ultimately to the band's big break when they were spotted by freelance talent scout and recording artist Mickie Most. Most supervised the recording of a demo which was submitted to Decca Records and brokered a deal in 1963. Decca issued a rather lacklustre cover version of Chuck Berry's 'Memphis Tennessee' as Berry and the band's début single and were rewarded with a surprise hit. It broke into the Top 20 at number 19, remarkably only 14 places below the reissued Chuck original.

It was some achievement, but The Cruisers would not benefit. Decca studio boss Mike Smith had deemed Berry's backing band inadequate for future recording work and replaced them with hired session pros like guitarist Jimmy Page and bassist John Paul Jones. Their playing was heard on a pair of pedestrian Elvis and Burt Bacharach cover versions, 'My Baby Left Me' and 'Baby It's You', that reached numbers 37 and 24 respectively but which lacked imagination and subtlety. Ironically, they could have easily been handled by The Cruisers themselves.

Berry was given a Geoff Stephens composition, 'The Crying Game', a tear-jerker ballad (later covered in the Eighties by Boy George) that swept to number five in August '64. A huge Decca press campaign followed and widespread TV exposure introduced Berry to a curious nation that were at once intrigued by his mysterious, somewhat sinister image. He had dyed his hair black and taken to wearing all black outfits, complete with leather gloves and capes. He had also perfected an evil manic stare that he would put to good use while pointing indiscriminately at female members of his audience. After flopping with Bacharach's 'One Heart Between Two', Berry scored his most-remembered and biggest hit (No. 5 in April '65) with a cover of Bobby Goldsboro's US hit, 'Little Things'. However, his biggest success came with a Ray Davies composition not commercially recorded by the Kinks, 'This Strange Effect', which had no effect whatsoever in England but was a number one in both Holland and Belgium where Berry made an award winning appearance at the 1965 Knokke Song Festival. He toured the continent extensively for the rest of the year and established himself as a major star across Europe, despite the fact that his next two singles flopped.

Returning to England at the end of '66 for his third Top Five placing – a cover of another US hit, BJ Thomas' saccharine 'Mama' – it was to be his last UK chart showing. The musical climate in England had changed dramatically by '67 and Berry, like many of his contemporaries, was finding himself looking and sounding like an anachronism. Europe afforded him a couple more years of the good life before he all but disappeared. A new contract with CBS in the Seventies did nothing to revive his profile or fortune, possibly due to the fact that his act had already been pinched, lock, stock, and gloves, by Alvin Stardust. In 1976, the fledgling Sex Pistols covered his punky 'Crying Game' B-side 'Don't Gimme No Lip Child' as 'No Lip' in their live act.

Berry still makes a respectable living on the UK nostalgia circuit and thanks to the Nineties revival of US interest in all things Sixties' British, he recently completed a series of American club dates as well as a 55-date tour of the UK as part of the 'Solid Silver Sixties' show.

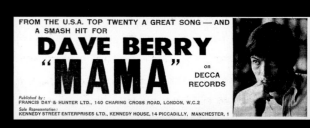

THE PETE BEST FOUR

For two years (between 1960-62) Pete Best was a Beatle, attracting his own rabid female following as the best looking one, which supposedly created jealousy in the ranks. It was always going to be a tough act to follow and the fact he tried at all is to his credit. Ousted in favour of Ringo Starr in the summer of 1962, Best dusted himself down and joined Lee Curtis & The All Stars before forming his own group, The Pete Best All-Stars. In a move where the words 'stable door', 'horse' and 'bolted' come to mind, they were signed by Dick Rowe at Decca in 1964 and re-named The Pete Best Four. Unfortunately their début single 'I'm Gonna Knock On Your Door' was promoted as an ex-Beatles project to a nation which, outside of Liverpool, knew practically nothing of the pre-Ringo Beatles. The single disappeared without trace as did Decca's enthusiasm, plans for a follow up were hastily shelved and tracks already recorded for an album remained in the vaults. Guitar player Wayne Bickerton, bassist Tony Waddington, and Frank Bowen (replaced by Tommy McGurk) had made up The Pete Best Four. Waddington and Bickerton went on to produce, amongst others, The Rubettes, with the latter recently becoming the chairman of the Performing Rights Society.

When his former group started to conquer the world, Best slumped into the depths of depression, eventually attempting suicide. He survived and was granted a second lease of life with the offer of a six-month American tour and an album deal with the American Mr Maestro label. Both were carried out under the new name of The Pete Best Combo, with a blatant cash-in, titled *Best Of The Beatles*.

Alas neither project would put Best back in the spotlight and in 1968 he retired from music and worked for the civil service. Best made news the same year when he successfully sued for libel after Ringo Starr's off the cuff remarks in a 1965 *Playboy* interview. A special guest at Beatles conventions over the intervening years, in 1995, Best finally got a hefty share of some overdue Beatle cash when early tracks featuring his playing were included on The Beatles' *Anthology* 1 multi-million seller.

(see also The Beatles)

THE BIG THREE

The Big Three have been immortalised as John Lennon's favourite contemporaries from the Mersey Beat era. Would they have received a similar seal of approval if they had been called Cass & The Casanovas? We think not.

The Cass in question was singer guitarist Brian Casser, who formed the group in 1959 with bass player Johnny 'Gus' Gustafson, drummer Johnny 'Hutch' Hutchinson and guitarist Adrian Barber. Apparently Cass wasn't the greatest of front men, so his mutinous bandmates disbanded and reformed without him. Casser moved to London and formed the equally pun-tastic Casey Jones & The Engineers who featured future Manfred Mann bassist Tom McGuinness and, for a few gigs, a young Eric Clapton, and later, Casey Jones & The Governors, who found great success in Hamburg, Germany.

Meanwhile, in Liverpool in 1961, the remaining Casanovas became the Hutchinson-led Big Three, who soon established a live reputation as a drum-driven, powerhouse R&B band. A second guitar player, Brian Griffiths (formerly of Howie & The Seniors) was added to the line-up, and while this may have turned The Big Three into a confusing Big Four it didn't stop them enjoying one of the most successful residencies at the Star Club, Hamburg. The group suffered a setback on their return when Barber remained in Germany but at least this made the band name make sense again! In August '62 Hutch sat in with rivals The Beatles for two gigs before Ringo arrived to replace Pete Best. In a further Beatle connection Brian Epstein became The Big Three's manager and Decca Records, swept up in their post-Beatles rejection gaffe, whisked the group off to London where they recorded a début single, a cover of Ritchie Barrett's 'Some Other Guy'. A poor representation of their true live sound, it only managed to reach number 37 in April '63.

Much to the group's anger, they were forced to record a Mitch Murray composition, 'By The Way', as their rush-released second single. Although commercial in a cheerful, Gerry & The Pacemakers way, it was again totally unrepresentative, but peaked higher at 22 in July. The chance to record a live document at the legendary Cavern Club provided an opportunity to capture the trio in all their raw panache. *Live At The Cavern* should have been the release that redressed the problem as to how the group should sound, and would have made a great album but for the unfortunate fact that Decca managed to lose or erase most of the tapes. While the EP eventually reached number six in December, Epstein, always at loggerheads with the group over image, dropped them.

The group moved to another agency but split soon in November '63 over financial disagreements, leaving Hutch to pick up the pieces. He recruited Bill 'Faron' Russley of Faron's Flamingos on

The Big Three

The Pete Best Four

The Pete Best Four

guitar and fellow Flamingo Paddy Chambers on bass. Opting to stick with the live approach, they taped a version of 'You Better Move On' for the *Live At The Cavern* compilation before this line-up also parted company, with Chambers blaming Hutch's hard drinking for the split in February '64. He joined King Size Taylor's remnants The Dominoes before forming Paddy, Klaus & Gibson, with German Beatle pal Klaus Voormann.

Hutchinson, meanwhile, soldered on, pulling yet another Big Three together with ex-Lee Curtis's All Stars bass player Paul Pilnick replacing Chambers. They recorded a cover of Sam Cooke's 'Bring It On Home To Me' (retitled 'If You Ever Change Your Mind') but despite its release coming a full year ahead of The Animals' successful version, it was still not the hit they desperately needed. After this line-up disbanded in October '64, Hutchinson resurfaced with yet another Big Three in September '65 with Roy Marshall (bass) and Barry Womersley (guitar) but, finally realising the writing was on the proverbial Cavern wall, and with no record deal, he broke the band up for good in Feb '66.

Johnny Gustafson joined The Merseybeats and played intermittently with Brian Griffiths as The Johnny Gus Set until Griffiths emigrated to Canada in the early Seventies. Gustafson carved out a successful session career as well as playing with Quatermass and brief spells in Roxy Music and Gillan. Pilnick played with Stealer's Wheel and Deaf School.

Hutchinson disappeared from the music scene altogether to become a builder and was conspicuously absent from the reformed Gustafson/Griffiths Big Three line-up in 1973, when Elton John's drummer, Nigel Olsson, sat at the back. At least he avoided being involved with one last Big Three disappointment: the album they recorded, *Resurrection*, bombed as well.

(see also Cilla Black, Faron's Flamingoes)

THE BIRDS

History has been unkind to The Birds, now chiefly remembered for being Ron Wood's first band and for the publicity that surrounded their Birds verses Byrds legal action and confrontation at London Airport in August 1965.

The West Drayton modsters slapped no fewer than seven writs on their visiting American counterparts, claiming that the US Byrds had no right to use the name. After all, the American version had been together for only a year, reaching number one with 'Mr Tambourine Man', had a hysterical girl following and knew Bob Dylan. The UK Birds, meanwhile, had slogged it out in an old Commer van for four years, living on egg and chips, released a minor hit, 'Leaving Here', and knew Bo Diddley. The writs made not a blind bit of difference to the Americans' tour and both bands henceforth kept a respectful distance.

The Birds recorded three 1964-65 Decca singles ('You're On My Mind', 'Leaving Here', 'No Good Without You, Baby') – each sublime,

definitive examples of tough, raw Brit R&B. The US Byrds stuck to their name and popularity, resulting in the English Birds changing their name to the even more confusing 'Birds Birds', winding up on Robert Stigwood's Reaction label in 1966 where their début single, a cover of the Who's 'Run Run Run', was scrapped due to contractual wrangles.

A superior cover of US group The McCoys' 'Say Those Magic Words' finally emerged, but the recess meant the group lost momentum and saw their following tail off. The same year, they appeared in a forgettable B-movie, *The Deadly Bees*, seen miming in a television studio to another unissued single, 'That's All I Need From You'. Long periods of inactivity and lack of recognition eventually brought about their disintegration in early 1967. Bass player Kim Gardner joined The Creation, where he was joined briefly by Ron Wood in 1968, during the latter's brief period out of The Jeff Beck Group. After returning to Beck's group for a final spell, 'Woody' and Beck vocalist Rod Stewart formed The Faces with the remnants of The Small Faces in 1969, and Wood officially became a Rolling Stone in 1976.

Of the other Birds, only Kim Gardner went on to make a name for himself. Following stints with Ashton, Gardner & Dyke, and pub rockers Badger in the early Seventies, he relocated to Los Angeles, opening and running Sunset Boulevard's most famous ex-pats hostelry The Cat & Fiddle, until his death from cancer in 2001. In a simple twist of fate, Ron Wood eventually did became mates with Byrds pal Bob Dylan, playing alongside him with fellow Stone Keith Richard in a memorably shambolic set at the climax of Live Aid in 1985.

(see also Jeff Beck, The Creation)

The Birds

CILLA BLACK

Cilla, nowadays one of the highest-paid stars on UK TV, was born Priscilla White in Liverpool. She studied at Anfield Commercial College, and was spotted in the Cavern Club in Mathew Street, where she worked in the cloakroom, as well as performing the occasional singing spot backed by The Big Three. It was during a Beatles concert in Southport in 1963, that she made her first professional singing appearance, substituting for The Fourmost. She was encouraged by John Lennon, who renamed her Cilla Black, and Beatles manager Brian Epstein signed her to his NEMS Enterprises stable of stars.

The Birds

Cilla's first minor chart success came in November 1963 when the Lennon/McCartney-penned 'Love Of The Loved' reached number 35. However, in February '64 she reached number one with 'Anyone Who Had A Heart', which sold 100,000 copies in one day, incurring the wrath of Dionne Warwick, who's original Cilla's cover trampled over. This success was followed three months later by an English translation of an Italian song 'You're My World' (another number one in May). Her fourth single, another Lennon-McCartney giveaway, 'It's For You', deserved better than its number seven chart placing in August, while her cover of 'You've Lost That Lovin' Feelin'' gave The Righteous Brothers' original a run for its money, not helped by Andrew Oldham (on behalf of The Rolling Stones) taking out an ad in the *New Musical Express* urging punters to buy the original. (Her version eventually reached number two in January '65).

Cilla complemented her chart successes with an appearance at the 1964 Royal Variety Performance, along with ritzy cabaret work on both sides of the Atlantic. In 1966, she sang the memorable theme tune to *Alfie*, written and conducted by Burt Bacharach. Her big screen début occurred in 1967 with her only film *Work... Is A Four Letter Word*. A year later, BBC Television rewarded her success with her own music series, titled simply *Cilla*. The theme tune, 'Step Inside Love', was written by her old Beatle pal Paul McCartney, which reached number eight in March '68. Cilla continued to score sporadic chart hits, such as 'Surround Yourself With Sorrow' (1969) 'Conversations' (1969) and 'Something Tells Me (Something's Gonna Happen Tonight)' (1971) into the Seventies and is now a mainstay of light entertainment television in Britain.

BLOSSOM TOES

The nucleus of Blossom Toes and their previous configurations, The Grave Diggers and The Ingoes, were guitarist Brian Godding and bass player Brian Belshaw, two scientific instrument makers from Highbury, Islington. As Ingoes members in 1966, the duo had persuaded Yardbirds manager Giorgio Gomelsky to take the band under his wing and on to a Yardbirds support tour of France. By all accounts the group, who also included guitar player Jim Cregan and drummer Kevin Westlake, were a competent and respected R&B unit. By 1967, however, they were called Blossom Toes and were living together, Monkees-style, in a house in Fulham, with The Action living next door. Their début album *We Are Ever So Clean* launched Gomelsky's Marmalade label and the group's individual members all had Teddy Bear names. Godding, or 'Little Brian', was now known as Wellington; Belshaw, or Big Brian was 'Scarlet'; Cregan was 'Bartholomew'; and Westlake was 'Plod'. It was all a tad twee and camp, even by 1967 standards. It was also a problem that manifested itself in much of the group's repertoire, especially on songs like 'Mrs Murphy's Budgerigar', 'I'll Be Late For Me' and 'Telegram Tuesday', all of which sounded naive and childish as opposed to psychedelic. The heavily orchestrated numbers were also impossible to reproduce live, so on stage the group had to rely mainly on covers.

A second album, *If Only For A Moment* (1969), marked the departure of Westlake, who was replaced by John 'Poli' Palmer (and in turn by Barry Reeves) and a return to a more basic rock format. However, the damage had been done and the group curled up its toes soon after. Godding and Belshaw regrouped with Westlake as B.B. Blunder with Action vocalist Reg King, while Cregan joined Family, Cockney Rebel and eventually Rod Stewart's post-Faces backing band.

(see also The Action, Family)

Blues By Five

BLUES BY FIVE

An obscure London-based group, not to be confused with another early Sixties group of the same name who featured original Rolling Stones Brian Knight and Charlie Watts among their ranks. Blues By Five's lone 1964 release was a cover of John Lee Hooker 'Boom Boom'. And yes they were on Decca...

BLUESOLOGY

Bluesology are a favourite with trivia gatherers for nurturing a future megastar, Pinner pianist Reginald Dwight aka Elton John. The nine-strong group, led by vocalist Stuart Brown, Freddie Creasey (bass), David Murphey (sax), Chris Bateson (trumpet) and Paul Gale (drums) actually had a fairly good innings forming in 1964 and lasting until 1969.

As well as playing their own gigs, they backed such visiting American R&B artistes as Billy Stewart, Patti Labelle & The Blue Bells, Major Lance, The Drifters, and Doris Troy. Two Fontana 45s, 'Come Back Baby' (1965) and 'Mister Frantic' (1966), and a Polydor single, 'Since I Found You Baby' (1967) credited to 'Stu Brown & Bluesology' – appeared but no one noticed. Now, of course, thanks to the Elton connection they are highly sought-after. In 1967, Long John Baldry hired the hapless outfit to back him on his chosen MOR path into cabaret. Elton John quit *Bluesoloogy* for a solo career in 1968, and went on to wear tiaras and make an advert for the Post Office.

(see also Long John Baldry)

THE BO STREET RUNNERS

This legendary Mod five piece from Harrow left the starting blocks at a lively pace by winning the first ever televised edition of *Ready, Steady, Go!'s* 'Ready, Steady, Win!' R&B contest, pipping rivals The Birds at the post. Their prize was an unprecedented £1,000 worth of equipment and a Decca recording contract. They were introduced as John Dominic (vocals), Gary Thomas (guitar), Royston Fry (keyboards), Dave Cameron (bass), and Nigel Hutchinson (drums). They all looked chuffed to bits and announced they were ready to chuck in their day jobs, turn professional and embark on a life of pop stardom. 'Bo Street Runner' from their self-financed Oak Records EP, which originally secured the Runners their *Ready, Steady, Go!* audition, was hastily re-recorded and issued as the group's début single, but when it failed to race up the charts despite the media glare, Decca quietly dropped them.

Hutchinson and Fry were rather unsportingly sacked and replaced by Glyn Thomas and Tim Hinkley respectively. The group also hired an extra member, Dave Quincy, on sax. Two further singles, 'Tell Me What You're Gonna Do' (a James Brown cover) and 'Baby Never Say Goodbye', followed in quick succession, issued by the more charitable Columbia in 1965, but as bad luck would have it the latter was in chart competition with Unit Four Plus Two's version. Next to make a sprint for it was Thomas, replaced by Mick Fleetwood, who took the drum stool in time for an opportunistic cover version of The Beatles' 'Drive My Car' (off *Rubber Soul*). With a surfeit of cover versions from the album floating around the charts' nether regions, the single got lost in the shuffle.

Patto stuck with Hinkley and formed the Chicago Line Blues Band which later evolved into Timebox and Patto, while Mick Fleetwood went on to play at US president Bill Clinton's inaugural ball, amongst other things.

(see also The Cheynes, Fleetwood Mac, The Peter B's, Shotgun Express)

Bo Street Runners

MARC BOLAN

The 'national elf' from Stoke Newington began his auspicious career modelling Mod threads for a fashion spread in *Town* magazine in 1962, under his real name of Mark Feld. As a face about town, he insinuated himself enough to secure a one-off Decca recording option, releasing a single, 'The Wizard', in 1965, which promptly went nowhere. Despite (or maybe because of) an irrefutable belief in his own talents, Bolan (like his contemporary, David Bowie)

Marc Bolan

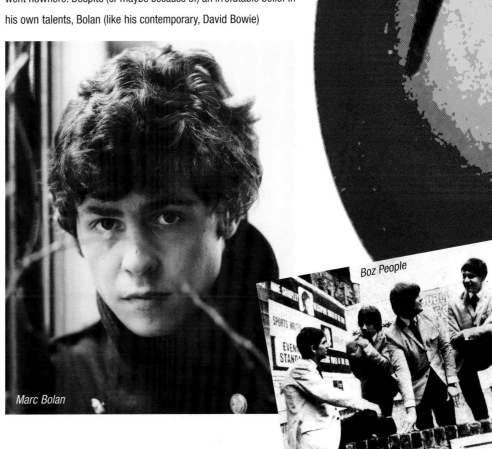

Boz People

19232

19236

19240

19233

19237

19241

19234

19238

19242

19235

19239

19243

continued to languish in obscurity. Two other singles from the period, 'The Third Degree' (Decca '66) and 'Hippy Gumbo' (Parlophone '66) are now worth a king's ransom. After a spell in Simon Napier-Bell's Mod shamsters, John's Children in 1967, he formed a hippy acoustic duo, Tyrannosaurus Rex, with percussionist Steve Peregrine Took, recording five singles ('Debora', 'One Inch Rock', Pewter Suitor', 'King Of The Rumbling Spires', 'By The Light Of A Magical Wood') and four albums (*My People Were Fair…*, *Prophets, Seers And Sages…*, *Unicorn*, *A Beard Of Stars*) for Regal Zonophone, which took him through to 1970 and the formation of T. Rex and superstardom. He died two weeks shy of his 30th birthday in a car accident on Barnes Common, London on September 16, 1977.

(see also John's Children)

of an innovator, being the first British musician to use the Hammond organ/Leslie speaker combination. He also built his own electric piano and was the first UK musician to use a Mellotron, which he demonstrated to a wide-eyed Cathy McGowan on TV's *Ready, Steady, Go!* in 1965.

Bond left Korner after only a year, taking the rhythm section of drummer Ginger Baker and bass player Jack Bruce with him. He cheekily set up The Graham Bond Trio (soon to be quartet) with the addition of guitar player John McLaughlin, in stiff competition with Korner. It was seen by most as a calculated act and one which typified Bond's somewhat antagonistic and bullish behaviour, characteristics that would eventually blight his entire career. McLaughlin left at the end of 1963 and was replaced by sax player Dick Heckstall-Smith, another veteran of Blues Incorporated.

The Graham Bond Organisation

THE GRAHAM BOND ORGANISATION

Organist Graham Bond, a widely recognised catalyst of the British R&B scene, is among scores of influential artists who never enjoyed a hit record. A purist of the highest order, commercial success wasn't exactly high on his list of priorities. Bond began his career not as an organist but as alto sax player with a jazz outfit, The Don Rendell Quintet, switching to organ in 1962 when he joined Alexis Korner's Blues Incorporated. As well as his obvious proficiency on keyboards, Bond also made a later name for himself as something

Another slight name change followed, this time to The Graham Bond Organisation, who made two highly impressive but commercially dismal albums, *The Sound Of '65* and *There's A Bond Between Us*. Both were a mixture of original material and interpretations of tracks like 'Wade In The Water' and the old chestnut 'Got My Mojo Working'. Columbia also forced the band to record such unrepresentative material as 'Tammy' (a version of the Debbie Reynolds hit) as singles, much to their chagrin. Despite being a formidable rhythm section Bruce and Baker were constantly at each others' throats, resulting in the latter sacking the former in

33

1965. Bruce joined John Mayall's Bluesbreakers, and the hit parading Manfred Mann, while the Graham Bond Organization limped on for several more months before Eric Clapton approached Baker about forming a new power trio Cream with his old nemesis Bruce.

Bond once more faced rebuilding his band almost from scratch. Jon Hiseman briefly occupied the drum stool but was soon gone, taking Heckstall-Smith with him to form Colosseum in 1968. (The band later covered Bond's composition, 'Walking In The Park' on their first album.) Bond disbanded his already-disbanded band, declared his disenchantment with the UK music scene and decamped to the US, vowing never to return. He also turned his back on his beloved jazz and R&B and made two progressive albums in 1968 for the American Pulsar label, *Mighty Graham Bond* and *Love Is The Law*, neither of which fared any better than his previous two efforts.

The label dropped him leaving a disheartened Bond no alternative but to return to the UK. Defiantly, he formed another band, this time The Graham Bond Initiation, which saw the inauguration of Bond's wife Diane Stewart. However, a poorly attended homecoming gig at the Royal Albert Hall put paid to any future plans and set Bond off on a downward spiral of drink and drugs. Next up came an ill-advised reunion with Ginger Baker, fresh (but not entirely happy) from the break up of Blind Faith, in Ginger Baker's Airforce, which flew only briefly in 1970. Then came a spell with The Jack Bruce Band, but this also dissolved acrimoniously, leaving Bond to step up his drink and drugs dependency, fuelling an already lethal depression, which led to the first signs of mental illness.

This manifested itself when Bond sidelined any immediate musical projects and announced he would now concentrate on his latest obsession, the study of black magic and the occult. He did manage one final musical interlude, a partnership with Cream songsmith, Pete Brown, which produced another failure of an album, *Two Heads Are Better Than One* in 1972. A complete nervous breakdown followed. By now, Bond was deep in debt, his marriage on the rocks and two further projects doomed. All of this undoubtedly led to his gruesome and premature death in 1974, aged 37, under the wheels of a tube train at Finsbury Park station.

(see also Cream, Alexis Korner's Blues Incorporated, Manfred Mann)

THE BOSTON CRABS

It was three falls and a submission for Cambridge's Boston Crabs. They had three mid-Sixties singles issued on Columbia, 'Down In Mexico', 'As Long As I Have You' and a cover of The Lovin Spoonful's 'You Didn't Have To Be So Nice', all of which failed to go the distance. Their best shot came via a worthy cover of the old blues standard 'Gin House' (also covered by Amen Corner) but this was hidden away on the flip side of the group's final single and thus

The Boston Crabs

missed the boat. For the record the Crabs were Fred Driedlin (vocals & guitar), Ian Jacks (guitar), Geoff Mott (guitar), Simon Jones (bass) and Alan Taylor (drums).

THE BOSTON DEXTERS

Edinburgh's Boston Dexters dressed up like Chicago gangsters, presumably to emphasise their love of Chicago blues. But that just raises the question of why not The Chicago Dexters? Whatever! The Dexters recorded three self-financed limited edition singles for their own Contemporary Records in 1964, which in turn resulted in an audition and a contract with Columbia in 1965. From that point on the group's R&B influences were sidelined in favour of mainstream pop, and after two singles, 'I've Got Something To Tell You' and 'Try Hard' the band was back in Edinburgh, blaming EMI's inappropriate choice of material for their failure, loss of audience, and their ultimate break up.

Guitar player Johnny Turnbull and singer Tam White formed The Buzz in 1966, while drummer Toto McNaughton and bass player Alan Coventry soldiered on for several months with a new line-up and without the gangster get ups. Which was a shame really because the whole country was just about to be swept up in a gangster chic frenzy following the massive success of the 1967 film *Bonnie And Clyde*.

(see also The Buzz)

DAVID BOWIE

Mod Mutation, Space Cadet, Glam Rock Chameleon, Thin White Duke, Punk Pioneer, New Romantic Godfather, Electronic Evangelist, and... well, the list is apparently endless, isn't it? One description is certainly apt though... a tryer.

A tryer who began his own personal musical 'oddity' in 1962 as David Jay, a sax player with the Peter Jay & The Jaywalkers-inspired

David Bowie

The King Bees

combo, The Konrads. Then came the short-lived Hooker Brothers before a succession of slightly lengthier projects – The King Bees, named after a Slim Harpo song, The Manish Boys, in homage to Muddy Waters, and The Lower Third – named after nothing of any importance as far as I know.

Jones released a series of unsuccessful singles with all three outfits from '64 to '66 on Decca, Parlophone and, eventually, Pye. In 1966, he changed his name in anticipation of the success of newcomer and namesake Davy Jones, the miniature Mancunian maracas shaker in the manufactured Monkees. He hit on David Bowie, apparently due to his fondness for the American hunting knife made famous by Kentucky fighting-man-of-action Jim Bowie, who died in the legendary battle at the Alamo – or so Richard Widmark would have us believe.

True to form he then assembled David Bowie & The Buzz, releasing two near-miss singles (with an uncredited Buzz) before going legitimately solo.

Through manager Kenneth Pitt, he re-signed to Decca via subsidiary outlet Deram. After starting off well with the cautionary Mod tale, 'The London Boys' (released December '66) he almost destroyed any credibility he had by releasing 'The Laughing Gnome' (April '67) – a thoroughly, hammed-up slice of music hall that Bowie sauntered through in his best 'cockernee' accent, cocking a snook at his London Mod contemporaries' power chord anthems and early forays into psychedelia.

In June a self-titled début album appeared, heavily influenced by Anthony Newley; the sleevenotes for which claimed that Bowie was already at least two years ahead of his time. However, being too early can be as disastrous as being too late and after a further flop with 'Love You Till Tuesday' (July '67) Bowie was left without a label. A few transformations later and he was back in 1969 on Philips, seemingly prophesying the failure of the upcoming Apollo 11 moon shot with a Top Five hit 'Space Oddity', a haunting ode to astronaut Major Tom who, at the song's finale, is left adrift in space. In his subsequent career Bowie has continued to be always ahead of the game with each re-evaluation and re-emergence, establishing a trademark of transfiguration that keeps his audience guessing almost forty years later. He's not short of a bob or two either.

(see also The Beatstalkers)

David Bowie & The Buzz

23529

23530

23531

23532

THE ALAN BOWN

CHRISTMAS to of the Better Groups of 1966 and the BEST GROUP OF 1967 THE ALAN BOWN SET from their Manager Richard Cowley UNIVERSAL ATTRACTIONS LTD.

Elkie Brooks & The Artwoods

the DERAM explosion!

THE ALAN BOWN! l as stone DM 259 ning new single—produced by Mike Hurst DERAM

THE ALAN BOWN SET

The Alan Bown Set are another of those outfits better known for the musicians who passed through their ranks than for their recorded output. Formed in 1965 by the trumpet playing Bown, formerly of The John Barry Seven, The Alan Bown Set were a long-standing soul revue that made their name as one of London's top live draws. This, however, was never reflected in any chart success. As well as Bown, the septet featured Tony Catchpole (guitar), John Goodsall (sax), Geoff Bannister (keyboards), Stan Haldane (bass), Vic Sweeny (drums) and Jess Roden (vocals).

Signed to Pye they released five singles including 'Emergency 999', now a Mod soul favourite and appeared on the showcase album *London Swings Live At The Marquee* with Jimmy James & The Vagabonds. Signing to MGM the group had a 1967 near miss with the single 'Toyland' but nothing else came close. As the decade wore on the group abandoned soul music and pursued a progressive route more suited to their singer's vocal abilities.

They dropped the Set from the title and became The Alan Bown!, recording for Deram in 1968. The band's biggest weakness lay in their inability to maintain a constant line-up or settle on a musical style – a problem that persisted right up until their eventual split in 1974. Roden left to form Bronco in 1970 and was replaced by Robert Palmer from CBS act Mandrake Paddlesteamer. Roden's next venture was The Butts Band (with ex-Doors Robbie Krieger and Jim Densmore) before a solo career beckoned. A saxophonist from the latterday Alan Bown! line-up John Anthony changed his surname to Helliwell and joined Supertramp. Bown worked as an A&R man for CBS Records, while Palmer went on to a successful career with Dada, Vinegar Joe and eventually solo.

THE BOYS

This Mod group from North London recorded a one-off 45, 'It Ain't Fair' for Pye Records and backed singer Sandra Barry on her one-off Decca 45, 'Really Gonna Shake'. Both sank without trace in 1964. A support slot to The Who at the Marquee lead to their own residency at this legendary central London club where their act of obscure soul and Motown covers was honed to perfection as The Action.

(see also The Action)

THE BRAIN

Bournemouth's Brain (better title) was a totally obscure project put together by the Giles brothers, Mike and Pete, and their guitarist pal Robert Fripp. Both brothers had been in Trendsetters Limited while Fripp had been in The League of Gentlemen. The trio recorded a solitary single for Parlophone, 'Nightmares In Red' in 1967 before going under their surnames as Giles, Giles & Fripp; recording two singles and an album for Deram in 1968.

Former Fairport Convention singer Judy Dyble came as part of the package for a short while before joining Trader Horne. Pete Sinfield joined as lyricist in time for the album *The Cheerful Insanity Of* which contained narrated stories such as 'The Saga Of Rodney Toady' and 'Just George'. It was all meant to be ever so trippy and funny in a Syd Barrett sort of way but ended up sounding self-indulgent, and amateurish. Not surprisingly it hardly sold, leaving a bitter aftertaste for Peter Giles who retired from the music business while Mike and Fripp formed King Crimson. Fripp is now better known for being one half of a celebrity couple; his wife being *Teletubbies* announcer Toyah.

ELKIE BROOKS

Thoughout the Sixties Elkie Brooks seemed to be cast in the demure shadow of Merseybeat songstresses such as Cilla Black and Beryl Marsden, but in actuality was rather more like Dusty Springfield with apochryphal offstage tales of hell-raising. The sister of Dakotas' drummer Mike Maxfield, Elkie was born Elaine Bookbinder (no really!) in Manchester, but unfortunately never enjoyed the same level of success as her contemporaries as single after single (mostly cover versions of the likes of Barbara Lewis and The Temptations) flopped. However Elkie's fortunes changed at the start of the Seventies, when she underwent a complete image and musical makeover, re-emerging as the raunchy rock chick that fronted 12-piece jazz-rock act, Dada and later, Vinegar Joe, with co-vocalist Robert Palmer and guitarist Pete Gage.

Elkie Brooks

DISC'S LP OF THE MONTH

The Crazy World of Arthur Brown

612 005   613 005
Mono   Stereo

TRACK RECORD

YOU LOOK
GOOD TOGETHER
recorded on Decca F 22568
by
THE BATS
Palace Music Co. Ltd.,
9 Albert Embankment, London SE1 Reliance
Sole Selling Agents: Southern Music

the crazy world of
ARTHUR BROWN

...put a spell on you

RECORD
MIRROR

Arthur Brown

The Batchelors

Arthur Brown was born plain Arthur Wilton in Whitby, Yorkshire but changed his name to the far more flamboyant Brown while studying philosophy at Reading University in 1965. It was here that he decided to pursue a career in music and formed his first student band, Blues And Brown, making his recording début with a self-financed University Rag Week flexi-disc credited to Arthur Brown & The Diamonds. This unbelievably rare artefact is now much sought after, as are the two tracks Brown recorded in Paris in 1966 as The Arthur Brown Set for French film director Roger Vadim's art flick *La Curee*. 'Baby You Know What You're Doing' and 'Don't Tell Me', were released on the French EP and American album versions of the soundtrack, housed in sleeves featuring a nude Jane Fonda – a crafty selling ploy in '66 if ever there was one!

Brown left university the same year and formed the first Crazy World Of Arthur Brown with fellow Reading student Vincent Crane on keyboards, Drachen Theaker (drums), and bass player Nick Greenwood. Their first official single, 'Devils Grip', released on Track Records and produced by Kit Lambert, slipped out unheralded and unnoticed at the end of 1967 but its 1968 follow up most certainly didn't. 'Fire' was a massive international hit that went straight to the top spot in the UK in June and to number two in the US, turning the group into a (relatively speaking) worldwide, overnight sensation before they'd even made a name for themselves. In order to maximise the overwhelming impact of 'Fire', Brown understandably wanted a bigger image for himself, one that would quite literally fire people's imaginations. He adopted the guise of a manic, almost satanic high priest with flames painted on his chest and face, fluorescent robes, and what looked like a small coal fire actually burning on his head. All of this brought him instant notoriety and a fanatical audience on the London underground club scene.

An album followed, titled simply *The Crazy World Of Arthur Brown*, which thanks to the inclusion of mostly familiar stage favourites sold well (despite the group's qualms with Lambert's production) and paved the way for their first US tour. It would also prove to be their last as mid-way though the trek both Theaker and Crane left and the band temporarily imploded. Crane did eventually return to the fold but Theaker was replaced by former Chris Farlowe & The Thunderbirds drummer Carl Palmer.

The flop follow-up to 'Fire', 'Nightmare', released in November, proved to be just that for Brown when Crane quit again, taking Palmer with him to form Atomic Rooster. Brown moved to a musical commune in Puddletown, Dorset, where he made an album of experimental music called *Strangelands*, but was unable to find the album a home label wise, and it remained unissued until 1988. Another group project followed, the theatrical rock outfit Kingdom Come, who recorded three albums for Polydor before disbanding in 1974, after which Brown resumed an erratic solo career. He made a memorable cameo appearance as the Priest in Ken Russell's film version of The Who's *Tommy* (1975) and briefly reunited with Crane on their reconciliation album project *Chisholm In My Bosom* on the Gull label in 1978.

Brown announced his semi-retirement from the music business in the Eighties and moved to the music capital of Texas: Austin. There he could continue to play small club dates along the city's famous Sixth Street and still concentrate on a house painting company he'd set up with former Mothers Of Invention drummer Jimmy Carl Black. Brown returned to England in 1997 and, fire restrictions permitting, continues to gig sporadically. Palmer became one third of Seventies prog rock behemoth Emerson, Lake & Palmer. Sadly Theacker drifted in and out of mental hospitals while Crane sadly passed away in 1989.

The Brumbeats

THE BRUMBEATS

It's thought there were in fact two Birmingham beat bands trading under the same name The Brumbeats. However there is very little evidence to substantiate this. What's likely, given that Birmingham was a relatively small city in the Sixties, is that they were one and the same. They possibly went through different line-ups but this is also unclear. What is known is that eventual Locomotive guitar player Norman Haines was a member and was certainly on board when the group signed a one off single deal with Decca and released 'Cry Little Girl, Cry' in 1964.

THE BUNCH OF FIVES

The first in a long line of one-off ventures created by drummer Viv Prince following his departure from The Pretty Things. This particular collaboration with ex-Hullaballoos guitar player Mick Wayne produced the Parlophone single 'Go Home Baby' in 1966. The band, like most of Prince's endeavours, disappeared directly after.

(see also The Hullabaloos, The Pretty Things)

ERIC BURDON & THE (NEW) ANIMALS

Following the demise of the original Animals in September 1966, Eric Burdon remained in New York, cutting an American-only album with various session musicians, entitled *Eric Is Here* (released March '67). Containing tracks from the songbooks of several contemporary composers, the album was only partially successful but included Randy Newman's 'Mama Told Me Not To Come' and a Scott English composition, 'Help Me Girl' (also recorded by US group The Outsiders) which peaked at number 14 when released as a single in October.

Burdon returned to England, retaining latterday Animals drummer Barry Jenkins for his next venture – a freewheeling, open-minded five-piece who would embrace the changing air as pop moved closer towards psychedelia. The New Animals consisted of ex-Steam Packet guitarist Vic Briggs, John Weider – guitar/violin, and Danny McCulloch – bass.

Ironically young Kent musician Noel Redding, who arrived to audition for the already-taken guitarist role, ended up playing bass in a new trio Burdon's ex-Animal compatriot Chas Chandler was assembling around an American guitarist named Jimi Hendrix.

Having fulfilled Burdon's contract with Decca The New Animals signed to MGM and the group's début single was a powerful Burdon original, the bittersweet 'When I Was Young', featuring Weider's viola to the fore. It reached number 15 in the US in April '67 but only a disappointing 45 in the UK.

The group toured the world and ended up at the Monterey International Pop Festival in June, playing a radically re-arranged version of the Stones' 'Paint It Black' and their next single, a gentle paean to the city where the nights were warm. Released in July, the pleasantly dippy 'San Franciscan Nights' provided the group with a Top 10 hit (nine – US; seven in the UK) in August.

It's US b-side the reflective 'Good Times' was hived off to create a seperate single in England (number 20 in September). While Burdon's singles embraced the hippie ethos of the time without straying too far into the cosmos, his albums such as *Winds Of Change* (1967) and *The Twain Shall Meet* (1968) were a different kettle of LSD. Both were insufferably pretentious in their propensity to sound hip and contemporary. Songs such as 'Winds Of Change', 'The Black Plague', 'Man-Woman', 'All Is One', 'Orange And Red Beams' sounded horribly contrived once the drugs wore off. *Winds Of Change* however contained a beautiful heartfelt ballad 'Anything' that was released as an American single while *The Twain...* spawned

Eric Burdon

'Monterey', an infectious horn-driven belter, with sitar touches, recounting Burdon's experiences at the legendary festival.

'Sky Pilot', a powerful anti-war epic spread over two sides of a single, was the group's last brush with the charts in February '68 and a US-only album *Every One Of Us* appeared mid-year when personnel changes occurred. Weider left and Andy Summers (ex-oot Money's Big Roll Band, Dantalion's Chariot) joined. The group continued to concentrate their attentions on America where they were disproportionately more popular than in England. By the end of the year the group had expanded to accommodate Zoot Money on keyboards. The New Animals recorded one last album *Love Is* (released as a double in the US in December) from which a cover of 'River Deep, Mountain High' was taken as a single – before the group imploded. Burdon remained in Los Angeles, fronting the six-piece, all-black funk ensemble War, scoring a fondly remembered hit 'Spill The Wine' in 1971. The victim of many a notorious music business manoeuvre Burdon stoically continues to gig around the globe with his own group. His autobiography I Used To Be An Animal, But I'm All Right Now was published in 1986.

(see also The Animals, Dantalion's Chariot, Family, Zoot Money's Big-Roll Band).

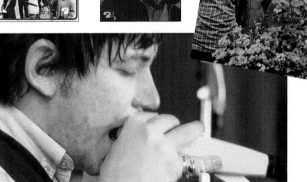

THE BUZZ

Despite EMI's mishandling of The Boston Dexters it didn't stop their guitar player, Johnny Turnbull, and singer, Tam White, returning to the label with a new group Buzz, with Brian Henderson (bass) and Mike Travis (drums) completing the Scottish four piece. It wasn't the company's longest running relationship, just one single to be exact, 'You're Holding Me Down', due to a notable production job by Joe Meek. Buzz are not to be confused with David Bowie's Pye-era backing band The Buzz. *(see also The Boston Dexters)*

Sky pilot
by
eric
burdon
and
the
animals

MGM
1373

CARTER-LEWIS & THE SOUTHERNERS

An early Sixties outfit, formed in 1961 and fronted by Birmingam vocalists-songwriters John Carter and Ken Lewis. The two had written hits for Mike Sarne ('Will I What', 1962) and The Marauders ('That's What I Want', 1963) and had a near miss the same year with their own 'Your Momma's Out Of Town' on Oriole. At one point, The Southerners featured young guitarist Jimmy Page and future Pretty Thing, Viv Prince. In 1964 Carter and Lewis joined up with session singer-pianist Perry Ford to form vocal trio The Ivy League.

(see also The Ivy League, The Pretty Things, The Yardbirds)

THE CASUALS

The Casuals enjoyed a long career, so to be remembered as one hit wonders seems a little unfair. This Lincoln group formed in 1961, and comprised Howard Newcombe (guitar, trumpet and vocals), Alan Taylor (bass), Johnny Tebb (keyboards) and Robert O'Brien (drums). They signed to Fontana Records in 1965, releasing one single, 'If You Walk Out' but spent most of their time touring the continent, concentrating mainly on Italy where they scored with several Italian language 45s.

A change of label to Decca in 1968 finally brought the group some homegrown exposure when they followed one more Italian release 'Adios Amor' with the single 'Jesamine', a beautiful slice of pure Sixties pop that rewarded the group with a well-deserved number two placing in October '68. It didn't, however, set a pattern; the follow-up, 'Toy', just edged into the Top 30, and each subsequent release: five singles and an album, *Hour World*, failed to even chart. Uncharacteristically, Decca stuck it out with the band for three years before eventually dropping them in 1971. Parlophone picked them up the following year but 'Tara Tiger Girl' continued the group's run of stiff's and signalled yet another label change in '74. The Casuals' last effort, 'Witch', appeared on the small Dawn label and did equally small business, forcing the band to call it quits in 1975, seven years after their brief spell in the limelight, and fourteen years after their formation.

CHAD & JEREMY

Chad Stuart and Jeremy Clyde were two ex-public school boys and drama students who met while studying at the London Central School of Speech & Drama. Inspired by a shared love of music they formed a singer/guitarist duo in the Simon & Garfunkel mould with Chad supplying the music to Jeremy's lyrics. They recorded a run of self penned folkie singles and albums for the Ember label between 1963 and 1966, including the minor hit 'Yesterdays Gone' in 1964 before capitalising on their quintessential English charm and moving to the US. The pair enjoyed four Top 30 singles stateside, plus massive TV and radio exposure which included the career high of a cameo role on the top-rated *Batman* TV show, playing, rather

unsurprisingly, an English pop duo. Chad also made records with his wife, Jill, and the two appeared together on such shows as *Shindig!* and *Hullabaloo*.

A badly-conceived concept album entitled *Of Cabbages And Kings*, which showcased a clumsy change in musical style, was released in 1967. Chad and Jeremy replaced their tried and tested brand of folk-influenced pop with psychedelic pretensions. This out of character disaster predictably flopped and effectively brought their recording career to a premature close.

Luckily the pair still had their acting skills to fall back on, and Clyde began making regular appearances on *Rowan And Martin's Laugh In* before landing the lead in *Sexton Blake*. He has forged a successful thespian career ever since. Stuart opted for the other side of the camera and took up writing and directing.

THE CHANCES ARE

Little is known of The Chances Are, except that their lone 1967 Columbia release was a mod-ified version of an obscure American single, 'Fragile Child' by The Golliwogs - later better known as Creedence Clearwater Revival.

The Chances Are

Carter-Lewis & The Southerners

The Casuals

Caravan

HERE IT IS! Their Great Follow-Up to YESTERDAY'S GONE
CHAD STUART & JEREMY CLYDE
LIKE I LOVE YOU TODAY

JEREMY CLYDE
I LOVE MY LOVE*
c/w Anytime 201823

HOUR WORLD
THE CASUALS

DECCA

The Chasers

THE CHASERS

The pride of Romford, The Chasers were a popular club act with a somewhat jazzy stage sound, but despite regular work in the south and the occasional foray to the continent, they never had success on record. The combos opening gambit, a raucous cover of Dee Clarks 'Hey Little Girl' produced by Chris Andrews for Decca in 1964, was probably their best recording. In 1966 they acquired a lead vocalist in Roger Pincott, and sporting a mod image signed to Parlophone for one single, 'Inspiration'. Pincott was subsequently replaced by Bobby Rio from the Revelles, and the group managed one further release, this time for Philips. Didn't they look smart though? Incidentally Len Tuckey was later in the Suzi Quatro Band and coincidentally became Mr Quatro for a time.

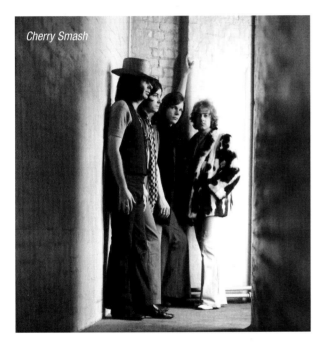
Cherry Smash

CHERRY SMASH

The Hampshire-based Cherry Smash made three singles between 1967 and 1969, the best of which was their first on Track Records, 'Sing Songs Of Love', written by Manfred Mann's Mike Hugg, which also featured in the classic 1968 film and soundtrack *Up The Junction*. The Smash's guitarist Bryan Sebastian was Hugg's brother. Previously, the siblings had collaborated on writing The Yardbirds' social commentary B-side, 'Mr. You're A Better Man Than I'. The Smash never did much, although their final Decca single, 'Fade Away Maureen' is another pop jewel, heavy on the harmony vocals.

(see also Manfred Mann)

THE CHEYNES

Formed in London in 1963, The Cheynes original line-up consisted Roger Peacock (vocals), Peter Bardens (organ/vocals), Eddie Lynch (lead guitar), Peter Hollis (bass) and Mick Fleetwood (drums). Lynch was replaced by Phil Sawyer in time for the group to make their début recording for Columbia, a cover of The Isley Brothers'

'Respectable'. Despite gaining a name as being one of the more robust R&B acts on the scene from numerous appearances at the Marquee and the like, the group couldn't translate it into record success. Two further singles 'Goin' To The River' ('64) and the Bill Wyman-produced 'Down And Out' (released January '65) failed to sell and the group split in April '65. Peacock joined The Mark Leeman Five, Sawyer joined (Les) Fleur de Lys and Bardens joined Them for a short spell before reuniting with Fleetwood in The Peter B's.

(see also (Les) Fleur de Lys, Fleetwood Mac, The Mark Leeman Five, The Peter B's, Shotgun Express, Them)

CHOCOLATE WATCH BAND

The English Chocolate Watch Band – a fairly ordinary acoustic duo who released two Decca singles in 1967 - are often confused nowadays with the US West Coast group of the same name. Although the English version was easier to identify, being that there were only two of them, it was the American version that are better remembered, thanks to a string of definitive punk-psychedelic genre' recordings and an appearance in the Roger Corman cult classic, *Riot On Sunset Strip*.

NEIL CHRISTIAN

Born Christopher Tidmarsh in Hoxton, east London, Christian is another example of an obscure performer nurturing the early careers of future renowned rock musicians in his backing group, The Crusaders. His first line-up included guitarist Jimmy Page who was later featured on the group's first Columbia single, 'Honey Hush'.

In 1965, Christian was signed to songwriter Miki Dallon's Strike label, getting off to a promising start with 'That's Nice' which reached the Top 20 in April '66 at 14. The Crusaders at the time were Ritchie Blackmore (guitar), Elmer Twitch (piano), Bibi Blange (bass) and Tornado Evans (drums), Follow-up singles 'Oops' and 'Two At A Time' were camper than a row of tents and flopped in England. Fortunately, Christian's foppish image went down a storm in Germany where he concentrated all his subsequent promotional efforts.

DAVE CLARK FIVE

If the phenomenon of the Beatles appearing on *The Ed Sullivan Show* brought the Fab Four to the attention of most Americans in February 1964, then it was the sight and sound of The Dave Clark Five on the same show that confirmed the 'British Invasion' had arrived in force. Clark's jackhammer beat proved to be just as infectious to American audiences as anything the Liverpudlians had to offer thus far.

The DC5's initial and hugely misleading publicity, however, may have had something to do with it. Promoted in the States by their

The Cherokees

The CHEYNES

Columbia DB 7368

GOIN' TO THE RIVER

Here come

The CHEYNES

Britain's most exciting R & B sound

Recording for Co

MARQUEE
90 Wardour St.,
London, W.1

THURSDAY, May 14th
THE CHEYNES
THE BLUEBIRDS

FRIDAY, May 15th
THE YARDBIRDS
THE AUTHENTICS

SATURDAY, May 16th
TUBBY HAYES
QUINTET
BOBBY BREEN
MICHAEL GARRICK TRIO

SUNDAY, May 17th
BIG BAND BASH
FORTY-TWO
BIG BAND
Directed by TOMMY WATT
(sponsored by Centre 42)

Y, May 18th
MANN

The Cheynes

The Clayton Squares

American record label Epic as 'The group with the Mersey sound and the Liverpool beat', this may have been testament to the popularity of The Beatles but it was a ploy that rankled with the London five-piece, who went to great pains to point out that the differences between the two cities were not merely geographical.

Formed in 1962 at the South Grove Youth Club, Tottenham, north London, the Five (part-time stuntman Dave Clark - drums, Mike Smith - organ, Lenny Davidson - guitar, Rick Huxley - bass, and Denis Payton- sax) were originally signed to Ember and Pye as an instrumental outfit, and had already released three singles before being discovered by an EMI A&R man during their weekly residency at the Tottenham Royal Ballroom. Signed to Columbia their first EMI release - a rock version of the nursery rhyme 'The Mulberry Bush' – rightly flopped while a version of The Contours 'Do You Love Me' barely made the Top 30 in October '63; all the more embarrassing in light of Brian Poole & The Tremeloes taking the same song to number one.

Fearing a premature end the group decided against another ill-advised cover for their third single. Instead they pushed for a Clark and Smith original called 'Glad All Over'. Released in November '63 it crashed to the top spot and 'the Tottenham Sound' according to the band's press agent was going to replace 'the Liverpool Sound'. Bizarrely, albeit momentarily, it did just that when, inevitably, the far superior 'I Want To Hold Your Hand' finally slipped from the top spot for 'Glad All Over' to usurp it. The single started a run of UK Top 20 chart entries - the stomping 'Bits And Pieces', 'Can't You See That She's Mine', 'Come Home', 'Catch Us If You Can', 'Everybody Knows' and 'The Red Balloon' - that lasted until 1970, making the Dave Clark 5 one of the most popular acts of the entire era.

It was an even greater story in America where the DC5 became the mop tops' biggest competitors, clocking up an impressive 24 consecutive hits ahead of Herman's Hermits, The Animals and even The Rolling Stones. The Five began their American onslaught in May '64 with a sell-out tour that kicked off with an appearance at New York's Carnegie Hall followed by a nationwide slot on *The Ed Sullivan Show* the following day. The group made their big screen début in mid-65 playing stuntmen escaping the big corrupt city with Barbara Ferris in John Boorman's comedy-drama *Catch Us If You Can. A Hard Day's Night* it wasn't but it did inspire the group to form their own company Big Five Films – a venture intended to make rock documentaries and music features although it seemed the only clients were the band themselves. The group continued to prosper in America throughout 1966, and into '67 despite the advent of psychedelia and its culling effects on dozens of similar bands. When their records stopped selling in the US thanks to manufactured groups like The Monkees, the group redevoted their attention to England where the MOR ballad 'Everybody Knows' managed a number two placing in December '67.

A rock and roll medley 'Good Old Rock 'n' Roll Part's 1&2' released during the brief Fifties revival of 1969 peaked at number seven, while 1970 saw them reach number 8 with a cover of 'Everybody Get Together'. In 1970 the DC5 eventually split. Clark continued to write and record with Smith as Dave Clark & Friends but the hits stopped coming and they dissolved the partnership in 1972. He then went to drama school and spent several years writing the musical *Time* which had a successful run at the Dominion

Dave Clark Five

Theatre in London in 1985 with Cliff Richard in the lead role.

Since then Clark's only musical venture was to issue the best-selling 1978 DC5 greatest hits compilation '25 Thumping Hits' and to acquire the rights to what little there was left of the classic ATV-Rediffusion television pop show *Ready, Steady, Go!*; the frequent television re-screenings of which annoyingly increase the profile of Clark's old group at the expense of more important artists. Unlike most of his Sixties contemporaries Clark remained a millionaire thanks to his shrewdly retaining the rights to the DC5's recordings and publishing, as well as being an astute investor.

Smith collaborated with ex-Manfred Mann singer Mike d'Abo and now lives in Spain where he writes jingles for television. Clark is rumoured to be preparing a Dave Clark Five boxed set and a documentary that has yet to see the light of day.

THE CLAYTON SQUARES

In the wake of The Beatles' global success, the world might have considered Liverpool the home of cheery, harmony-laden pop, but the locals preferred something grittier, and groups like The Clayton Squares and Wimple Winch epitomised the soulful R&B/freakbeat second wave of Merseybeat circa 1965/66. This horn-dominated combo made two singles for Decca, including a cover of The Lovin' Spoonful's 'There She Is' in 1966, but were otherwise a short-lived local phenomenon. Members went on to the art-rock ensemble, Liverpool Scene.

THE CLIQUE

This North London five piece were formed in 1964 and signed up by Kinks manager Larry Page to the Pye label after hearing their demo cut at the Marquee studios. The group's first single, a strong beat number 'She Ain't No Good', was also covered simultaneously by The Knack on Piccadilly. A further single 'We Didn't Kiss' was released in May '65 but also failed to make The Clique click and the group disbanded. Lead guitarist Jesse Hector went on to form the Hammersmith Gorillas in the mid Seventies.

JOE COCKER

Sheffield gas fitter Joe (real name John) Cocker started his musical career in 1959 as a singing drummer in The Cavaliers skiffle group. He then called himself Vance Arnold and fronted a rock and roll covers band called The Avengers. By 1962 rock had pretty much given way to a diluted and sentimental form of pop so Vance went looking for the blues. The group's big break came after playing at two of Peter Stringfellow's club nights held at the Sheffield City Hall in December '63. Stringfellow had invited record company A&R men to witness first hand some of the city's best bands supporting Wayne Fontana & The Mindbenders and The Rolling Stones.

According to Sheffield newspaper *The Star* The Avengers stole the show while *The Telegraph* predicted a star of the future. In fact

Joe Cocker

the group generated enough positive local press that Decca's A&R man Dick Rowe and producer Mike Leander travelled up north to catch the group at a gig in Manchester, and offered them a one-off single deal. In time honoured record company tradition The Avengers found they were surplus to requirements and only the singer need stay. Cocker recorded a cover of the Beatles 'I'll Cry Instead' accompanied by session vocalists The Ivy League and guitarist Big Jim Sullivan. Released into a 1964 world of Beatles cover versions the single did absolutely nothing and Cocker was quickly dropped. Unsurprisingly his old band repaid his lack of loyalty by dispersing. Cocker then formed Joe Cocker's Big Blues with Dave Hopper (guitar), Dave Green (bass), Dave Memmott (drums), and pianist Vernon Nash. They did several rounds of gigs at US army bases in France before packing it in due to lack of interest. Cocker rejoined the gas board and avoided performing for over a year.

In 1966 the determined Cocker put together another group; initially recalling Hopper (replaced by guitarist Frank Miles) and Nash and recruiting drummer Freddy Guite and Cocker's long-standing musical partner, bass player/pianist Chris Stainton. He called them The Grease Band after reading an article in which jazz man Jimmy Smith described a musician as "having a lot of grease". The new band hit the road and worked solidly for a year in the pubs and clubs of northern England. A demo was passed to Move-Procol Harum producer Denny Cordell via DJ friend Tony Hall. The song, a band composition entitled 'Marjorine', resulted in another recording opportunity, but in a case of déjà vu, without Nash, Miles and Memmott. A deal with Regal Zonophone was quickly signed and Cocker and Stainton moved to London in 1968 with a new Grease Band featuring Tommy Eyre – keyboards, Tommy Reilly – drums, and Mickey Gee – drums. 'Marjorine' (released March '68) only just managed to break into the Top 50 at 48, and Reilly and Gee were sent packing. However it was only a temporary setback because the follow up, a powerful rearrangement of The Beatles 'With A Little Help From My Friends' recorded with a little help from sessionmen Jimmy Page, and Procol Harum drummer B.J Wilson, shot straight to number one in November. Ex-Eire Apparent guitarist Henry McCullough and drummer Kenny Slade were hastily recruited and the single and accompanying album also broke Cocker in the States where Cordell's Straight ahead acts were issued on A&M Records.

In the New Year, a new-look Grease Band featuring Bruce Rowland – drums, Alan Spenner –bass (both from Wynder K. Frogg), and Stainton moving to keyboards, toured Britain and embarked upon their first US tour in April, and played a show stopping performance at the Woodstock festival in August 1969. In October, Cocker scored another Top 10 hit with 'Delta Lady', and a second, self-titled album, produced by American musician, arranger and producer Leon Russell.

Cocker continued into the Seventies backed by an ungainly 21-piece US band led by Russell, known as Mad Dogs & Englishmen. More hits followed Stateside including 'The Letter' and 'Cry Me A River' but Cocker eventually burnt himself out, being busted on an Australian tour and consequently barred from his cash cow America. The band inevitably fell apart and the singer descended into a self-destructive drink and drugs lifestyle.

He did, of course, sort himself out eventually and made several successful comebacks in the Eighties and Nineties. In 1989 he was invited to perform at the inauguration concert for President George Bush Senior. Nowadays he lives a healthy life in California.

COPS AND ROBBERS

This Watford based covers band were a popular live draw for a while during the mid-Sixties. They had one near miss with a take on Bob Dylan's 'Its All Over Now Baby Blue' in 1965, but all their other releases weren't as well thought out, the appalling 'I Could Have Danced All Night' (from *My Fair Lady*) being a case in point. Presumably singer Brian 'Smudger' Smith, and organ player Terry 'the Fox' fancied themselves as the Robbers, while drummer Henry Harrison and bass player Steve Smith, were happy being cops. After the band broke up Harrison formed The New Vaudeville Band who achieved novelty success with singles 'Winchester Cathedral' (1966) and 'Peek A-Boo' (1967).

CREAM

Eric Clapton, Jack Bruce and Ginger Baker are possibly the most famous rock trio ever. They only played together for a little over two years yet are widely regarded as one of the world's most influential bands. They got together at the height of the swinging London era in 1966 and effortlessly filled a void between R&B and the dawning of Rock.

Each member was deemed to be such a world class exponent of his chosen instrument that the name Cream was acknowledged as wholly appropriate, although they originally played their first gig billed with their surnames alone.

Baker and Bruce had played together in the Graham Bond Organization but despite respecting each others talents had got on so badly that Baker eventually fired Bruce in 1965. Bruce joined John Mayall's Bluesbreakers and subsequently Manfred Mann. By chance Bruce joined Mayall just prior to Clapton's departure but no recordings took place. The Graham Bond Organization carried on for a short while without Bruce but Baker was ready to leave. He approached Clapton with a view to starting a band together and the guitar player agreed. There was one proviso however - Clapton insisted Bruce be the bass player. Baker had no option but to make his peace and resolve his differences. So with pride suitably swallowed Clapton, Baker and Bruce were ready to roll.

The trio played a couple of unannounced gigs including one at The Twisted Wheel club in Manchester before Clapton dubbed them Cream and they accepted an invitation to perform at the July 1966 Windsor Jazz and Blues festival. Fans of the individual players expected the group to pursue a straightforward blues direction. What they got was a unique blend of influences ranging from Delta blues and rock through to pop and extended, proto-psychedelic wig-outs. For the next 26 months Cream reigned supreme. However, their début single, 'Wrapping Paper', a barrel piano driven ditty by Bruce and co-songwriter Pete Brown (released October '66) was totally out of character and confounded listeners. The group's début album *Fresh Cream* was more fitting, and reached four on the album charts in January '67, while the infectious 'I Feel Free' demonstrated the group's unexpected pop abilities, reaching eleven the same month. Cream were one of the country's top draws – the groups' group – and word filtered across the Atlantic. The band made their first visit to New York in March – playing on a farcical multi-artist Murray the 'K' bill where they were given just ten minutes to do their act - and recording their next album *Disraeli Gears* with producers Tom Dowd and Felix Pappalardi.

A taster from the album, 'Strange Brew' was released in June, and the summer was spent completing the album and breaking the States, where the audiences at underground halls like the Fillmore West in San Francisco and Detroit's Grande Ballroom encouraged the group to push the boundaries with virtuostic displays of instrumental prowess. The live side of the double album *Wheels Of Fire* is a testament to this, but also highlights the level of self-indulgence involved. In 1968 the group were seemingly indestructible with a fanatical following, enviable album sales and two further hit singles, 'Sunshine Of Your Love' and 'White Room'. But on tour Clapton had been exposed to the rustic charms of The Band's *Music From Big Pink* album. This, together with a scathing

Cops & Robbers

THE COPS 'N ROBBERS
I Could Have Danced All Night

7N 15870

The Creation

Rolling Stone review that described him as 'the master of the cliché, made Clapton decide he didn't want to continue. Cream announced they were splitting and two emotional farewell concerts were staged at the Royal Albert Hall in November 1968, while a posthumous single 'Badge' and album *Goodbye* reached 18 and one respectively in April 1969.

All three members went on to enjoy successful careers in both rock and jazz. In 1969, Clapton and Baker joined forces with Traffic's Steve Winwood and Family's Rick Grech in the short-lived supergroup Blind Faith while Bruce embarked on a solo mission. Following Blind Faith's split Baker went on to form Ginger Baker's Airforce with Winwood, and the Baker-Gurvitz Army. Clapton had a backseat role with Delaney and Bonnie's touring outfit, members of whom joined him in Derek & The Dominoes in 1970.

Clapton dropped from sight in the early Seventies, addicted to heroin, but emerged to reclaim his reputation as one of the world's foremost guitar heroes. He is now something of a British institution, playing a yearly residency at the Royal Albert Hall. Baker experimented with African music and is a celebrated polo player and Bruce still records as a solo artist. In 1992 a Cream reunion of sorts occured in New York when the group were inducted into the Rock and Roll Hall Of Fame. Clapton could not be convinced a tour or album was a good idea so Baker and Bruce formed an ill-fated partnership with Gary Moore in the early Nineties as BBM (Baker, Bruce and Moore).

(see also Graham Bond Organisation, Manfred Mann, John Mayall, The Yardbirds)

THE CREATION

Originally The Mark Four, Kenny Pickett – vocals, Eddie Phillips – guitar, Bob Garner – bass, and Jack Jones – drums, changed their name in 1966 to the snappier sounding Creation and announced that their music was 'red with purple flashes'. The Creation were at the forefront of the mid-Sixties Mod movement, wearing matching purple button-down shirts and embraced the earliest aspects of the pop art trend pioneered by The Who, a band to whom The Creation were constantly compared. That's not to say they were Who copyists, far from it. In fact, The Creation proved to be every bit as innovative as their West London counterparts, even sharing the same producer in Shel Talmy, who had parted acrimoniously with the Shepherd's Bush mob and was looking for a band that could fulfil the same credos of visual and musical power.

The Creation

The Creation's 1966 début single on Talmy's independent Planet label (distributed via Philips), was the epic 'Making Time' which, although only reaching number 49, was a ground breaking record. It was notable for an ear-splitting guitar solo performed by Phillips, who played his Gibson 335 with a violin bow two years before Yardbird and Zep man Jimmy Page did the same thing.

The band's live shows were also something of an event, and took pop art gimmickry even further. A theatrical element was introduced to the set, whereby singer Pickett would action paint, using brightly coloured aerosols on large canvasses set up on the sides of the stage, which he would then burn down. This progressed to painting the bodies of semi-naked girls and members of the audience. The band also pioneered an early form of big screen projection performance, hanging a huge back drop above the stage on which a film was shown of the group playing live from a previous show. It was meant to give a 3-D effect but this was only partially successful.

Despite such antics, on the whole, the British music press largely ignored the group. They managed to get a front-page ad in the *New Musical Express*, announcing a follow up single 'Painter Man' in October '66. However this fared little better than their début and only managed to reach number 36. It was left to the Germans to recognise The Creation's true genius which they did by sending it straight to number one.

One major flaw the band didn't address was that they all hated each other. Members started to come and go at an alarming rate in '67, starting with the sacking of Jones. He was replaced by Dave Preston, an acquaintance of Garner's. Jones was reinstated but then a more serious development occurred when Pickett left. Garner took over vocals and Kim Gardner (ex-Birds) was brought in on bass. The band switched to Polydor in 1967 and released three singles that were as equally quirky and idiosyncratic as their Planet output; even more so. 'If I Stay Too Long' was a slower, moodier number composed by Garner, while 'Life Is Just A Beginning' utilised an inspired string arrangement. Perhaps their finest moment, 'How Does It Feel To Feel' featured Phillips violin bow flourishes to the fore, with prominent feedback squeals on the US mix of the single.

When these fantastic records performed poorly chartwise in the UK, the band decided to practically quit live work in their homeland and concentrate solely on Europe, Germany in particular. The result paid off and after several successful tours (including one supporting The Rolling Stones in April '67) The Creation were one of the biggest live bands on the Continent. A German-only album *We Are Paintermen* featured the Polydor singles as well as several other songs that were their equal such as 'For All That I Am', and a fine cover of The Capitols 'Cool Jerk'. The quality level was blighted only by pedestrian covers of 'Hey Joe' and 'Like A Rolling Stone'.

In 1968, a restless Phillips departed to be replaced by another ex-Bird, Ronnie Wood, who had been fired from The Jeff Beck Group. Garner then left for Pickett to rejoin. These constant personnel changes cost the band its identity and momentum, and after one last Polydor single, 'Midway Down', The Creation broke up in mid-68. Tragically, the band were on the verge of signing an American record deal with United Artists, that could have arguably turned them into one of the biggest bands of the era.

Phillips quit the music industry for a period, working as a bus driver among other things, but re-emerged as guitar player with P.P. Arnold, before pursuing a low-key solo career. He still periodically plays and records with ex-Mark Five bandmate John Dalton and ex-Kink Mick Avory in Cuckoo's Nest. Jones left the music business and now owns a shop. Pickett became a roadie for Led Zeppelin, and achieved dubious success as the co-writer (with renowned session bassist Herbie Flowers) of the Clive Dunn hit 'Grandad' in 1970.

The classic Phillips, Pickett, Garner and Jones line-up of The Creation reformed in 1993, releasing a live album *Lay The Ghost*, followed by a single ('Creation') and album *Power Surge* for the Creation label in '95. Work began on a second studio album in 1996 but this never reached fruition due to the tragic death of Kenny Pickett from a heart attack on January 10, 1997. In 1999 Phillips and Garner scored a surprise hit as the fictional line-dancing group featured in the TV show *Emmerdale Farm*. The pair also played a sold-out, one-off club gig in New York as part of a new Creation line-up in 2001.

(see also Jeff Beck, The Birds, The Mark Four)

The Cryin' Shames

THE CRYIN' SHAMES

A Liverpudlian outfit originally known as The Bumblies, featuring two lead singers in Paul Crane and Joey Keen. The group released three Decca singles; the first of which, a cover of The Drifters' 'Please Stay', hit the Top 30 in mid-1966. However, the band's crowning achievement was 'Come On Back' (credited to Paul Ritchie & The Cryin' Shames), a brooding slice of menace which, with its wobbly organ and otherworldly fuzz, is probably the closest any British act has come to emulating the sound of the classic American garage bands. Not surprisingly, the record was produced, as were all The Shames' releases, by the quintessential English maverick Joe Meek. Crane later joined the highly regarded Gary Walker & The Rain.

(see also The Escorts, Gary Walker)

THE CYAN THREE

Not much is known about this nattily-attired outfit and their lone single for Decca in 1966 - an appealing version of The Temptations' 'Since I Lost My Baby', also covered outstandingly (albeit as a B-side) by The Action on Parlophone.

It's a real cool chew... and that flavour lasts and lasts through a stack of swinging pops! So get with Beatmint—eight great pieces for only 3d.

ANGLO BEATMINT

8 BIG PIECES 3D

The Cryin' Shames

Dantalion's Chariot

DANTALION'S CHARIOT

Formed following the break-up of Zoot Money's Big Roll Band in 1966, Dantalion's Chariot was the unashamedly psychedelic creation of keyboardist Zoot and his big rollers, Andy Summers (guitar), Pat Donaldson (bass) and Colin Allen (drums). The interestingly titled 'The Madman Running Through The Fields', their sole release for Columbia in 1967, was an out-and-out flop, albeit undeservedly so. With its backward cymbal flourishes and complicated structure, the track is widely regarded as one of the finest recorded examples of British psychedelia.

The band made a name for themselves playing London hippie havens like the Middle Earth and the UFO club. There they would take to an all-white stage dressed in white, with white instruments (including a B3 Hammond) and play while bathed in a glorious Technicolor light show provided by Jeff Dexter's Light and Sound Show. Their weird world was also the subject of a Fred Marshall documentary entitled *Pop Down* which also featured Blossom Toes and The Idle Race. When the Summer of Love ended, so did the band. Summers joined The Soft Machine on an American tour with Jimi Hendrix in 1968 before both he and Money joined Eric Burdon in the final stages of the equally far-out New Animals, who re-recorded 'Madman' and included it on the album *Love Is*. Colin Allen joined John Mayall followed by Stone The Crows. A posthumous 1997 collection of unreleased Dantalion's Chariot recordings, *Chariot Rising*, paid testament to the group's inventiveness in that halcyon year of 1967.

(see also John Mayall, Zoot Money's Big-Roll Band)

DAVID & JONATHAN

David's real name was Roger Cook, Jonathan's was Roger Greenaway which beggars the Biblical question why not Roger and Roger? We'll never know, but what we do know is these two were a pair of singer-songwriters that got together in 1965, finding instant chart success when The Fortunes recorded their composition, 'You've Got Your Troubles' – a number two hit in July.

David and Jonathan achieved a number 11 hit with a cover of The Beatles' 'Michelle' (The Overlanders competing version shot to the top slot) in January '66, before scoring a second time with the self-penned 'Lovers Of The World Unite' which made a creditable number seven in September. The duo kept on recording until 1968 but sampled further success only when their songs were covered by other artists; the best example being The New Seekers' 'I'd Like To Teach The World To Sing'. Cook went on to form Blue Mink with he and Greenaway providing the material.

(see also The Fortunes)

THE CYRIL DAVIES RHYTHM & BLUES ALL STARS

North London harmonica player and panelbeater Cyril Davies started playing professionally in the mid-Fifties while with Chris Barber's Jazz Band and Beryl Bryden's Back-Room Skiffle. He and guitar player Alexis Korner left Barber's band in 1961 to form Alexis Korner's Blues Incorporated. The pair also set up the famous Ealing Club, below the ABC bakery opposite Ealing Broadway station, in March 1962 and recorded the live album *R&B From The Marquee* (featuring Long John Baldry on vocals) at the club's old Oxford Street address, released on Decca's Ace of Clubs label. As the band's front man Davies was never happy with the way the band was billed so he quit to form his own band including Baldry, and for a time, guitarist Jimmy Page and pianist Nicky Hopkins, making sure everyone knew who was boss.

The quartet made two 1963 singles for Pye – the first authentic British R&B single, 'Country Line Special' and 'Preachin' The Blues' before Davies' premature death from leukaemia in January 1964. Baldry took over the band and renamed them The Hoochie Coochie Men. *(see also Long John Baldry, Alexis Korner's Blues Incorporated)*

SPENCER DAVIS GROUP

This talented quartet comprised Spencer Davis, a former Birmingham University student, teacher and part-time blues musician, drummer Pete York, and the Birmingham-born Winwood brothers, bassist Mervyn, nicknamed Muff after the television character 'Muffin The Mule', and younger sibling Steve. The four met at the city's Golden Eagle pub and started life as The Rhythm & Blues Quartet, before being spotted by Chris Blackwell of Island Records on June 1, 1964. Unable to fully support his acts at the time, manager Blackwell became the group's publisher while the group signed to Philips subsidiary, Fontana. Their first release in April '64 was a cover of John Lee Hooker's 'Dimples', but it sank without trace. However, it more than ably demonstrated that aged only 16, young Steve Winwood had a voice that belied his years; sounding blacker and more soulful than any of his contemporaries with the possible exception of another Steve (Marriott).

In November of 1964, their second single, a cover of The Soul Sisters' 'I Can't Stand It', reached number 47, followed by a cover of Brenda Holloway's 'Every Little Bit Hurts' (number 41 in March 1965). The group's début album, imaginatively titled *Their First Album*, was a strong collection of the group's diverse influences, and featured Island labelmate, Millie Small warbling away on a cover of The Ikettes 'I'm Blue'. The group's fourth single, a cover of The Malibus' 'Strong Love' stalled at number 44 in June.

Despite not gaining the chart recognition they deserved to date, The SDG were the toast of the country's more discerning musicians. On August 8, the group played on the final day of the fifth annual National Jazz & Blues Festival at the Richmond Athletic Ground near London. The festival ended with The Animals bill-topping appearance and Steve returned onstage to bawl along with admirers Eric Burdon, Long John Baldry and Rod Stewart. In September, The SDG began a 24-date UK tour as special guests of The Rolling Stones who took quite a shine to the group, even going so far as to loan them their limousine and driver Tom Keylock while the Stones were away on an Australian tour.

The breakthrough hit came in January '66 when 'Keep On Running', with it's sprightly rhythm, fuzz-box riff, and undeniably

THE SPENCER DAVIS GROUP
"STRONG LOVE"
TF 571
fontana

catchy chorus, reached number one, displacing The Beatles double A-side 'We Can Work It Out'/'Day Tripper'. The song was written by Blackwell's Jamaican protégé' Jackie Edwards, who also penned follow-ups, 'Somebody Help Me', (another number one in April), and 'When I Come Home' (number twelve in September).

On July 11, the group entered the world of pop movies when they begin shooting, alongside Dave Berry and quiz host Nicholas Parsons, the trashy *The Ghost Goes Gear* on location in Windsor and Chiddington Castle in Kent. Released to cinemas in December, supporting *One Million Years BC*, the film has rarely been seen since - no doubt to the band's relief. The band's second and third albums, *Their Second Album* and *Autumn '66* (which creative genius was responsible for dreaming up such titles?!) were still dominated by reverential covers of various blues, soul and jazz numbers but the group's confidence was strong enough to attempt releasing their own composition as an A-side.

Released in November of '66, 'Gimme Some Loving' was only kept off the number one spot by The Beach Boys masterpiece 'Good Vibrations'. Built around a solid bass hook riff (pinched from Homer Bank's soul classic '(Ain't That) A Lot Of Love'), Winwood's roaring Hammond, and enhanced by Jimmy Miller's superb production, 'Gimme Some Loving' made inroads into the American charts where the group were already a cult name.

In January of 1967, The Spencer Davis Group released 'I'm A Man' – another infectious, Latin-style groover, later covered in extended form by US group Chicago - which reached number nine, and also perked further interest in the States. However any impetus created was lost when in April, both Winwood brothers left the band; Muff to become a promo man at Island, and Steve to help form

Billie Davis

fellow Brummie collective Traffic. "Here we were with two of the biggest records of our lives and no band," Davis recently lamented. Davis stoically soldiered on and replaced the Winwoods with organist Eddie Hardin, formerly of A Wild Uncertainty and ex-Cheynes, Fleur de Lys and Shotgun Express guitarist Phil Sawyer, who was later replaced by Ray Fenwick, formerly of The Syndicats, and Dutch group, After Tea.

The new line-up's first single, 'Time Seller' was very similar in feel to Procol Harum's blockbuster 'A Whiter Shade Of Pale' and reached number 30 in August '67. In November, the group made an appearance during a dance sequence in the period piece *Here We Go Round The Mulberry Bush*. The film's theme tune was somewhat ironically performed by Traffic. The SDG also wrote six songs which appeared on the film soundtrack and album. Another stab at the charts, 'Mr. Second Class' and an album *With Their New Face On* were relatively unsuccessful and in October 1968, Hardin and York both departed from the group to form 'the smallest big band in the world' dubbed (surprise, surprise) Hardin-York.

In November of that year, with the additional line-up of ex-Mirage Dee Murray on bass and Nigel Olsson (ex-Plastic Penny) on drums, a version of the SDG began a North American tour. Olsson was replaced by Dave Hynes but in July of 1969, Davis sensibly decided enough was enough. Murray and Olsson went on to join Elton John's band, while Davis relocated to California to work as a soloist and A&R man.

In 1973, a version of The Spencer Davis Group reconvened to record two albums for Vertigo, *Gluggo* and *Living In The Back Street*, featuring a line-up of Davis-York-Hardin-Fenwick and Charlie McCracken (ex-Taste) on bass.

Pete York set up a drum clinic and moved to Germany to play at various jazz and blues festivals, and occasionally plays with Davis in a reformed version of The Spencer Davis Group. Eddie Hardin continues to release the occasional album of new age music. Fenwick worked with various members of Deep Purple. Muff Winwood became head of A&R at the London office of CBS (now Sony), while his brother continues to enjoy an acclaimed career as a solo artist.

(see also The Cheynes, Fleur de Lys, Shotgun Express, The Syndicats, Traffic)

DAVE DEE, DOZY, BEAKY, MICK & TICH

Although often derided by many of their (mostly less successful) peers as pantomime pop pretenders, DD,D,B,M&T were still one of the biggest selling pop acts of the Sixties. They began their collective career in Salisbury, Wiltshire, in 1961 as Dave Dee & The Bostons. Dave Dee (born David Harmon) had been a trainee police cadet and was one of the first to arrive on the car accident scene that killed Eddie Cochran in 1960, retrieving Cochran's beloved Gretsch '57

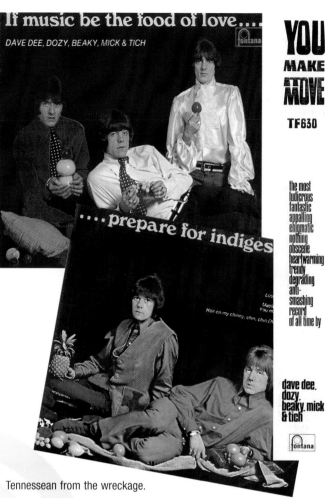

Tennessean from the wreckage.

The rest of The Bostons comprised Trevor Davies (Dozy-bass), John Dymond (Beaky – guitar), Michael Wilson (Mick – drums) and Ian Amey (Tich – lead guitar).

The quintet learnt their trade in much the same way as most English bands did in 1962 by visiting Germany. They also established a risque reputation due to Dee's routine of smutty storytelling and audience fraternising. They changed their name in 1964 to the all-accommodating Dave Dee, Dozy, Beaky, Mick and Tich at the suggestion of their management and song writing team, Alan Blaikley and Ken Howard, who would dramatically change the fortunes of the Hamburg-honed five piece.

Over the next five years Blaikley and Howard supplied the band with no fewer than twelve consecutive chart hits. After false starts with 'No Time', 'All I Want' and 'You Make It Move', the duo found the hit-making touch with 'Hold Tight' (number four – March 1966), 'Hideaway' (number ten – June 1966) and the saucy *Zorba The Greek* pastiche, 'Bend It' (number two – September 1966, which had to be re-recorded with new lyrics for the prurient American market). Three more hits followed throughout 1967 – 'Touch Me, Touch Me', 'Okay', and 'Zabadak'; the latter which, when roughly translated, apparently mean't 'refuse', 'swill' or 'rubbish' – how apt!

Every release was perfectly performed with the charisma and excitement of an end of pier music hall act, allied to a musical gimmick of one sort or another, e.g 'Hold Tight' was built around a football chant, 'Save Me' used a Latin cha-cha rhythm, 'Okay' – a Balearic gypsy dance, etc.

The band achieved their only number one with the almighty 'The Legend Of Xanadu' in February 1968, giving Dee the opportunity to dress up in kinky leather boots and brandish a bullwhip on *Top Of The Pops.* None of this won the group any serious critical acclaim or respect, not that it worried the band as they (or at least their management) were raking it in. More hits followed through 1968 into '69 with 'Last Night In Soho', a heartfelt ode to a biker's grizzly fate in London's famous square mile (number eight in July), 'The Wreck Of The Antoinette' (number 14 in October) and a return to Xanadu territory with 'Don Juan' (number 23 in March '69).

By now the group's total lack of credibility was gnawing away at Dee who decided he wanted a more dignified solo career. He also fancied a bit of acting, so he gave the other lads his notice, recording one last execrable 45 with the band, 'Snake In The Grass' (number 23 in May) and then he was gone.

Dee's solo musical career wasn't the success he hoped it would be; neither was his acting career. He released around half a dozen singles, of which only 'My Woman's Man' charted at number 42 in March 1970. He was co-presenter for a spell on German TV's *Beat Club* (DD, D, B, M & T were astronomically popular in the Fatherland) and made a few minor TV and film appearances. Dee got a proper job in 1973 as head of A&R at WEA Records, and was astute enough to turn down The Sex Pistols in 1976.

Meanwhile, Dozy & Co. soldered on leaderless for another three years, changing their style to a rockier approach for their singles and 1970 album, *Fresh Ear* before disbanding. In 1974 a reformed Dave Dee, Dozy, Mick & Tich, released a single, 'She's My Lady', on the small Antic label. There were a couple of successful reunion tours in the Seventies and Eighties which encouraged the band to reform on a semi-permanent basis, without Mick who now runs a driving school in Wiltshire. They were last seen on stage at the London Palladium in 2001.

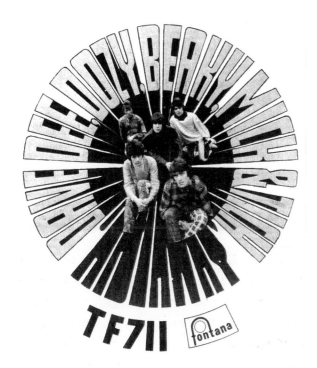

KIKI DEE

Born in Bradford as Pauline Matthews, Kiki sang with various dance groups before recording her first disc, 'Early Night', produced by Mitch Murray, in 1964. She released a string of unsuccessful singles for Fontana and appeared in a dreadful pirate radio crime caper *Dateline Diamonds* in 1965, alongside Kenny Everett, Dave Cash, The Caravelles, and Small Faces.

It was not until 1968 that she recorded her first album, *I'm Kiki Dee*, for Fontana and a single 'Now The Flowers Cry'/'On A Magic Carpet Ride' is much in demand from the cultish Northern Soul fraternity (as are many of her earlier recordings).

In 1969, Kiki achieved the extraordinary feat of becoming the first British female singer to sign for the legendary Detroit based Tamla-Motown. Although the resultant album *Great Expectations* was a pleasant and well-performed set of covers from the Motown stable, the record failed to live up to the sales standards expected and she was subsequently released from her contract. Fortunately, help was at hand from long-time friend and admirer Elton John, who signed her to his Rocket label in 1973. In November of that year, she reached number 13 with the track 'Amoureuse' (aka 'Loving And Free'), written by French chanteuse Veronique Sanson. However her real taste of success and for what she will forever be associated came in 1976 with a number one duet with her label boss, 'Don't Go Breaking My Heart'.

THE DENNISONS

One of the late-starting Merseybeat bands and another outfit inevitably signed to Decca, The Dennisons had three stabs at the singles chart and achieved two minor hits in 1963/4. Their début single was a self-penned original called '(Come On) Be My Girl' which reached number 46. Their second 45 - a cover of the Rufus Thomas classic, 'Walkin' The Dog' - made it to number 36 in May 1964, while their final Shel Talmy-produced single 'Nobody Like My Babe' missed completely. The band's drummer, Clive Hornsby is now better known as Jack Sugden in the soap opera *Emmerdale.*

THE DEVIANTS

London hippies who in 1967 formed what can only be described as the first communal band led by afro-headed freak Mick Farren, with Sid Bishop (guitar), Cord Rees (bass) and Russell Hunter (drums). Originally known as The Social Deviants the anarchic collective got together in the Notting Hill area of West London and ambled through a two-year escapade that somehow threw up three Fugs-influenced albums; the first *Ptooff!* - released on their own Underground Impresarios label - was distributed via mail order through IT magazine and reissued by Decca in 1969. The second *Disposable* (1968), released on Stable (containing the Deviants' anthem 'Let's Loot The Supermarket') featured Duncan Sanderson replacing Rees. Paul Rudolph was added following Bishop's departure for the third

Mick Farren of The Deviants

self-titled album appearing rather bizarrely on folk label Transatlantic.

The Deviants dispersed in 1969 when Farren was fired and left stranded during an American tour. Rudolph, Sanderson and Hunter formed arguably the first British punk band The Pink Fairies with ex-Fairies, Tomorrow and Pretty Things drummer Twink. In 1970 Farren released his solo album *Mona The Carniverous Circus*, and continued a multi-facted career as novelist, musician and primarily music journalist. He is now based in Los Angeles.

THE DIMPLES

Hard to believe that such a mod-looking Scunthorpe soul outfit spawned the founding members of Seventies prog heavies Methuselah and medievalists Amazing Blondel - vocalist John Gladwin and guitarist Terry Wincott. The Dimples were handled by Don Arden's Galaxy Artists and were regular faces on the London college/ballroom circuit, releasing one single, 'The Love Of A Lifetime', for Decca in 1966, before becoming ye olde worlde folkniks.

DONOVAN

Donovan remains the era's most prolific and pastoral song poet and credit is due for surviving his poor man's Dylan tag. Originally from Glasgow, Donovan Leitch was discovered busking around London and given a residency on *Ready, Steady, Go!*

He cut a distinctive image as wistful folkie in beatnik cap and denims, with an acoustic daubed 'This Machine Kills...' taken from Woody Guthrie's slogan 'This Machine Kills Fascists'. Donovan can also be seen in the Bob Dylan 1965 documentary film *Don't Look Back*, prostrating himself before his idol. Don's regular TV slots boosted record sales and sent his first single 'Catch The Wind' to number four in April 1965. His début album *What's Bin Did And What's Bin Hid* belted to number three and a second single 'Colours' was another number four in July.

That was pretty much his set pattern throughout the Sixties, apart from a bit of a hiccup around the time of his second album. The reflective and fanciful *Fairytale* peaked at number 20 and the 'Turquoise' single number 30, but a quick change of musical direction put a harder edged Donovan back on track by 1966. He brought in the producer and management team of Mickie Most and John Cameron and released the superb single 'Sunshine Superman' (featuring Jimmy Page's guitar) which went straight to the top in the US in August and to number two in the UK upon its belated release in December. However legal disputes between his old management agency and Most delayed the release of the accompanying album in Britain. In July 1966 Donovan became the first high profile rock star to be busted for drugs and at the dawn of the psychedelic era he became something of a hippie hero.

His individual status was further assured when 'Mellow Yellow' (featuring Paul McCartney on backing vocals) was another

Donovan & Jimmy Saville

international hit in August 1966 (reaching two in the US and eight belatedly in the UK in February '67). The *Sunshine Superman* album was finally released in Britain in July '67 and the songs 'Season Of The Witch' and 'Fat Angel' were covered respectively by Vanilla Fudge and Jefferson Airplane. The plain daft 'There Is A Mountain' followed (US number eleven in August; UK number eight – November '67) and the rest of the year was spent touring America, where the *Mellow Yellow* and live *Donovan In Concert* albums both made the Top 20.

1968 was an equally good year, kicking off with a number five hit, 'Jennifer Juniper' (supposedly written for Jenny Boyd, Patti's sister) in March (which in a reversal of his territorial fortunes only made 26 in the US), and 'Hurdy Gurdy Man', which reached four in June (five in the US).

Donovan also released the quintessential flower-power double album boxed-set, *A Gift From A Flower To A Garden*, something of a

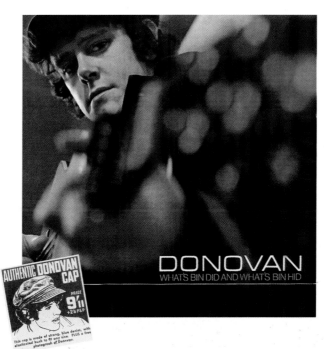

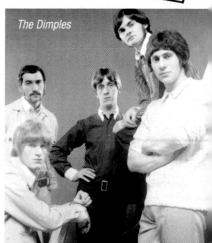

The Dimples

whimsical concept with one disc full of songs for children and the other tracks for their parents. The album came packaged with a photo of the Maharishi Mahesh Yogi, at whose Rishikesh ashram Donovan had studied Transcendental Meditation with The Beatles in early 1968. 'Atlantis' featuring McCartney on drums and Stephen Stills on backing vocals, stalled at number 23 in December (US - number seven) when, in 1969, there was another change in direction and stance. Denouncing the use of drugs, he joined forces with The Jeff Beck Group to record what is arguably his finest single 'Goo Goo Barabajagal (Love Is Hot)' which, unusually, was a bigger hit in England (where it reached number 12) than it was in the States (36).

Donovan's popularity began to wane with the onset of the Seventies. His next album, *Open Road*, sold reasonably well and made the Top 30 but there were no hit singles. Then came *HMS Donovan*, his first non-charting album and a several poor selling singles – one of which, 'Celia Of The Seals' was a beautiful anti-seal culling lovesong. *Donovan's Greatest Hits* was rushed out to bolster his bank account but financial problems forced him to seek tax exile in Ireland. He later moved to Joshua Tree, California, and concentrated on writing musical scores for the movie industry, including *If It's Tuesday It Must Be Belgium*, *Brother Sun Sister Moon* and *The Pied Piper*, in which he starred. His last album to gain any sort of commercial and critical success was 1973's *Cosmic Wheels* which reached number fifteen. Now based in Ireland Donovan continues to tour the world on a regular basis.

DOWNLINERS SECT

Contemporaries of The Rolling Stones and The Pretty Things, The Downliners Sect were the descendants of an earlier Twickenham group called simply, Downliners. They were led by guitar player Don Craine (real name Michael O'Donnell), but split up after a brief tour of US air force bases in 1962. Craine and drummer Johnny Sutton then reshaped the group with bass player Keith Grant and guitar player Terry Gibson, renaming it The Downliners Sect. By 1963 the group's brash brand of R&B had gained them a sizeable following and residencies at Eel Pie Island and at London's Studio 51 Club, where their self financed EP *A Nite In Great Newport Street* was recorded. Featuring rough 'n' ready interpretations of Chuck Berry, Jimmy Reed, and Booker T's 'Green Onions', the recording led to the Sect signing with EMI.

Harmonica player Ray Sone was added to the line-up, beating off competion from Rod Stewart and Steve Marriott for the role. He arrived in time for their début 1964 single release, a cover of Jimmy Reed's 'Baby What's Wrong' which made a low UK chart entry but whipped up some European interest. This was most noticeable in Sweden where the group's second single, a cover of The Coasters 'Little Egypt', topped the charts. Although serious musicians, the group had an irreverent and fun loving attitude towards their image and choice of material. This was evident on the band's first album, *The Sect*, which had them decked out in Victorian country gent finery, Craine in his ever present deerstalker hat, and showcased tracks like 'Be A Sect Manic', 'Sect Appeal' and 'One Ugly Child'. Unfortunately, this alienated blues and R&B purists who contemptuously denounced the Sect as charlatans.

The group responded with a complete change in musical direction. Their second album, *The Country Sect* (1965) incorporated country and folk influences that got them credited for inventing country rock (in Canada anyway). *The Rock Sects In* (the Sect's third album, released in 1966) is notable for the track 'Why Don't You Smile Now', a song by US group The Primitives, written by Lou Reed and John Cale prior to their founding The Velvet Underground. *The*

Downliners Sect

THEY'RE FAB!
A HIT WITH THEIR FIRST DISC
DOWNLINERS SECT
BABY WHAT'S WRONG?
Columbia DB 7300
Publisher:
CAMPBELL-CONNELLY & CO. LTD.
10 DENMARK STREET, W.C.2.
TEM 1653
Representation:
MALCOLM NIXON AGENCY,
5 CONDUIT STREET, W.1.
HYD 6846

THE SECT DOWNLINERS SECT

Sect Sing Sick Songs, a 1965 EP of ghoulish tunes that included 'I Want My Baby Back' ('Over there was my baby, and over there was my baby, and way over there was...'), 'Now She's Dead' and 'Leader Of The Sect', inspired by The Shangri-Las' death disc classic 'Leader Of The Pack' landed the group with a blanket BBC ban that wrecked their already shaky commercial footing.

When five more singles, including the Graham Gouldman composition 'The Cost Of Living' and 'Glendora' – a tale of love between man and mannequin, featuring Marty and Joyce Wilde on backing vocals - all failed to chart, the Sect began to slide. Gibson and Sutton left and were respectively replaced by Bob Taylor and Kevin Flanagan, while ex-Screaming Lord Sutch keyboardist Matthew Fisher fleshed out the line-up. The group, renamed Don Craine's New Downliners Sect, steeled themselves for one last hurrah. Unfortunately the Pye one-off, 'I Can't Get Away From You', wasn't it and Sect boss Craine hung up his deerstalker and departed in '67. He went on to join Finnegans Wheel and was later one half of a duo called Loose End. Grant reunited with Sutton and had another stab at the Swedish market but after recording a handful of unsuccessful tracks for juke box-only release they too quit. Fisher, who had been replaced by Barry Cooper, went on to Procol Harum. That should have been the end of it, but Craine and Grant reactivated the band in 1976; recording the single 'Show Biz', and reissuing the first Downliners Sect album.

In the early Nineties the British Invasion All-Stars were formed that, aside from Craine and Grant, featured Yardbird Jim McCarty, Nashville Teen Ray Phillips, and The Creation's Eddie Phillips. They recorded two albums, *Regression* and *United*, which also featured contributions from Pretty Things' Phil May and Dick Taylor, Pirate Mick Green, and Matthew Fisher. Craine and Grant have continued to record and perform in various similar projects, including The Yardbirds Experience, which included Noel Redding, and their most recent ensemble, a new version of Art Wood's Quiet Melon.

JULIE DRISCOLL

This former secretary first came to prominence in 1965 when the svengali-like manoeuvring of Yardbirds manager Georgio Gomelsky got her a job in the vocal line-up of Steam Packet. Not that she was a total novice.

Julie had already released a little known single, 'Take Me By The Hand', on Columbia the year before. However, it was Steam Packet that got her noticed. Although the group was a relatively short-term project, it gave Driscoll the profile and opportunity to continue a solo career and from there gain exposure as vocalist and sex symbol with Brian Auger & The Trinity. Her time with Auger was equally brief and is best remembered for the 1968 hit version of Bob Dylan's 'This Wheels On Fire'.

When the Trinity imploded in 1969 'Jools' married jazz pianist Keith Tippett and limited her recorded work to occasional appearances on his avant-garde recordings. Still regarded as one of the best British female vocalists from the Sixties Julie's last high-profile appearance was duetting on a reworked version of 'This Wheels On Fire' with comedian Adrian Edmondson for the theme tune to the Nineties hit TV show *Absolutely Fabulous*. When plans were made for its release as a single she pressured to have it withdrawn – the reappearance of a past hit was obviously the last thing she wanted.

(see also Brian Auger, Steam Packet, Rod Stewart)

SIMON DUPREE & THE BIG SOUND

Hailing from Portsmouth this popular sextet, originally known as The Roadrunners, didn't actually have a Simon Dupree in their ranks. The name was tagged to lead singer Derek Shulman, whose brothers Ray (guitar) and Phil (sax/trumpet) were part of The Big Sound with Pete O'Flaherty (bass), Eric Hine (keyboards) and Tony Ransley (drums).

As well as being a popular soul show band on the South Coast, the group became big in London's clubs, alongside similar outfits like The Alan Bown Set, and were signed to Parlophone in '66. 'I See The Light', a frantic, organ driven belter and a minor hit for The Five Americans in the US was their first release in December but this and follow-ups, 'Reservations' and the Mike Hugg composition 'Daytime, Nightime' (recorded by Manfred Mann as 'Each And Every Day') failed to click despite the group being big favourites with audiences around the country.

Their frenzied female fanbase was immortalised in a 1967 BBC *Man Alive* special The Ravers at this time, which caught the group sweating up a storm while lapping up their braying banshees' advances.

The group's début album *Without Reservations* (August '67) was a predictable nod to their soul influences but an unexpected hit arrived with the atmospheric 'Kites' – reaching number nine in December '67. The group had recorded it reluctantly and now found themselves plugging it on *Top Of The Pops*. The soul feel went out the window as the group released paisley confections like 'For Whom The Bell Tolls' (which barely cracked the Top 50 at 43) in March '68, 'Part Of My Past' (May '68) and 'Thinking About My Life' (September '68), Without doubt their most psychedelic moment was 'We Are The Moles', recorded as alter-egos The Moles and so redolent of *Magical Mystery Tour*-era Beatles, that some poor souls were fooled into thinking it was the Fabs behind a pseudonym.

After two more unsuccessful singles Dupree suffered a nervous breakdown and The Big Sound disintegrated in 1970. The Shulman brothers stayed together throughout the Seventies in proggers Gentle Giant.

Julie Driscoll

SAVE ME
JULIE DRISCOLL
AND BRIAN AUGER
WITH THE TRINITY
MARMALADE 598004
Distributed by Polydor Records Ltd.

63

Simon Dupree & The Big Sound

THE EASYBEATS

Like The Zombies The Easybeats were one of the most inventive and under-rated groups of the era. Although they remain irrevocably linked with Australia, their international hit 'Friday On My Mind' and some of their most original (and ignored) recordings were made in Blighty. Besides all five were of English, Scottish and Dutch origin, whose parents had emigrated 'down under' in the early Sixties. Formed at the Villawood Migrant Hostel in Sydney in 1964 Stevie Wright (from Leeds) George Young (from Glasgow) and Gordon 'Snowy' Fleet (a Liverpudlian who had played in an early line-up of The Mojos before boarding the boat) joined forces with Dutchmen Harry Vanda – guitar and Dick Diamonde- bass.

After paying their dues in the harbour city's rougher clubs the group acquired a manager in Mike Vaughan, signed to EMI (Australia) in 1965 and within a year 'Easyfever' swept the whole country with the classic singles 'For My Woman', 'She's So Fine' (the first of four homegrown number ones), 'Wedding Ring', 'Sad And Lonely And Blue', a double A-sider 'Women'/'In My Book', 'Come And See Her' and 'Sorry', along with a top-selling EP *Easyfever* and three class albums *Easy*, *It's 2 Easy* and *Volume 3*. Most of the group's originals were initially written by Young and Wright, although the latter's role was taken over by Vanda once he'd commanded English.

In July 66, finding themselves big fish in a small pond, the group and Vaughan set their sights on England. They arrived in London where their English record company United Artists had released 'Come And See Her' (admittedly not their strongest card) to minimal effect. The group were paired with Kinks/Who producer Shel Talmy and the follow up 'Friday On My Mind' was a classic piece of power pop, which deserved to have gone all the way, but stopped at number six in December. Despite the group's absence it inevitably reached the top in Australia and broke through in the US where it made number 16 in April '67. While subsequent singles failed to match the immediate commerciality of 'Friday' The Easybeats boldly experimented with 'Who'll Be The One', 'Heaven and Hell' and 'Falling Off The Edge Of The World' – the latter, like 'Do I Figure In Your Life?' by The Honeybus, dealing with the uncommon pop subject of marital breakdown.

Unfortunately for all their brilliance they failed to sell as did the group's 1967 début album *Good Friday* – the recording of which soured their working relationship with Talmy. While their fortunes may have been fading in Britain the Easybeats returned to Australia in May '67 for a triumphant tour as homecoming heroes. However Fleet had tired of the pop star lifestyle and quit after the last gig in Perth, his replacement being Englishman Tony Cahill of local legends The Purple Hearts. When 'The Music Goes Round My Head' and its superior flip, 'Come In You'll Get Pneumonia' failed in December '67 the group drastically resorted to the big ballad treatment that was all the rage at the time with 'Hello, How Are You' which made it to number 20 in May' 68. It was a hollow reward as the group's heart

lay with rockers like 'Good Times' (a follow-up single which featured admirer Steve Marriott on backing vocals). Both tracks appeared on the group's second English album *Vigil* which displayed Vanda and Young's studio expertise having spent their extra-curricular time with various pet projects like My Dear Watson and Grapefruit (who featured Young's elder brother Alex).

A change of style to harder rock and a new record label in Polydor produced 'St. Louis' and the album *Friends*. The Easybeats were running on empty in England and returned to Australia to play their final gigs in 1969. Vanda and Young stayed together forming their company Albert Productions, releasing a variety of records under pseudonyms and producing various young hopefuls, including Young's little brothers, Malcolm and Angus in AC/DC. The pair received massive success from composing and producing the John Paul Young hit 'Love Is In The Air'. Fleet became a builder in Perth, Diamonde a drug fiend. Wright seemed set for a successful solo career, scoring a number one with the epic 'Evie (Parts 1&2)' but a serious heroin habit debilitated his progress. In 1986 to mark the anniversary of 'Friday On My Mind' the original members reunited for one last nostalgic Australian tour.

(see also Grapefruit)

THE END

Sometimes the old adage 'It's not what you know, it's who you know' just doesn't cut the mustard and The End are a perfect example. They were the young protégés of Rolling Stone Bill Wyman and as such they seemed destined for recognition.

Formed by Colin Giffin (guitar/sax) and Dave Brown (bass), previously with The Innocents (who met their benefactor on a 1964 Stones tour support slot), the early line-up was completed by Nicky Graham (organ), John Horton (sax) and Roger Groom (drums). Ironically The End's career was summed up by the title of their Glyn Johns produced début 45, 'I Can't Get Any Joy', released on Philips in September 1965. It sank without trace. Regular support slots on Stones dates and a move to Decca in 1967 looked promising but did nothing to help commercially. Groom and Horton were replaced by Hugh Atwooll and Gordon 'Goldie' Smith respectively.

Another single 'Shades Of Orange', a ghostly psychedelic number recorded in November '67 featured Charlie Watts playing

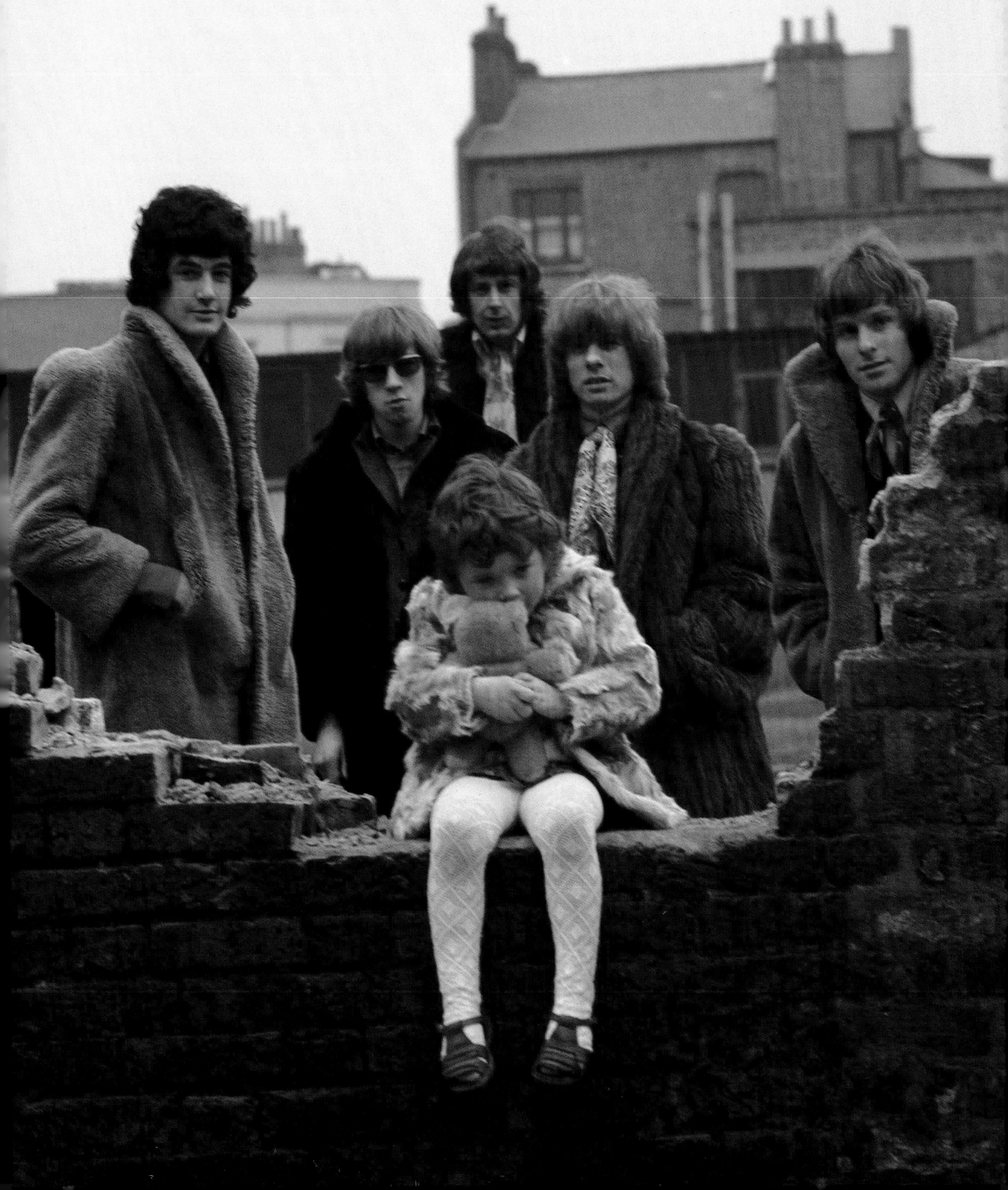

The Eyes Of Blue

tabla and a phased Lennonesque vocal so convincing that it turned up on Beatles' bootlegs in the Seventies. The single went nowhere when released the following March. The End relocated to Spain where they were quite popular and released a number of records exclusive to that market. Gordie was replaced by guitarist Terry Taylor and then in early 69 both Giffin and Atwooll quit.

In December 1969, Decca belatedly released the album *Introspection* (featuring the Stones rhythm section and keyboard whizz Nicky Hopkins) containing tracks recorded and stockpiled over the preceding two years. Thanks to 'Shades Of Orange' The End's reputation has been reassessed by beat and psychedelic collectors over the years, resulting in three collections by Sixties reissue specialists Tenth Planet – *In The Beginning…*, *Retrospection* and *The Last Word* licensed from Wyman's company, Ripple Productions.

The End have since reformed for the odd one-off appearance, most recently on the Isle of Wight for the New Untouchables weekender in 1998.

THE EQUALS
BABY COME BACK
No 27 THIS WEEK   PT 135
PRESIDENT RECORDS
25, DENMARK STREET, LONDON. W.C.2. 01-240 3026

THE EQUALS

Along with The Foundations, skinhead fave raves The Equals were one of England's first hitmaking interracial groups, remembered mainly for the involvement of guitarist Eddie Grant. The north London five-piece consisted of three West Indians – Grant (lead guitar/vocals), twins Dervin and Lincoln Gordon (vocals and rhythm guitar respectively) plus Englishmen John Hall (drums) and Patrick Lloyd (guitar). Grant cut a bit of a dash with his bleached white Afro and the group stomped into the number one position in July '68 with a reissue of the pounding 'Baby, Come Back'.

The group were even more popular on the Continent, particularly in Germany where they enjoyed a three-year run of chart action with singles like 'I Won't Be There', 'I Get So Excited' and 'Softly Softly'. 'Viva Bobby Joe' was adapted by football terraces up and down the country and 'Black Skin Blue Eyed Boy' was one of 1970's biggest tunes. Their fair-selling albums included *Unequalled Equals* (1967) and *Equals Explosion* (1968). Grant left in '71 and the hits stopped coming, however that didn't deter The Equals from continuing recording and performing in cabaret. Grant became a successful producer and scored several solo hits in the early Eighties. He now lives in the Caribbean where he runs a studio.

THE ESCORTS

The Escorts formed in 1962, featuring Ray Walker (vocals), Terry Sylvester (guitar, vocals), John Kinrade (guitar), Mike Gregory (bass) and original drummer John Foster, aka Johnny Sticks. In April '63, Walker quit to get married while Foster was replaced by Pete Clarke.

Like compatriots The Merseybeats, The Escorts were signed to Fontana by A&R man Jack Baverstock. The group's début single, a raucous cover of Larry Williams' 'Dizzy Miss Lizzy', appeared in April 1964. Their second single, 'The One To Cry', was a minor hit in June but despite being one of the more accomplished second-generation Merseyside outfits, The Escorts failed to click with a public besotted by the likes of Gerry and Freddie.

Perhaps it was their choice of cover versions. The Drifters' 'I Don't Want To Go On Without You' was also covered by The Searchers and The Moody Blues while The Everly Brothers' 'Let It Be Me' was competing against Peter & Gordon. Clarke left and rejoined The Escorts on two occasions; his 1964/65 replacement being Kenny Goodless, who ended up in The Merseys' backing band The Fruit Eating Bears.

In January 1966 Sylvester left to join another Liverpudlian band on the rocks, The Swinging Blue Jeans, before taking over from Graham Nash in The Hollies three years later. His erstwhile bandmates signed to Columbia, replacing Sylvester with ex-Big Three, Paddy Klaus & Gibson guitarist Paddy Chambers and Clarke with Tommy Kelly for their swansong release, a version of the Miracles 'From Head To Toe', produced by Paul McCartney who played tambourine. Kelly was replaced by Paul Comerford (ex-Cryin' Shames) before The Escorts finally split in July '67.

(see also The Cryin' Shames, The Fruit Eating Bears, The Hollies, The Swinging Blue Jeans)

THE EYES

Formed in Ealing in 1964, The Eyes were originally called The Aces, then The Arrows, who became Dave Russell & The Renegades, and, in turn Gerry Hart & The Hartbeats. Led by vocalist Terry Nolder, Chris Lovegrove and Phil Heatley (guitars), Barry Allchin (bass) and Brian Corcoran (drums), they settled on the name The Eyes (equally as crap a name as the others!) in 1965 in time to cash in on the pop art movement pioneered by The Who. The Eyes used the obligatory wail

The Eyes

The Eyes Of Blue

The Fairies

of feedback and distortion but combined it with a backing track of police sirens and sound effects such as skidding cars, alarm clocks and a gong Corcoran had bought for £2 down the Portobello Road which he would hit indiscriminately throughout their set.

The group failed to have even a minor hit despite being the first to advertise their efforts on railway hoardings and on London buses in January 1966 with the saying 'The Eyes Are Smashed To Fragments'. The first of three Mercury singles, 'When The Night Fails' was a moody piece of freakbeat with eerie sound effects, wailing harp and power chords, while the flipside, 'I'm Rowed Out' was a blatant rewrite of the Who's 'I Can't Explain' riff, in turn pinched from 'You Really Got Me' and 'Louie Louie'. The single failed to chart, as did three other singles for Mercury: 'The Immediate Pleasure', with 'My Degeneration' – a Who parodic ode to 'coffee', Mod slang for sex – on the flip, The Everly Brothers 'Man With Money', filched from The Who's live act, and its powerhouse underbelly, 'You're Too Much' – 'borrowed' (again!) from The Birds' 'How Can It Be'. A BBC ban thanks to 'The Immediate Pleasure' didn't help their commercial prospects. A final single – a cover of the Fabs' *Revolver* tune, 'Good Day Sunshine' - and an album of Rolling Stones' covers as The Pupils, ended things on a desultory note.

The Arrival Of The Eyes (1966) must rank along with The Artwoods' *Jazz In Jeans* as one of the rarest UK-pressed EPs from the Sixties Beat era. As for The Eyes, they were last seen sporting London Underground uniforms which may offer a clue as to their eventual destination.

THE EYES OF BLUE

Along with The Bystanders, this group were part of a Welsh attempt to match the West Coast sound, but in their early period, Neath's Eyes Of Blue were a stomping soul band, more akin to their Welsh brethren Amen Corner. In their 'Stax-Volt' period they made two singles for Deram in 1966/67, 'Heart Trouble' and 'Supermarket Full Of Cans'. From there the group recorded two progressive-psych LPs for Mercury and even a movie cameo in *Connecting Rooms*.

THE FAIRIES

One of the all-time great raving British R&B outfits, The Fairies were responsible for a genre classic in 'Get Yourself Home', a cacophonous Pretties-styled thrash full of frantic percussion and cavernous echo. (In fact The Pretty Things, who shared the same management, had recorded a demo of the song for possible single release.)

The combo typified the arrogantly hirsute, maracas-shaking end of the beat boom, a transcendent moment in 1964-65 when punkified white boy rhythm'n'blues made a small but significant chart impact. Originally known as Dane Stephens & The Deepbeats, the Colchester-based Fairies released their first single on Decca, the peppy 'Anytime At All', in 1964 with Stephens (vocals), Fred Gandy (guitar), John Acutt (guitar), 'Wimp' Weaver (bass) and John 'Twink' Alder (drums). Stephens (real name Dougie Ord) was temporarily replaced by the Jagger-ish Nick Wymer, formerly of The Nix-Nomads, for 'Get Yourself Home', before returning for a more melodic final single, 'Don't Mind', in 1965. Alder went on to fill the drum stool in The In Crowd, Tomorrow, and, ultimately, The Pretty Things.

(see also The In Crowd, The Pretty Things, Tomorrow)

MARIANNE FAITHFULL

Within weeks of meeting Andrew Oldham at a party thrown in Easter 1964 by the Stones svengali to launch singer Adrienne Posta, Reading convent school educated Marianne had recorded and released 'As Tears Go By' - a song specially tailor-made for her, marking the start of the Jagger/Richards songwriting partnership.

Born in Hampstead, London, the daughter of the Austro-Hungarian Baroness Erisso, Eva Sacher-Masoch and a professor of Italian Renaissance studies, Dr. Robert Glynn Faithfull, Marianne's success with 'As Tears Go By' – number nine in August 1964 - prompted Decca's unique move to simultaneously release her first two albums on the same day. After the follow-up, a Joan Baez-style reading of

Marianne Faithfull

71

Marianne Faithfull

'The House Of The Rising Sun' flopped, Marianne reached number four with her follow-up, Jackie De Shannon's 'Come And Stay With Me' in February 1965, following through with 'This Little Bird' (number six), 'Summer Nights' (number 10) and, finally, a cover of 'Yesterday', which reached number 36 in November.

By then, she had married Cambridge undergraduate John Dunbar, giving birth to their son Nicholas which to all intents and purposes put her pop career on hold. Her final chart success was 'Is This What I Get For Loving You?' which reached No. 43 in March 1967.

With her straight blonde hair and demure dresses, Marianne was initially promoted as a shyly innocent beauty but her subsequent relationship with Mick Jagger (that began in December 1966) changed all that, and her reputation for notoriety wasn't helped when she became infamous as the 'Mars Bar' girl following the infamous police drugs raid at Keith Richard's Redlands home in February 1967.

In 1968 she recorded 'Sister Morphine', co-written with Jagger and Richards, paired with Goffin-King's 'Something Better' (performed for *The Rolling Stones' Rock And Roll Circus* television special). However, Decca executives objected to the song's so-called drug content (actually about a car crash victim waiting to be administered a final pain-killing dose) and withdrew the record from sale shortly after its release in February 1969. Her talents were not confined to music, Marianne also appeared on the London stage, playing Irma in *Three Sisters* (1967), Ophelia in *Hamlet* (1969), and also made excursions into film with *I'll Never Forget Whatsisname?* (1967) and the notorious *Girl On A Motorcycle* (*Naked Under Leather* in the US) in 1968.

Marianne closed out the Sixties with a failed suicide attempt in Sydney, Australia, in July, 1969, while Jagger was filming Ned Kelly there. It marked the beginning of the couple's estrangement and over a decade of rough living for the baroness's daughter. Putting disastrous affairs and drug addiction behind her, Marianne has in recent years returned recovered and rejuvenated, with new recordings, acclaimed concerts and her autobiography *Faithful*, published in 1993. Sharp of wit and with a croak that only a million cigarettes could produce, she is now a grande dame of rock, appearing regularly on chat shows to dispense the wisdom of her altogether unique experiences.

GEORGIE FAME

Lancashire lad Clive Powell began his long musical career playing piano at Butlins holiday camp where he was spotted by drummer Rory Blackwell who persuaded him to join his group and move to London in 1959.

There Powell was spotted by songwriter Lionel Bart and recommended to rock impresario Larry Parnes. Parnes' management stable already boasted a Wilde (Marty), a Fury (Billy)

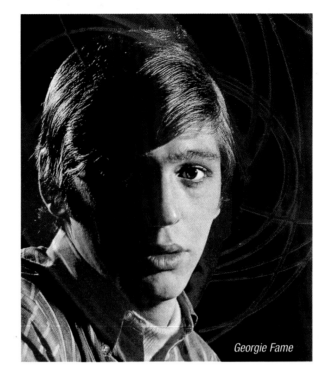
Georgie Fame

and a Power (Duffy) so Powell was renamed Georgie Fame. As well as auditioning to back Gene Vincent Fame acted as a backing musician for Parnes' top names, including the aforementioned Marty Wilde, and Vince Eager before joining Billy Fury's band the Blue Flames in 1961. Fury eventually replaced the band with The Tornadoes and Fame assumed leadership as Georgie Fame & The Blue Flames.

In January 1962 the band began a residency at the Flamingo club in the basement of the Whiskey A Go-Go in Wardour Street, run by Rik Gunnell, who became Fame's manager. The club was a haven for visiting American servicemen and one evening a visiting GI turned Fame on to Jimmy Smith and Mose Allison. Smith's sound featured the distinctively powerful Hammond B3 organ while Allison's cool, smoky delivery and jazzy piano arrangements were equally revelatory. The next day Fame went out and ordered a Hammond. The Flamingo wouldn't be the same and the Blue Flames built up a large following amongst the capital's mod fraternity playing a potent mix of Jazz, R&B and Jamaican Blue Beat.

Record company ears began to hear of the buzz that Fame was creating in Soho and on the recommendation of Ian Samwell (who had composed Cliff Richard's best ever single, 'Move It') Fame signed to EMI in 1963. Fame's first batch of Columbia 45s failed to sell beyond the Flamingo faithful as did his début album *Live At The Flamingo Club* which remains an accurate and evocative record of an all-nighter in the sweaty basement.

The second 1964 album *Fame At Last* did exactly what it said on the sleeve and reached the Top 20 paving the way for 'Yeh Yeh' which sailed to the number one spot in January 1965. It became a million seller and set Fame up as one of the leading exponents of the British R&B scene. Fame went from strength to strength as a musician and performer but follow-ups like 'In The Meantime', 'Like We Used To Be' and 'Something' (a John Mayall song) failed to

create the same impact. In January 1966 Fame achieved his second number one with 'Get Away', which was originally written as a petrol advertisement. By now The Blue Flames featured ex-Riot Squad, and future Jimi Hendrix Experience drummer, Mitch Mitchell. A cover of Bobby Hebb's 'Sunny' and Billy Stewart's 'Sitting In The Park' were unsuccessful and when Fame's EMI contract ended, on the advice of manager Gunnell, he elected to ditch the band in order to go solo. He also rather surprisingly turned his back on R&B and chose to pursue a career in mainstream pop, recording for CBS.

Fame's third number one came with the Callender-Murray song, 'The Ballad Of Bonnie And Clyde' in January 1968 and his only US hit; number seven in March 1968. An album with the Harry South Big Band and a partnership with Alan Price at the end of the decade took him perilously close to cabaret career death but Fame pulled back with yet another hit 'Rosetta' under his belt in 1971.

Since then he has continued to divide his time between writing for television and a low-key solo career as well as guest appearances, including stints in Van Morrison's live set-up. Fame continues gigging with his son in a latter-day version of The Blue Flames.

(see also Jimi Hendrix Experience, Alan Price Set)

FAMILY

More underground heroes in the shape of Leicester five piece Family - Roger Chapman (vocals), Charles Whitney (guitar), Rick Grech (bass/violin) and Rob Townsend (drums) - who secured their place in rock lore as the inspiration for the anonymous band featured in Jenny Fabian's 1968 cult paperback *Groupie*.

Originally known as The Farinas, American scam merchant Kim Fowley suggested the name change to The Family and devised an advertising campaign that asked "Are you in the family way?" The group moved south to London as Family in 1967 and signed a one off single deal with Liberty who released the classic 'Scene Thru' The Eyes Of A Lens' – one of the high water marks of English psychedelia. The single bombed completely but the group became one of the most raved-about groups on London's underground scene. In contrast to most of his peace n' love contemporaries Chapman was a genuinely confrontational performer, drawing praise from the likes of John Lennon who marvelled at Chapman's tattoed knuckles spelling 'Love' and 'Hate'. The group's live reputation paved the way to a deal with Reprise and their début album *Music In A Dolls House*, released in August 1968 and produced by Traffic's Dave Mason was a huge critical success, peaking at number 35, while the follow-up *Family Entertainment* reached number 6 in April '69.

With a healthy home profile seemingly secure they embarked on a US tour that would prove disastrous, with American audiences less than enamoured with Family's brand of theatrical rock. An altercation with top US promoter Bill Graham did nothing for their

chances either. Grech left to join supergroup Blind Faith in May '69, being replaced by ex-Eric Burdon and The Animals guitar/violinist John Weider while sax player Jim King was sacked for a display of rock star behaviour. King's replacement was ex-Blossom Toes, John 'Poli' Palmer. Family enjoyed unexpected single successes with 'No Mule's Fool' (number 29 - November '69), 'Strange Band'/'The Weaver's Answer' (11 - October '70), 'In My Own Time' (4 - August 71 and 'Burlesque' (13 - November '72). Late additions to the Family were King Crimson guitarist John Wetton and pianist Tony Ashton.

Drummer Rob Townsend picked up sticks with Medicine Head and The Blues Band. Chapman and Whitney formed Streetwalkers. Grech appeared alongside Eric Clapton, Ginger Baker and Steve Winwood in the short-lived Blind Faith but died of kidney and liver failure in 1990, apparently destitute. Chapman is now based in Germany where he still enjoys tremendous popularity with *that* voice.

(see also Blossom Toes, Eric Burdon & The Animals)

CHRIS FARLOWE & THE THUNDERBIRDS

When singer John Deighton changed his name to Chris Farlowe and swapped skiffle for R&B he embarked on one of the longest running careers in British Rock. He also put together one of the most formidable backing bands of the early Sixties, The Thunderbirds. The group featured (at various times) the brilliant young guitarist Albert Lee, organist Dave Greenslade, pianist Nicky Hopkins, bass player Ricky Chapman, and drummer's Johnny Wise and Carl Palmer. The Thunderbirds became instant mod favourites and a semi-permanent fixture at clubs like the Flamingo and Klook's Kleek in Hampstead with a potent mixture of blues and soul covers.

A one-off deal with Decca produced the single 'Air Travel' (credited to 'Chris Farlow') in 1962 but despite the group's huge live appeal it didn't sell. A switch to Columbia in 1963 produced a year's run of excellent releases like 'I Remember', 'Girl Trouble' and a cover of Jimmy Clanton's 'Just A Dream' but precious little chart action.

A period of confusion followed early in 1965 when the single 'Buzz With The Fuzz' was withdrawn due to some suspect lyrics referring to 'joint rolling' and mod slang regarding our boys in blue. Then Farlowe released the single 'Stormy Monday Blues' under the pseudonym Little Joe Cook, on the legendary Sue label in an aborted effort to pass himself off as an American black artist. If that wasn't enough to put the anchors on an already precarious career then Farlowe's next gaffe was priceless.

Farlowe had just been dropped by Columbia but had been thrown a lifeline by the new Immediate label. It was an open secret that Farlowe needed a hit single and was on the look out for offers. Paul McCartney, well pleased with how a new song he'd written had turned out, arrived on the singer's doorstep and gave him first refusal on it. Farlowe unbelievably declined 'Yesterday' and opted instead for the appropriately titled 'The Fool' which became yet another non-charter. Realising the magnitude of such a Fabs-related *faux pas* label boss Andrew Loog Oldham strongly suggested the next best thing and Farlowe was given the Jagger-Richards' 'Think', produced by Jagger which the Stones had recorded for their *Aftermath* album. Released in January '66 a Farlowe single finally cracked the Top 40 reaching number 37. It coincided with Immediate's first EP release *Farlowe In The Midnight Hour* – a best-selling selection of cover versions - clocking in at a respectable sixth place on the EP charts. The album *14 Things To Think About* made number 19 but Farlowe's finest moment followed in July when Jagger's production of another *Aftermath* offcut 'Out Of Time' swept to the top spot. Columbia responded by reissuing 'Just A Dream' and a compilation of Farlowe & The Thunderbirds output for the label but with the artist condemning them in the music press unsurprisingly, they failed to sell. Farlowe was riding high among his peers, being invited along to *Ready, Steady, Go!* in September as a personal guest of Otis Redding, with whom he duetted.

It was a case of third time unlucky as a third Jagger-Richards song 'Ride On Baby' unexpectedly stalled outside the Top 30 in November, while a second Immediate album *The Art Of Chris Farlowe* (released in December) got to 37. Small Faces' Steve Marriott and Ronnie Lane took over the producer-composer roles for 'My Way Of Giving', for which they sang back-up vocals with Jagger, but the single only managed one week in the chart at 48 in February '67. Jagger returned to produce 'Yesterdays Papers' but this fared even worse, and by mid-'67 it was becoming obvious Farlowe was losing ground. There would only be three more minor hits – a sitar-tabla driven cover of jazzman Jon Hendricks 'Moanin', Mike D'Abo's composition 'Handbags And Gladrags', and a gypsy-like arrangement of the Stones' 'Paint It Black', released in 1968, that had been recorded two years before.

Farlowe returned in 1970 with a new look and a new band The Hill. Gone were the sharp mod togs of the early to mid-Sixties; replaced by long hair and buckskin. The band recorded one album before Farlowe rejoined Dave Greenslade in Colosseum.

Since then Farlowe has flitted from one group project to the next including spells with Atomic Rooster, Stone The Crows, and a reformed Thunderbirds, as well as singing on Jimmy Page's *Nightrider* album in 1988.

He still owns and runs an antiques business in Islington, North London and recently enjoyed some of the best reviews of his career playing and touring with Van Morrison.

FARON'S FLAMINGOS

Yet more Merseybeat also-rans Faron's Flamingos (singer-guitarist Nicky Crouch, Billy Jones – guitar, Eric London - bass and Trevor Morais – drums) were a popular live attraction around Liverpool's dancehalls.

Originally called The Ravens they changed their name following the arrival of singer Bill (Faron) Roughley in 1961 when Cavern Club DJ Bob Wooler suggested the new name. London left to be replaced by 'Mushy' Cooper and after a tour of US air force bases in France further changes saw Jones leave and Paddy Chambers join in 1962. When Cooper left Faron took on the additional role of bassist in 1963.

This line-up recorded two tracks, 'Let's Stomp' and 'Talkin' Bout You' for the Oriole Records compilation album *This Is Mersey Beat* (1963). Faron's Flamingos had two non-charting singles 'Shake Sherry' and a cover of the Contours' US hit 'Do You Love Me' which only just lost out to Brian Poole & The Tremeloes' version. The group split at the height of Merseymania in November '63. Faron and Chambers joined the equally unsuccessful Big Three, Crouch went to The Mojos, while Morais later joined The Peddlers.

(see also The Big Three, The Mojos)

GARY FARR & THE T-BONES

Hailing from the South Coast, blond haired blue-eyed Farr was the son of boxer Tommy Farr. His five piece T-Bones took over The Yardbirds residency at the Crawdaddy Club at Richmond Athletic Ground in 1964, and like the 'Birds also gained a contract with Columbia. The group released several unsuccessful soul covers for the label and unissued Giorgio Gomelsky-produced recordings from this time were issued as *London 1964/65* in 1977.

When the original line-up disbanded at the end of '65, Farr formed a new T-Bones including former Who roadie Dave 'Cyrano' Langston (guitar), Lee Jackson (bass) and Keith Emerson (organ). When they split in '67, Jackson and Emerson went on to form The Nice. Farr then hooked up with Gomelsky's newly-formed Marmalade label, joining up with former Blossom Toes drummer Kevin Westlake in a short-lived duo The Lion And The Fish. He issued two albums for Marmalade, *Take Something With You* (1969) and *Strange Fruit* (1971) before emigrating to America in '72 where he cut *Addressed To The Censors Of Love* at Muscle Shoals.

Little was heard from Farr until his premature death in 1994. His brother Rikki was originally a successful club promoter and manager, and co-staged the 1969 & 70 Isle of Wight Festivals. He now runs a health food restaurant in Los Angeles.

(see also Blossom Toes, The Nice)

FIRE

If nothing else, Fire's place in Sixties Brit freakbeat is assured with 'Father's Name Is Dad', a dynamic, riff-laden pop-rocker that's as catchy as a cold. Its Who-like B-side, 'Treacle Toffee World', is almost equally impressive. Hailing from Hounslow, the trio (Dave Lambert – guitar, Bob Voice – drums and Dick Dufall - bass) were originally

Fire

known as Friday's Chyld and were an early signing to The Beatles' Apple publishing company by plugger Mike Berry. The initial response to their 1968 début was encouraging - luckily as the band had re-recorded the vocals on the advice of Paul McCartney, resulting in two different mixes of the single - but the group was coerced into allowing an appalling pop ditty, 'Round The Gum Tree', as the follow-up. Subsequently, Fire and their record label/publisher parted company and the group worked up fresh material that was to become *The Magic Shoemaker* concept album for Pye in 1970. Lambert joined The Strawbs in 1972.

In 1997, Sixties reissue specialists Tenth Planet released *Underground And Overhead: The Alternate Fire*, consisting of unissued demos from the 1967-68 period, that hinted at the group's potential if they'd been allowed to develop naturally.

FIVE DAY WEEK STRAW PEOPLE

Not really a group, rather a side project connected to The Attack. In early 1968 Attack guitarist John DuCann was commissioned to record an exploitative psychedelic album for Saga Records, a label that specialized in budget cash-in albums for the likes of Woolworths.

Ironically, as Five Day Week Straw People, Du Cann and fellow musicians Mick Hawksworth (bass) and Jack Collins (drums) crafted a remarkably interesting record that, despite its murky sound thanks to a bad pressing, is filled with intriguing pop-psych. The album went on to survive the bargain bins and has become something of a collectors item. Bizarre!

(see also The Attack)

FLEETWOOD MAC

One of the great institutions of British Rock were formed in 1967 as Peter Green's Fleetwood Mac. The Fleetwood in question was ex-Cheynes, Bo Street Runners drummer Mick Fleetwood, who had known singer-guitar player Green since teaming up together in The Peter B's (aka Peter B's Looners), Shotgun Express and John Mayall's Bluesbreakers. They were joined by second guitarist Jeremy Spencer and bass player Bob Brunning. The band got their name from an instrumental composition Green and Fleetwood recorded along with Mayall bassist John McVie while still in The Bluesbreakers.

Right from their conception they were an ideal choice to record for Decca producer Mike Vernon's new Blue Horizon record label, and their début single - a cover of Elmore James' 'I Believe My Time Ain't Long' – was sung by James' acolyte Spencer. The four-piece made their live début at the Windsor National Jazz and Blues Festival in August '67. Brunning departed to form the Brunning-Hall Sunflower Blues Band and McVie rejoined his erstwhile bandmates Green and Fleetwood in December. Peter Green's Fleetwood Mac,

released in February '68 was an unadulterated tribute to the blues greats that inspired them but without being slavishly interpreted the performances were stamped with the musicians' individuality. The album belted up the charts to number 4 and put the group at the forefront of the British Blues Boom that was about to sweep the country for the next year. It marked the beginning of phase one of Fleetwood Mac's incredible yet bizarre career.

Now abbreviated to Fleetwood Mac single success followed hot on the heels of the album with Green's 'Black Magic Woman' making number 37 in April and 'Need Your Love So Bad' number 31 in August. In mid-68 in an effort to subtly change the band's musical direction Green decided to expand the line-up by adding a second guitar player, 18-year-old Danny Kirwan. Kirwan had come under Green's wing as part of a Brixton three piece named Boilerhouse, in whom Green took a managerial interest. When over 300 applicants auditioned to replace bassist Trevor Stevens and drummer David Terry none were deemed suitable by the hard to please Green so Kirwan simply joined the Mac.

The band began to move away from the restrictions of playing simple 12-bar blues, although this approach was still evident on the group's second album *Mr. Wonderful* (released in September, reaching number 10), augmented by Chicken Shack's piano player, Christine Perfect. Green's haunting and timeless instrumental 'Albatross' flew to the top spot in January '69 and was followed by the chillingly autobiographical 'Man Of The World' - a number 2 hit in May, released on stopgap label, Immediate. Fleetwood Mac signed to Frank Sinatra's Reprise Records and found themselves in the enviable position of being able to achieve hit singles without losing their credibility with the underground albums market. 'Oh Well

Fire

First Gear

FLEETWOOD MAC 7-63200
FIRST BLUE HORIZON ALBUM

Manufactured and distributed by
CBS Records, 28-30 Theobalds Rd., London WC1

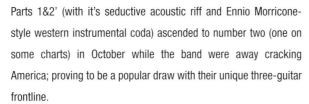

Parts 1&2' (with it's seductive acoustic riff and Ennio Morricone-style western instrumental coda) ascended to number two (one on some charts) in October while the band were away cracking America; proving to be a popular draw with their unique three-guitar frontline.

Their début album for Reprise *Then Play On* was the perfect tool to crack the market wide open but with it came disaster. Kirwan and Green fell out on a European tour, while the latter had fallen in with a bad crowd in Denmark, ingesting some particularly bad acid which left him profoundly affected. Green made the decision to quit and announced his intention in May 1970 just as his last contribution to the band 'The Green Manalishi' climbed the charts to number 10. Fleetwood Mac played on and entered yet another phase. Now married to John McVie Christine Perfect joined as a permanent member and the group concentrated their attention almost solely on the US market. Their early Seventies albums *Kiln House*, *Future Games*, *Bare Trees*, *Penguin*, *Mystery To Me* and *Heroes Are Hard To Find* were reasonably successful across the Atlantic but were all but ignored in the UK. Jeremy Spencer disappeared in 1971, mid-way through an American tour only to turn up as part of a fervent religious cult called the Children of God.

Danny Kirwan was sacked for drunken behaviour in 1972 and several configurations of the band followed. In 1973 a bogus Fleetwood Mac toured the States and in 1974 American duo Lindsey Buckingham and Stevie Nicks joined the splintered line-up. By the mid-to-late Seventies inter-band marriages and outrageous Rock Star behaviour became the norm; a few colossal selling albums *Fleetwood Mac*, *Rumours* and *Tusk* meant they could do it in style! After many years of mental illness Peter Green finally returned to the musical fray and now plays regularly with his own Splinter Band.

Mick Fleetwood now co-owns the successful London auction house Fleetwood Owen.

(see also The Bo Street Runners, The Cheynes, Elmer Gantry's Velvet Opera, John Mayall, The Peter B's, Shotgun Express)

(LES) FLEUR-DE-LYS

A name that inspires awe when uttered in the presence of British mod and psych enthusiasts, on the basis of a handful of singles the group recorded between 1965 and 1968. The labyrinthine twists of line-up changes and pseudonyms is complicated to say the least so pay attention!

Forming in Southampton in 1964 the original Fleur-de-Lys (translated 'flower of leaves') comprised Frank Smith (guitar/vocals), Alex Chamberlain (organ), Gary Churchill (bass) and Keith Guster (drums). (Guster was the only constant throughout the constant personnel upheavals). Signed to Immediate, their first single - an uncharacteristic remake of Buddy Holly's 'Moondreams', produced by Jimmy Page, was released in November 1965 and promptly vanished. Disillusioned the group folded with Guster resuscitating a new line-up with three London musicians, Gordon Haskell (bass), Phil Sawyer (guitar), and Pete Sears (keyboards). The group's style was best exemplified by their second release, 'Circles', a Pete Townshend composition – also recorded by The Who – featuring a searing guitar solo from Sawyer, released by Immediate in March 1966.

More changes occurred when vocalist Chris Andrews' (no relation to the 'Yesterday Man' hitmaker) made the group a five piece, only for Sawyer and Sears to leave and guitarist Bryn Haworth to join. The brash brand of Who-like pop-art, continued with 'Mud In Your Eye', a hard-hitting number (the first of three 1966-68 singles

Les Fleur-De-Lys

The Flys

The big Ivy League and Flowerpot Men mix-up

IT'S all a bit unfortunate, really.
I mean, when the Flowerpot Men's first record came out. Everyone said, "Well, it's only your actual Ivy League, innit."

But they were only wrong, weren't they?

But wrong or not, it certainly effected the Ivy League — so I spoke to Perry Ford to try to find out what it was all about.

"When the Flowerpot Men first appeared on the scene, most people seemed to think that it was in fact the Ivy League with a new name — the general opinion was that there was no more Ivy League. Two or three club-owners in places we'd been booked rang up to cancel our dates.

"At one place we went to — right out in the jungles of England — we went onstage, and three little dollies came rushing over and said 'Where are they?' I asked them what they were on about, and they said: The Flowerpot Men — where are they?' Apparently they thought that the Flowerpot Men were our backing group!

"I don't really know whether it did us harm or good — perhaps the only bad thing about it was that people thought the group had disbanded. We certainly got a lot of publicity out of it though.

"Anyway, we're still very much alive — we've been doing cabaret for about a year, and we're fully booked up until next March. But we want to get back onto the pop scene, and that's why the publicity we've been getting, on the whole, has been quite useful.

"I'm not knocking cabaret though—it's nice and steady, not as hectic as pop. But the pop scene is the most interesting thing in the world. It's really exciting and we'd like to get back into it — we've been working like mad, writing and rehearsing. And I think we'll get there soon — the two new guys in the group are great. Just what we needed in fact. It's like the early days of the Ivy League all over again.

"I'm pleased that Tony and Neil left us to form the Flowerpot Men. I'm not being nasty or anything — we're still the best o[...] I'm glad they're doing so well. It was a good [...]nd the two new guys [...]t great ideas, and no[...]
Ken Lewis le[...]
"In fact th[...] much of ear[...] them now a[...]
John and K[...] sort of feel[...]
"A lot o[...] singing on[...]
The first I[...] [...]ing at th[...]

WAYNE FONTANA AND THE MINDBENDERS
STOP, LOOK AND LISTEN
TF 451
fontana

wayne fontana and the mindbenders
THE GAME OF LOVE

for Polydor) with Haworth's clanging guitar, Guster's heavily compressed drums, and Andrews' resigned vocals.

Off record Fleur de Lys lead a double life as a soulful Stax/Volt influenced group; acting as a backing band to such visiting dignitaries as Aretha Franklin and Isaac Hayes. Around mid-67, through producer/manager Frank Fenter, the group were hired to work with South African blue-eyed soulstress Sharon Tandy, backing her on the coruscating Atlantic singles 'Hold On' and 'Daughter Of The Sun' and on Tony and Tandy's, 'Two Can Make It Together'. 'Hold On' was originally layed down by Fleur de Lys alter ego, Rupert's People, another brainchild of Fenter's, featuring guitarist friend Rod Lynton. Lynton had also composed a dreamy, Procol Harum-style number to go with it called 'Reflections Of Charles Brown'. However, only Andrews was enthused with it so the group left him to form a proper Rupert's People with Lynton; both tracks being issued as a Columbia single.

Now down to a three-piece their next releases came (in September '67) 'I Can See The Light', with Haworth on vocals, was passable, while 'Tick Tock' was issued under the pseudonym, Shyster. The next in line, 'Gong With The Luminous Nose', written by Haskell based on Edward Lear's famous nonsense poem was a tour-de-force of Haskell's dispassionate vocal, Haworth's crunching guitar, and Guster's drum fills. An album recorded with Polydor artist John Bromley was issued by Polydor while the group kept busy backing Donnie Elbert, and William E. Kimber on albums as well as the mysterious Waygood Ellis for a single.

Constant studio work and lack of commercial success hastened Haskell's departure in 1969, while the group switched labels from Polydor to Atlantic, with new members Tony Head (vocals) and Tago Byers (bass).

The group's uptempo horn-ridden side displayed itself on the commercial 'Stop Crossing The Bridge', and 'Butchers and Bakers' under the pseudonym Chocolate Frog. However, for many their best single was the last to arrive in February '69.

'Liar', co-written by Haworth, was a negative tour de force performance with soaring harmonies and Haworth's brilliant light and shade tones through guitar harmonics and blistering solos. Needless to say it joined the fate of all the group's other singles and the Fleur de Lys were finally at an end.

Of all the myriad line-up changes, Sears joined Sam Gopal, Stoneground, Silver Metre, before relocating to the West Coast to join John Cippolina in Copperhead. Sears then found success with Journey and Jefferson Starship. Sawyer joined Mark II of The Spencer Davis Group, Haworth pursued a solo career, while Haskell joined King Crimson at the end of '69 and had freak success with a self-produced number one 'How Wonderful You Are' in December 2001.

(see also Rupert's People, Spencer Davis Group)

THE FLIES

East London combo The Flies emerged in late 1966 with a blistering version of the garage rock perennial '(I'm Not Your) Stepping Stone'. They had been together since 1964, playing variously as The Rebs, The In-Sect (under which name they recorded a rare LP for the British-besotted US market), The Decadent Streak and No Flies On Us. Decca insisted the group shorten the latter to The Flies for release, but after a second single ('House Of Love'), the company dropped them. The more psychedelic follow-up, 'The Magic Train', released in 1968 on Decca-distributed RCA, marked the addition of songwriting drummer Peter Dunton to The Flies' ranks, but the group did not survive the year, and members splintered off to Gun, Please, Bulldog Breed and T2.

In their 1967 heyday, The Flies had a notorious stage act inspired by The Who and The Move that involved detonating bags of flour in the heat of the moment. When they appeared at the 14-Hour Technicolour Dream at London's Alexandra Palace in April of that year, wearing painted faces and palm leaf skirts, they managed to cover most of the audience in white powder (as seen in a BBC *Man Alive* television documentary 'What Is A Happening?'). Flour Power indeed.

THE FLOWERPOT MEN

The Flowerpot Men were the archetypal one hit wonders - the brain wave of session singer and original Ivy League man Perry Ford. As Scott McKenzie had done in the US, Ford, his brother Peter, and two latter-day Ivy Leaguers Tony Burrows and Neil Landon cashed in on the Californian centre of all things flower power, when 'Let's Go To San Francisco' reached number four at the fag end of the Summer of Love in September '67.

Of course they wouldn't let it lie and rather than go out on a glorious in-joke they ruined it by releasing a handful of follow-ups that were painfully poor and deservedly flopped. A name change to Friends in 1968 didn't win them any, and the whole thing came to a sorry end in 1969.

Burrows went on to Edison Lighthouse and Landon joined Fat Mattress. Ex-Artwood and future Deep Purple keyboardist Jon Lord led the studio musicians.

(see also The Artwoods, The Ivy League, The Searchers)

WAYNE FONTANA & THE MINDBENDERS

Wayne Fontana - known to his family as Glyn Ellis but apparently renamed in honour of Elvis Presley's legendary original drummer- signed to (where else?) Fontana Records after being spotted by A&R man Jack Baverstock, with Ellis' first group The Velfins at Manchester's Oasis club in 1963.

Bizarrely enough only Fontana and drummer Ric Rothwell bothered to attend the band's first run through. Session players Eric Stewart (guitar) and Bob Lang (bass) were hastily recruited and Fontana christened them The Mindbenders after the current cult horror film. The group cut their début single, a cover of Fats Domino's 'Hello Josephine' which although not a hit still made the bottom end of the Top 50 at 46. The new line-up, buoyed by the near miss, decided to stick together and recorded the even less successful 'For You For You'. Things began to look decidedly bleak when this was in turn followed by another non-starter 'Little Darlin''.

However a fourth single, a cover of Ben E. King's 'Stop Look And Listen' stopped the rot setting in when it squeezed the group back into the charts at number 37. Their breakthrough came with a fifth release and another cover with the Curtis Mayfield composition, 'Um,Um,Um,Um,Um', originally recorded by Major Lance and a number five, released in October 1964. The following year the band clocked up a further hit with a cover of Lavern Baker's 'The Game Of Love' – a UK number two in February and American number one a month later. The group were at the pinnacle of their success when suddenly things began to unravel, due to two significant factors. First they were temporarily prevented from seizing upon their American success due to a visa situation which left them stranded in the UK. Secondly the group turned down the Hank Ballard Jnr. song 'I'm Alive' as a follow-up to 'The Game Of Love'. They left it for fellow Mancs, The Hollies to take the song to the top spot while Fontana and The Mindbenders put out the inferior and ominously titled 'It's Just A Little Bit Too Late'. One more single - the self-penned original 'She Needs Love' – followed before singer and band parted acrimoniously at the end of 1965, sniping at each other through the pages of the music papers.

While The Mindbenders elected to remain together as a three piece, Fontana attempted a patchy solo career, which yielded only two minor hits – 'Come On Home' (number sixteen in June '66, written by Jackie Edwards, who composed 'Keep On Running' and 'Somebody Help Me' for The Spencer Davis Group) and the Graham Gouldman fantasy composition 'Pamela Pamela' (number eleven, January 1967). Fontana still performs as a solo act on the revivalist circuit and was last seen opening the 'Solid Silver Sixties' show at the London Palladium in 2001.

(see also The Mindbenders)

FORCE FIVE

An early Sixties beat group that had five members (singer Ron Gent, Bert Pulham and Pete Gosling - guitars, Dave Osbourne - bass and Dave Skates – drums), five singles, and five flops between 1964-66. They started in 1960 rather naively calling themselves The Shadows, then The Whirlwinds and after a quick count, Force Five. The group got a deal with United Artists and began a dismal run of singles luck with 'Don't Make My Baby Blue'. Follow up 'Yeah, I'm

Waiting' earned them a spot on *Ready, Steady, Go!* while the next three singles 'Baby Don't Care', 'I Want You Babe' and the apt 'Don't Know Which Way To Turn' took them struggling through to 1966. The following year Force Five backed American slush pot and fellow UA artist, Bobby Goldsboro on a single 'No Fun At The Fair'. Eventually another name change was decided upon - the delightful Crocheted Doughnut Ring.

DEAN FORD & THE GAYLORDS

A popular north of the borders showband, Dean Ford & The Gaylords formed in 1963. The original line-up featured singer Ford (real name Thomas MacAleese), William 'Junior' Campbell and Pat Fairlie (guitars), Graham Knight (bass) and Ray Duffy (drums).

A Glasgow covers band formed along the same lines as The Alex Harvey Soul Band, they played a mixture of Stax and Motown standards and secured a weekly guest spot on the BBC Scotland TV show *Come Thursday*. The band ventured to London, and thanks to a connection with Peter Walsh, the manager of Brian Poole and The Tremeloes, the group got a deal with Columbia. The group issued four singles kicking off with a limp version of Chubby Checker's 'Twenty Miles'. An early Gallagher and Lyle composition 'Mr Heartbreak's Here Instead' came next and showed little promise for neither band or songwriters.

A third cover released in 1965 was a rendition of Shirley Ellis's 'The Name Game'. Needless to say all three 45s sank, but it didn't deter the group from abbreviating their name to The Gaylords in 1966 and having one last stab with the moddy-sounding 'He's A Good Face (But He's Down And Out)'. The group's decision to relocate to London forced Duffy to leave (he later turned up in Matthews Southern Comfort) and his place was taken by ex-Attack drummer Alan Whitehead - a Sassenach hailing from Shropshire – who answered an ad placed in *Melody Maker*.

(see also The Attack, Marmalade).

THE FORTUNES

This long-lasting Midlands-based harmony group are something of a British pop institution, still going strong with Rod Allen (nee Rodney Bainbridge) at the fore. Formed in 1963 as The Cliftones, because of their membership at Clifton Hall, the Midlands pop academy, the group (Allen – bass, Glen Dale and Barry Pritchard - guitars, David Carr - keyboards and Andy Brown - drums) were managed by impresario Reg Clifton, who suggested the new name and secured them a Decca contract.

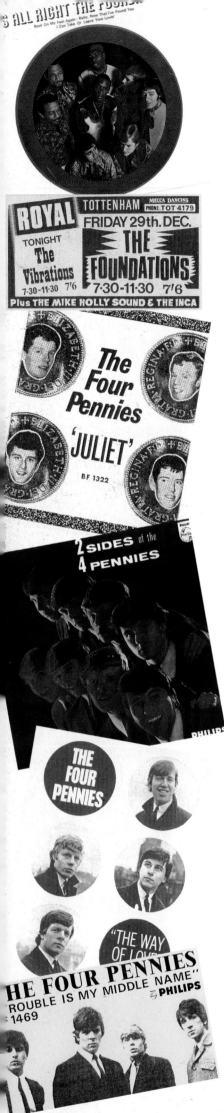

After flops with singles like 'Summertime, Summertime' (credited to 'Fortunes and Cliftones') and 'Caroline' (which the pirate radio station adopted as their theme) the lack of fortune changed in 1965, when their fifth single, the horn-laden weepie 'You've Got Your Troubles', written by duo Roger Cook and David Greenaway got to number two in July and seven in the US in September. 'Here It Comes Again' reached number four in October but subsequent '66 singles in a similar style, such as 'This Golden Ring' and 'You Gave Me Somebody To Love' (also recorded by Manfred Mann) failed to capitalise on the early hits. However from a musical point of view The Fortunes continued to record worthy, Moody Blues-style R&B on their flipsides. The group switched labels to United Artists in 1967 with 'The Idol', an accurate reflection of what fame can do to one's head, but aside from prolonging the band's popularity on the continent, the record was not the hit it deserved to be.

Good fortune arrived again in 1971 when 'Here Comes That Rainy Day Feeling' made the US Top 20 while 'Freedom Come, Freedom Go' and 'Storm In A Teacup' were Top 10 hits in the UK.

(see also David & Jonathan)

THE FOUNDATIONS

In the mid-Sixties, Britain had few convincing home-grown soul acts; relying on imports such as Geno Washington and Herbie Goins to provide some authentic grits n' gravy in the clubs. But like The Equals, the multiracial Foundations provided a breath of fresh air to the British pop scene.

Led by vocalist Clem Curtis, the line-up featured Alan Warner (guitar), Tony Gomez (organ), Pat Burke (tenor sax/flute), Mike Elliot (tenor sax), Eric Dale (trombone), Peter Macbeth (bass) and Tim Harris (drums). The group were discovered by record-shop proprietor Barry Class rehearsing in the basement below his office. The success of the Foundations in November 1967 with the Tony Macauley and John MacLeod-penned number one 'Baby, Now That I've Found You' proved that Blighty could successfully export a competent, commercial, yet soulful sound when the record reached number nine in America the following January with global sales exceeding three million.

The identikit Macauley-Macleod follow-ups to 'Baby…', 'Back On My Feet Again' and 'Any Old Time You're Sad And Lonely' deserved to flop but 'Build Me Up, Buttercup', co-written by Macauley and Manfred Mann's Mike D'Abo, with vocals by Curtis's replacement Colin Young, reached number two in December 1968. It was also successfully revived in America (where it originally reached number three in January '69) in the Farrelly Brothers 1997 comedy, *There's Something About Mary*. The Foundations scored one last top-ten hit with 'In The Bad, Bad Old Days' in March 1969 before the group's rhythm section splintered to form progressive outfit Pluto.

The Foundations are a textbook example of a group not being able to assimilate their record success into a career of any permanence. Their hits are fondly remembered, if not the actual members.

THE FOURMOST

From Liverpool and originally known as The Blue Jays, then The Four Jays, followed by The Four Mosts, singer-guitarist Mike Millward, Brian O' Hara (guitar), Billy Hatton (bass), and drummer Brian Redman (replaced by Dave Lovelady), became part of Brian Epsteins second division of bands in his frankly overcrowded NEMS stable.

Eppy took them on in 1963, shortened their name to The Fourmost and got the group signed to EMI. Sound familiar? He also ensured the band had a decent song or two courtesy of Messrs. Lennon and McCartney, and 'Hello Little Girl', previously offered to Gerry and the Pacemakers, made the Top 10 in October. The Fourmost's Beatle connection carried on throughout the year with various support slots and another song 'I'm In Love'. The Beatle magic didn't work so well second time around; the single only made the Top 20 in February 1964 while it did reach eight on some charts. The group enjoyed a further hit 'A Little Loving' (number six in May '64) and appeared with Gerry and Co. in the film *Ferry Cross The Mersey*. Their chart success eventually petered out with the passing of Merseybeat in 1965.

Sadly Millward died of leukaemia in 1966, leaving the group to carry on for a couple of barren years with replacement Bill Parkinson before drifting in to cabaret. One of their last CBS singles, 'Rosetta', (released in 1969), was produced by Paul McCartney.

THE FOUR PENNIES

Originally known as The Lionel Morton Four this Blackburn, Lancashire group was fronted by singer-guitarist Lionel Morton, Fritz Fryer (bass), Mike Wilsh (piano) and Alan Buck (drums).

Their first 45, asking the musical question 'Do You Want Me' was answered with a number 47 placing but its follow up - the soppy, Morton-composed ballad 'Juliet' - hit the top spot in May 1964. Ironically it was actually the B-side of the less commercial 'Tell Me Girl' that was flipped once it began to attract airplay. Unfortunately 'Juliet' labelled The Four Pennies as one hit wonders due to their subsequent releases falling short of the mark. Morton was the first to leave in 1966 and the group disbanded shortly after. Morton became a children's television personality and married actress Julia Foster while Fryer moved into production. Buck actively tried to re-form the band to work the cabaret circuit in the mid-Seventies but luckily failed to convince the others.

FOUR PLUS ONE

Not to be confused with Unit Four, nor Unit Four Plus Two this London R&B group (Keith Hopkins aka Keith West -vocals, Les Jones and John 'Junior' Wood – guitar, Simon 'Boots' Alcot - bass and Ken Lawrence – drums) added up to five. They recorded a solitary cover of 'Time Is On My Side' for Parlophone in 1964 before renaming themselves The In Crowd

(see also Aquarian Age, The In Crowd, Tomorrow)

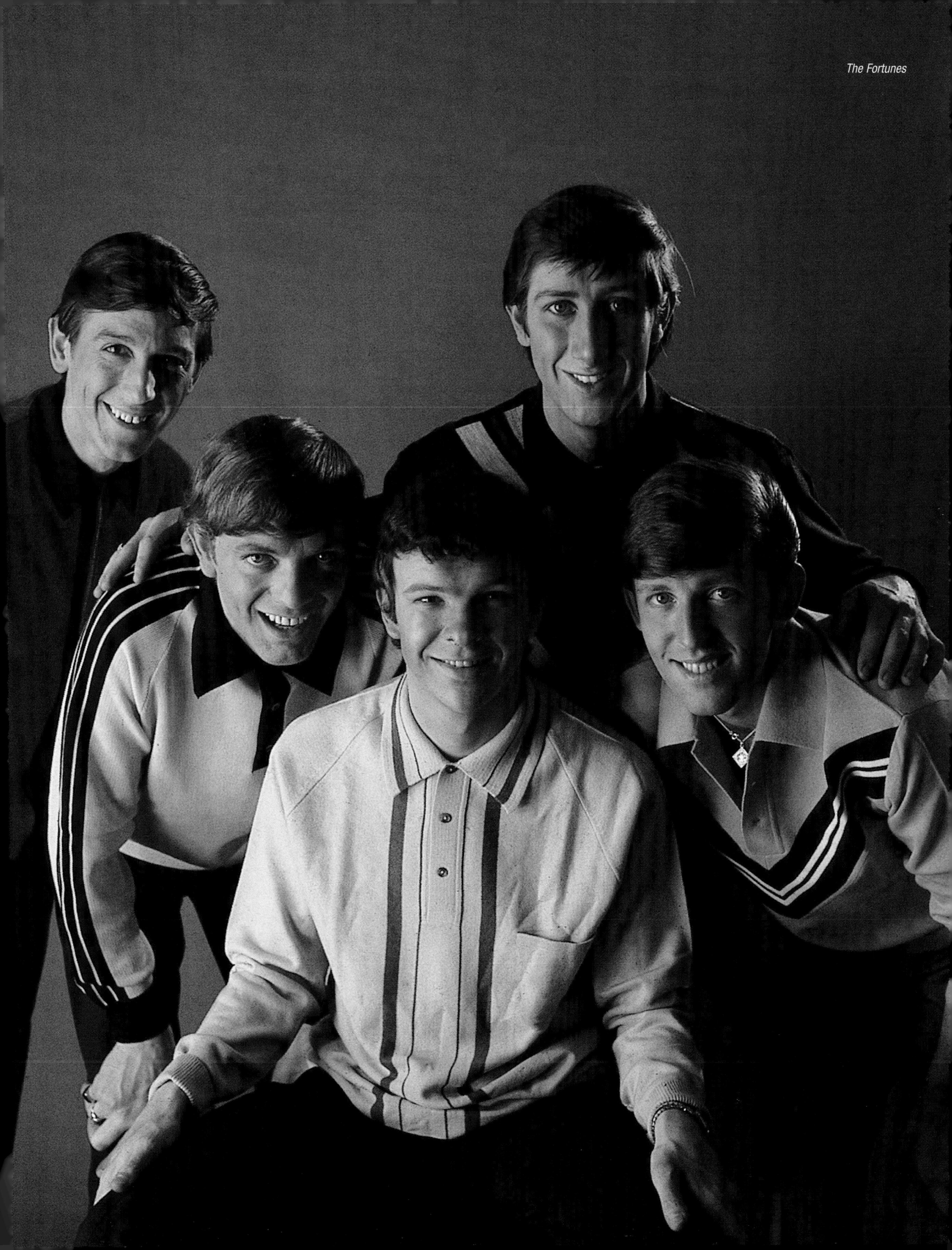

The Fortunes

THE FOX

No relation to another Fox who recorded for CBS or Noosha Fox's Seventies outfit The Fox were a Brighton band who got together in 1968. Each member had seen local action in a variety of south coast outfits. Organist Alex Lane had fronted soul scene veterans The Alex Lane Group, guitarists Steve Brayne and Winston B Weatherill had been in Beatroute and Gary Farr and the T-Bones respectively, while bassist Dave Windross and drummer Tim Reeves had been in Omega Plus. Originally there had been a sixth Fox in percussion player Nick Apostiledes.

The Fox built up a strong following which in turn got them some heavy duty London management with the Meehan Brothers, Tony and Pat. The Meehans whisked the group off to the capital and a début album *For Fox Sake* was knocked out in double quick time. The LP, acknowledged as a psychedelic classic was snapped up by Fontana and the group were given a Radio One session. DJ and fellow Brighton native Anne Nightingale tipped them for the top and a US tour was imminent. Of course nothing happened and the group broke up on the eve of playing the Plumpton Jazz, Blues, and Pop Festival in August 1969. Tim Reeves went on to Mungo Jerry and the other members can still be found playing the South Coast R&B pub circuit.

The Frays

THE FRAYS

A Putney, South West London, group who débuted with the wailing R&B number 'Keep Me Covered' on Decca in 1965. When the original singer wanted to pursue a folk/blues direction, he was replaced by Martin Hummingbird, who steered the group back to soulful R&B. The Frays second single thus features a moody Them-like interpretation of Jerry Butlers 'For Your Precious Love', backed by a beaty take of The Vibrations' 'My Girl Sloopy', that is sadly marred by fake screams. The group were popular on the London scene as an authentic soul act, Hummingbird outdoing himself with knee-drops and falsetto screams, and they even got to open for Wilson Pickett at the Flamingo Club. The departure of guitarist John Patten hastened their demise in 1966.

FREDDIE & THE DREAMERS

As evidenced the cabaret graveyard was the only option for many of the Sixties beat bands, performers and one hit wonders. This wasn't the case for Freddie & The Dreamers; they started out as cabaret!

Ex-milkman Freddie Garitty began his musical career singing in Manchester skiffle groups The Red Sox, The John Norman Four, and The Kingfishers, before forming Freddie & The Dreamers in 1959. The group (guitarists Roy Crewsdon and Derek Quinn, Pete Birrell on bass, and drummer Bernie Dwyer) received an early break on the radio programme Beat Show in 1961, and played intensively in and around the north of England.

Freddie developed a comic stage act that was pure slapstick, often dropping his trousers, leaping in the air and inventing step routines for the band. In the wake of The Beatles the group were swept up by EMI and enjoyed a two-year run of catchy hit singles for Columbia. The first, a cover of James Ray's 'If You Gotta Make A Fool Of Somebody', reached three in June 1963, followed by 'I'm Tellin' You Now' (number two – August '63) and 'You Were Made For Me' (number three – December '63). In 1964, the group returned to the Top Five with a Xmas single, 'I Understand'.

In 1965 they achieved the unthinkable and actually cracked the American market, appearing on *Hullaballoo* and *Shindig!* taking 'I'm Telling You Now' to the top of the charts in March. The Americans lapped up Freddie's mad cap stage act and a US-only single 'Do The Freddie' started a nationwide dance craze and gave the group another US Top Five in May. Back in England they appeared in the banal feature films *Every Day's A Holiday* (1964, with John Leyton and Mike Sarne) playing a bunch of singing chefs at a holiday camp, and a group of boy scouts in Cuckoo Patrol (1965). As the year wore on the group's record releases became decreasingly successful and their live appearances were restricted to pantomime. When chart success finally ran out in 1966 they took to the cabaret circuit like ducks to water, finally bowing out in 1970.

Freddie went into children's television and was a favourite on the weekly series *Little Big Time*. He put a new version of the Dreamers together in 1976 and played successful tours in the US and Australia. He continued to work the nostalgia market until serious heart problems forced him into early retirement.

The Fox

Freddie & The Dreamers

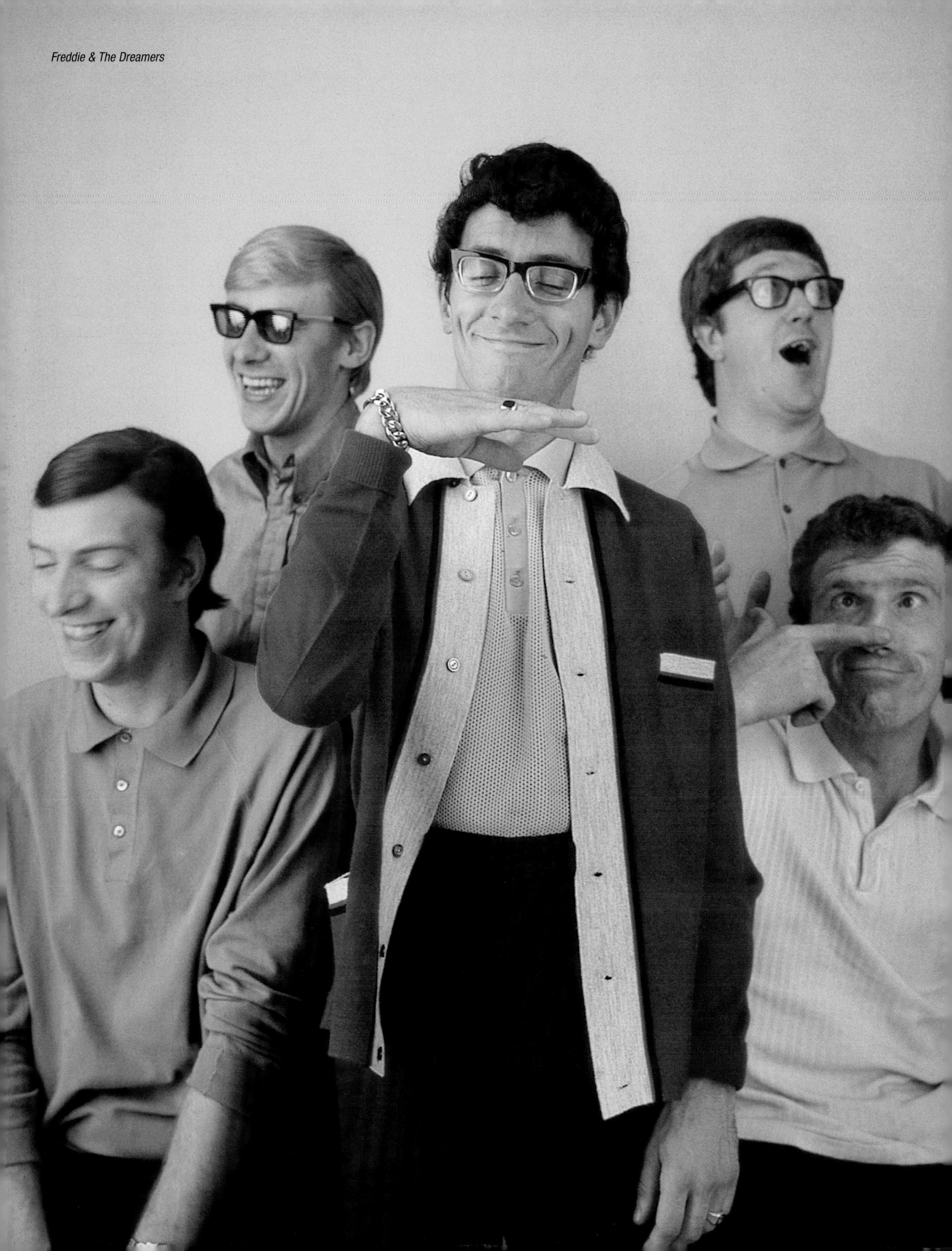

Goldie & The Gingerbreads

THE GAMBLERS

The early Sixties were awash with the discarded backing bands of old school rockers like Adam Faith, Marty Wilde and Billy Fury. The Gamblers (Jim Crawford – vocals, Tony Damond – guitar, Alan Sanderson – bass, Alan George – keyboards, Ken Brady – sax, Andy Mac – drums) had been Billy Fury's abandoned lot.

They were sportingly kept on at Decca and recorded four singles between '63 and '66 including covers of 'You Really Got A Hold On Me', 'Nobody But Me' and a lame version of The Supremes' lame theme to a US teen exploitation movie *Doctor Goldfoot (And His Bikini Machine)*. Decca eventually had no choice but to let them go at the end of '66 to gamble with Parlophone by releasing a telling last single 'Cry Me A River' backed by 'Who Will Buy'. Alas no one would.

THE GAME

The Game, from Mitcham, Surrey, featured Terry Boyes (vocals/harmonica), Terry Spencer and Tony Bird (guitars), Alan Janaway (bass), and Jimmy Nelson (drums). Bird left to be replaced by Jimmy Nelson in early '65, and the group honed their sound and image, influenced by such Mod heavyweights as The Birds and The Who.

Through an association with singer Jeanie Lamb, the group came to the attention of Kenny Lynch, who got the group a deal with Pye. A one-off single written by Lynch and Clive Westlake, 'But I Do' was released in July 65, which, despite pirate Radio Caroline plays, sold poorly. Having co-penned a hit 'Sha-La-La-Lee' for The Small Faces and having his subsequent song submissions thrown back in his face by the mod midgets, Lynch was eager to turn The Game into suitable replacements without such churlish behaviour. Lynch's first move was to replace a hapless Boyes, whose voice he felt wasn't strong enough with singer Reg Charsley for a second single, the moddy 'Gonna Get Me Someone', released on Decca in 1966.

The Game parted company with Lynch and temporarily disbanded. Spencer, Janaway, and Bird regrouped with drummer Terry Goodsell at the end of 1966 and moved to Parlophone for two sublime, distortion-driven pop-art singles that cemented their status as freakbeat legends. 'The Addicted Man' (released Jan '67), actually an anti-drug song, was condemned on TV's *Juke Box Jury* as glamourising drug use, resulting in the record being withdrawn due to adverse publicity. 'It's Shocking What They Call Me', (released a month later in Feb '67 to try and capitalise on the surrounding furore), married delicate, English vocals with Creation-style pyrotechnics. Unsurprisingly, the record went unpromoted, directly resulting in The Game's premature ending the same year. In the mid-Nineties, the original members reformed and released a new CD *Still On The Game*.

ELMER GANTRY'S VELVET OPERA

Now better known for his involvement in one of the more ludicrous scams perpetrated by the backroom boys in the rock business, vocalist Gantry's original Velvet Opera featured Colin Foster (guitar), John Ford (bass) and Richard Hudson (drums).

In 1967 Elmer Gantry's Velvet Opera built up a promising reputation from regular club appearances and slots on John Peel's *Top Gear* radio show. Signing to CBS and recording for their offshoot Direction, the group's début single was a catchy pop song with a hard-psych edge, but despite the radio plugs, 'Flames' failed to ignite, nor did follow-ups, 'Mary Jane' (1968) and 'Volcano' (1969). The group's sole album *Elmer Gantry's Velvet Opera* (1968) was a patchy affair but included highlights like 'Mother Writes' and 'Intro'.

Gantry was replaced on vocals by Paul Brett for the 1969 CBS album *Ride A Hustler's Dream* as Velvet Opera and the group pre-dated glam rock by about three years, with painted faces, feather boa's and big girls hats.

After the group finally split in 1973, Brett formed the Paul Brett Sage, and John Ford and Richard Hudson put together The Strawbs and Hudson-Ford. Gantry was somehow persuaded to take to the road fronting a band billing itself as Fleetwood Mac; accepting illicit dates right across America until blocked by litigation brought by the real Fleetwood Mac against ex-manager Clive Davis who had masterminded the whole scam. Gantry emerged once more as the singer in Stretch, scoring with the ironic single, 'Why Did You Do It', in 1975.

DAVID GARRICK

Blonde-haired pretty boy David Garrick was a mid-Sixties prototype David Cassidy whose real name was Phillip Darryl Core. He came from Liverpool where he'd been a choirboy and an operatic student for four years. He arrived in London around 1965 and snagged a record deal with Pye subsidiary Piccadilly. His knockers sniped this was based solely on his innocent good looks which was a little unfair

Gerry Marsden
& passenger

Wayne Gibson Dynamic

given his earlier pedigree. He was given Jagger-Richards' 'Lady Jane' to record after his first two singles failed to chart. It reached number 28 in July '66 while the excruciating follow-up 'Dear Mrs Applebee' did a bit better at 22 in October. For around six months Garrick was splashed across the pages of every teen magazine in circulation. Yet nothing much happened music wise. His 1967 début album *A Boy Called David* was a thrown together affair featuring the two minor hits and a collection of all-to-familiar covers like 'Groovy Kind Of Love' and 'Dandy'. It didn't sell and Pye gradually lost interest in Garrick, who continued to release records well into 1969 but he never graced the charts or a bedroom wall again.

GERRY & THE PACEMAKERS

When The Beatles came first in *Mersey Beat*'s 1962 popularity poll, only a few votes behind were Gerry & The Pacemakers – a fairly accurate reflection of both groups' status, which remained constant for at least two years.

Formed in 1958 by singer-guitar player Gerry Marsden, his drummer brother Freddie, and pianist Les Chadwick, they were originally called The Mars Bars until Gerry saw a television athletics programme mentioning pacemakers.

The group were joined by bassist Les Maguire and played at various dancehalls around Liverpool, often sharing the bill with The Beatles as well as enduring the inevitable National Service stint in Hamburg,

In 1963 they became the second group to sign to Brian Epstein's NEMS management company and were signed by EMI producer George Martin to record for Columbia. A Mitch Murray song The Beatles had recorded but rejected – 'How Do You Do It' – became their début single; going straight to number one in March. Two more chart toppers, 'I Like It' (another Murray composition) and 'You'll Never Walk Alone' (from the musical *Carousel*) followed in quick succession earning them the distinction of being the first group to achieve three consecutive number ones with their first three releases. 'You'll Never Walk Alone' also received the dubious honour of becoming Liverpool Football Club's terrace chant.

The Gerry-penned 'I'm The One' couldn't make it a fourth, being kept off the pole position in January '64 by fellow Scousers The Searchers with 'Needles And Pins'. While anything with a Liverpool accent was a license to print money Gerry and the boys made a big initial impact in the US, appearing on *The Ed Sullivan Show* and peaking at number 4 in June with 'Don't Let The Sun Catch You Crying' (not the Ray Charles song but one of Gerry's own compositions). The band embarked on a lengthy American tour, and a US only album of the same name made the *Billboard* chart at number 29.

It had been a successful run for the group but in the ever changing musical climate, it wasn't to last. In England they remained

in the public eye throughout the rest of '64 and although 'It's Gonna Be Alright' could only muster a number 24 chart placing, 'Ferry Cross The Mersey' – the title theme to the band's feature film, made while the dust from *A Hard Day's Night* was still settling – reached eight.

Ferry Across The Mersey was released to cinemas in February 1965 and featured the band playing themselves in a simple plot whereby Gerry & The Pacemakers enter a talent contest and (surprise, surprise) win it. Of course you got to see the other entrants, some of whom (The Fourmost, Cilla Black) just happened to be Liverpudlian and signed to NEMS. A cover of Bobby Darin's 'I'll Be There' gave Gerry & The Pacemakers their last Top 20 entry (15 – April '65). A final 1965 single, the ballad 'Walk Hand In Hand' sold only modestly while 'La La La' (as dreadful as its title suggests) and 'Girl On a Swing' flopped entirely the following year.

By 1966 it was obvious that the Liverpool beat bands (Beatles excepted, of course) faced musical extinction by failing to keep abreast of the times and as such were now considered passé. Gerry's solution was to cut his losses and head out solo. He signed a deal with CBS but none of his three 1967-68 singles caught on. In 1968 he wisely sidelined his musical exploits in favour of acting. He took over the cheeky chappie lead role from Joe Brown in the musical *Charlie Girl* (featuring Derek Nimmo) and stayed with it until 1970. Next came a decade working in children's television, most notably *The Sooty Show*.

There have been inevitable Gerry-led versions of The Pacemakers since, including a sell-out 'British Invasion' performance at New York's Madison Square Gardens in 1973. Two of the group's biggest hits have since returned to the top of the charts, both in unfortunate connection with football tragedies. The first was in 1985, following the Bradford City stadium fire, when an all-star cast re-recorded 'You'll Never Walk Alone', while a new version of 'Ferry Cross The Mersey' was released in 1989 after the Hillsborough ground disaster. The profits from both went to the charities involved.

Gerry continues performing, fronting a version of The Pacemakers on the nostalgia circuit, whilst his brother Freddie runs Pacemakers driving school in Liverpool. Maguire was last heard of working as a tour guide in the Middle East.

THE GLASS MENAGERIE

With a name like The Glass Menagerie these Lancashire lads (Lou Stonebridge –vocals, Alan Kendall – guitar, John Medley – bass, Bill Atkinson – drums) were obviously hoping to get in on some psychedelic action when they arrived in London in 1968.

They got a deal with Pye but showed a distinct lack of imagination by releasing a cover of The Rolling Stones' 'She's A Rainbow' as their début single. Of course it flopped as did their other two releases – a cover of The Lovin' Spoonful's 'You Didn't Have To

Gerry & The Pacemakers

Herbie Goins & The Night-Timers

Be So Nice' and a psychedelic original 'Frederick Jordan' – and eventually they were dropped. They managed to release another two singles with Polydor in 1969 but nothing happened chart wise there either. Kendall went forth to join Toe Fat while Stonebridge joined McGuinness Flint and Paladin.

THE GODS

Formed in 1965 in Hatfield, Hertfordshire The Gods featured future Rolling Stones guitarist Mick Taylor, Ken Hensley (keyboards), John Glassock (bass) and brother Brian Glassock (drums) and at one point, Tony Monroe (ex-Birds guitarist) within their ranks. The original line-up broke up when Taylor replaced Peter Green in John Mayall's Bluesbreakers in mid '67.

Hensley reformed a new Gods featuring Joe Konas (guitar), Paul Newton (bass) and Lee Kerslake (drums). Greg Lake replaced Newton but left in 1968, turning up the following year in King Crimson. John Glassock rejoined the group in time for their relocation to London and a recording contract with Columbia. The group's first single, 'Baby's Rich' was an infectious pop number with strident guitar stabs but failed to make an impression as did a version of The Beatles' 'Hey Bulldog'. Two albums *Genesis* (1968) and the posthumous *To Samuel A Son* (1970) sold extremely poorly and are now collectors items, particularly to Uriah Heep completists as Kerslake, Hensley and Newton formed the Seventies behemoth after a stint in Toe Fat. *(see also Cliff Bennett & The Rebel Rousers, The Birds, The Rolling Stones)*

HERBIE GOINS & THE NIGHT-TIMERS

Originally one of the many vocalists with Alexis Korner's Blues Incorporated Florida-born Goins remained in Britain after being demobbed and was one of the few authentic soulsters Britain had in the mid-Sixties. His English backing group The Night-Timers were a consistently in-demand attraction on the club and ballroom circuit. Their recorded legacy consists of a couple of singles and a 1967 album for Parlophone, *Number One In Your Heart*, the Motownesque title track of which was probably Goins' finest moment. The group broke up the following year.

GRANNY'S INTENTIONS

An Irish combo signed to Deram in 1967, with a brace of singles and one album, *Honest Injun*, released in 1970. Their style was blues-rock and the album is notable for featuring Gary Moore as guest guitarist on several tracks.

GRAPEFRUIT

With strong pop connections to The Beatles and The Easybeats, Grapefruit - John Perry (vocals, guitar), Pete Sweetenham (vocals, guitar), Geoff Sweetenham (drums), and George Alexander (nee' Alex Young – bass, vocals) - seemed poised for success.

Alexander was previously in My Dear Watson, protégé's of The Easybeats who included his younger brother, George. Thanks to Perry and the Sweetenham brothers' previous connection with Tony Rivers & The Castaways (a fine Beach Boys/Four Seasons-style harmony group from Essex who released several singles on Columbia & Immediate), Grapefruit's records had impeccable harmonies and polished production courtesy of noted LA producer Terry Melcher.

John Lennon named them after his future paramour Yoko Ono's book, Beatle aide and mentor Terry Doran signed the group to Apple Publishing, securing a recording deal with RCA and Grapefruit were launched with great fanfare in January 1968 at a Mayfair reception attended by three Beatles, Cilla Black, Donovan, and Brian Jones. Things looked promising when début single, the charming 'Dear Delilah' landed just short of the Top 20 a month later, but 'Elevator' failed to rise and apart from another modest chart entry in August with a Four Seasons cover, 'C'mon Marianne', the group never regained momentum. Grapefruit possessed the same pop sensibility as The Honeybus and the pre-Badfinger Iveys, though they unwisely left one of their best songs, 'Breaking Up A Dream', on the recording studio floor. After an enjoyable first album *Around Grapefruit* in 1968, Grapefruit decided to change tack the following year in a misguided soul/rock direction with Deep Water, featuring additional member, keyboardist Mick Fowler while Geoff Sweetenham was later replaced by Bobby Ware.

In 1971, Alex joined his brother George and Easybeat songwriting partner Harry Vanda in their various appellations such as Paintbox and Haffy's Whisky Sour. Various other members ended back up with old mucker Tony Rivers in RCA artists, Harmony Grass. *(see also The Easybeats)*

Granny's Intentions

Grapefruit

Deep Water GRAPEFRUIT
Come Down To The Station

YES and ELEVATOR A DOUBLE HIT BY GRAPEFRUIT
RCA 1677
RCA VICTOR

DEAR DELILAH FIRST RELEASE BY GRAPEFRUIT ON RCA VICTOR

C'MON MARIANNE b/w Ain't It Good
RCA Victor 1716
GRAPEFRUIT
RCA VICTOR

The Habits

THE HABITS

The Habits released one 1966 single during their lifetime. 'Elbow Baby' was produced by Spencer Davis and Stevie Winwood, who had noticed The Habits acting as backing group for vocalist Charles Dickens on a Rolling Stones tour. The trio were from London and drummer Brian Davison went on to play in The Attack and The Nice. *(see also The Attack, Spencer Davis Group, Charles Dickens, The Nice)*

ALEX HARVEY (SOUL BAND)

With the passing of skiffle, the 'Scottish Tommy Steele', aka Alex Harvey reinvented himself as a Glasgow soulman. He put together the visionary Alex Harvey Soul Band in 1959 as a sort of touring house band for hire. They did several Scottish tours backing visiting American artists like Gene Vincent, Eddie Cochran and Little Richard before heading south and hitting the London R&B circuit. The group's original line-up featured brass, timbales and congas which was all quite experimental for the time. They also cut a bit of a dash visually, appearing in gold and silver lamé suits and ties, red shirts and white winkle picker boots.

Their 1964 début album, *Alex Harvey And His Soul Band* was a faithful representation of the group's live show, which was a collection of early rock'n'roll and Motown covers. Harvey had dispensed with his band altogether and used King Size Taylor's backing band, The Dominoes, instead. He repeated the snub on the follow up and when The Blues was released in '64 featuring only Harvey and his little brother Leslie, the Soul Band broke up and went home.

Harvey stayed in London and signed to Fontana as a solo artist, releasing two singles in 1965: a version of Edwin Starr's 'Agent 00 Soul' and the traditional 'Work Song', neither of which made any impact. When psychedelia flowered in 1967 Harvey formed an appropriately trippy group called Giant Moth who signed to Decca and released two giant flops in 'Maybe Some Day' and 'Midnight Moses'. By 1968 Harvey's career as a recording artist appeared to have come to an end. He became a jobbing musician and accepted work as the in-house guitar player at the 800 Club playing regular six hour shifts, and also did a lengthy stint as guitarist in the pit for the musical *Hair*. He returned to Glasgow in 1971 and set about putting a new group together, taking control of a local outfit called Tear Gas and modestly renaming them The Sensational Alex Harvey Band. Harvey died of a heart attack on February 4, 1982.

HAYDOCK'S ROCKHOUSE

Bass player Eric Haydock was sacked from The Hollies in June 1966 but was shown uncharacteristic record company loyalty by EMI, who retained him for Columbia. He put together Haydock's Rockhouse – a six piece soul band that released two singles. First was a cover of Sam Cooke's 'Cupid' which flopped and the second, a cover of The Lovin' Spoonful's 'Lovin' You' which flopped too. Good deed done, EMI dropped them in 1967. Haydock now owns a musical instrument shop in Stockport. *(see also The Hollies)*

JIMI HENDRIX EXPERIENCE

There are rock guitarists and there is Jimi Hendrix. Over three decades on from his tragic premature death in 1970 the legacy of Jimi's unnatural ability as a technically gifted and wildly innovative guitarist has been safely carved into legend for succeeding generations. However it often overshadows his abilities as a truly original lyricist and arranger.

Although American Jimi's inclusion in this book rests upon the fact that he was deliberately brought to England by his manager, ex-Animal Chas Chandler, in 1966 and the period of his initial success and most enduring recordings, spanning 1966-68, were made in England.

He was born John Allan Hendrix in Seattle, Washington (his father later changed his son's name to James Marshall Hendrix) and self-taught himself to play guitar. He joined the 101st Airborne Division but was discharged after breaking his ankle in a parachute jump. For the next three years Jimi paid his dues as a back-up musician on the south's 'chitlin' circuit backing such names as The Isley Brothers, Little Richard, King Curtis and Curtis Knight. Relocating to New York, Jimi formed his own band Jimmy James & The Blue Flames, playing at various cafés and clubs, including the Café Wha? where an unsuspecting Chas Chandler, acting on a tip-off by Keith Richards' girlfriend Linda Keith, caught Jimmy's act and persuaded him to come to England.

Chandler became Jimi's manager and Jimmy became Jimi on the transatlantic flight. Arriving in London in September '66 word soon spread of the freakish prowess of this flamboyant foreigner. Auditions roped in ex-Loving Kind guitarist Noel Redding (who originally arrived to audition for Eric Burdon's reconstituted Animals) and ex-Riot Squad, Georgie Fame drummer John 'Mitch' Mitchell. The trio started playing around London's trendiest clubs, leaving audiences gobsmacked while knocking the likes of Eric Clapton, Pete Townshend and Jeff Beck into flabbergasted silence. A song that Chandler had seen Tim Rose perform in

Herbal Mixture

New York became Jimi's début single. 'Hey Joe' was promoted with an appearance on the penultimate edition of *Ready, Steady, Go!* which helped push it to number six in January '67. Television viewers in staid England were not used to seeing a wild black man playing his guitar with his teeth, behind his head and his back on *Top Of The Pops* and the 24-year old became an overnight sensation. 'Purple Haze' was another success (number three in April) while the group were shunted onto a hilariously mismatched package tour with Cat Stevens, Engelbert Humpedinck and The Walker Brothers. The group stole the show almost every night with Jimi's literal pyrotechnics thanks to a can of lighter fuel and a flambed Stratocaster. The quieter, reflective 'The Wind Cries Mary' followed in May (reaching number six) while the Experience's classic début album *Are You Experienced?*, appeared the same month and sounds as devastating now as it did then. Stage favourites like 'Foxy Lady', 'Manic Depression', and 'Fire' were delivered with a red hot intensity while studio experiments like 'I Don't Live Today', 'Third Stone From The Sun' and 'Are You Experienced?' were the ultimate in '67-style English acid rock. Even a 12-bar blues on 'Red House' was turned upside down, rewriting the rules in the process. 'Was that OK?' Jimi asks a stunned engineer at its conclusion. The album reached number two in June, the same month that the Experience made a show-stopping appearance at the Monterey International Festival. For Jimi it must have been a personal triumph to return to his homeland as a conquering hero. The group spent most of the summer in America, enduring a short spell on a tour supporting The Monkees, while starting to record tracks for their second album. 'The Burning Of The Midnight Lamp' wasn't as successful as previous singles, only reaching 18 in September, but like the other power trio Cream, singles were being considered less important than albums and concerts.

Axis: Bold As Love was released in December and in many ways improved upon the first album with an increasing use of the studio as an experimental palette on songs like 'EXP', 'If Six Was Nine' and 'Bold As Love', thanks to the expertise of engineer Eddie Kramer. 'Up From The Skies', 'Spanish Castle Magic', 'Little Wing', 'Castles Made Of Sand' were further evidence of Jimi's imaginative songwriting while 'She's So Fine' marked the songwriting emergence of Redding. The Experience spent most of '68 on arduous tours of America and Canada that eventually rent them asunder. Jimi was tiring of having to employ the usual gimmicks to please audiences. Tracks for the group's third album were started in London and finished at the Record Plant in New York. 'All Along The Watchtower' featured Traffic guitarist Dave Mason and an unused Brian Jones piano part, while a lengthy jam on 'Voodoo Chile' featured guests such as Steve Winwood, Jack Casady (from Jefferson Airplane) and Jimi's old buddy, Buddy Miles. Elsewhere the record played host to 'Crosstown Traffic', 'Gypsy Eyes' and the wah-wah extravaganza of 'Voodoo Chile (Slight Return)', released posthumously as a single, which ironically became Jimi's only number one. The tortuous creation of *Electric*

Ladyland made Chandler quit in disgust mid-way through the sessions due to the countless hangers-on. The album was released in November '68 in a sleeve depicting nude models – against Jimi's wishes. The Experience made an infamous appearance on *Happening For Lulu* in January '69 where they were put off the air after running over time with an impromptu 'Sunshine Of Your Love' tribute to Cream. After more gruelling road work, Redding threw in the towel in June. Jimi formed various different backing vehicles – such as Gypsies Sons and Rainbows, and later, The Band Of Gypsies, retaining Mitchell or Buddy Miles, with old army buddy, Billy Cox on bass. On September 18, 1970 Jimi died in London, aged 27. An open verdict was recorded with death caused by inhalation of vomit.

Redding had formed and been fired from Fat Mattress – an extracurricular group featuring ex-Loving Kind/Flowerpot Men singer Neil Landon. He disappeared to America and turned up in various dead-end outfits before finally settling in Ireland, forming The Noel Redding Band in 1975. His autobiography *Are You Experienced* was published in 1991 at the same time that Mitchell's Hendrix memoirs appeared. Redding continues to play and record periodically with different versions of his band as well as guesting with many others. His most recent ensemble was the Nineties group Shut Up Frank, featuring ex-Animal Dave Rowberry and ex-Kink Mick Avory. Thirty years on Jimi Hendrix continues to be among the most profitable artists in the world, with countless posthumous archive releases and tributes, proving the old maxim that nothing enhances an artist's collectability more than his death. In September 1997, a blue plaque was erected at his old flat in Brook Street, London, cementing his status as an honorary Englishman.

(see also Eire Apparent, The Flowerpot Men, The Loving Kind, The Riot Squad)

HERBAL MIXTURE

Herbal Mixture was a short-lived and bizarre interlude in the otherwise long-lived career of Tony McPhee & The Groundhogs, one of Britain's most venerable blues outfits. After a handful of recordings, including a stint backing John Lee Hooker, guitarist McPhee and bassist Pete Cruickshank temporarily disbanded John Lee's Groundhogs in 1966 and formed Herbal Mixture (named because of McPhee's interest in alternative medicine) with drummer Mike Meeham. During their ensuing year or so of operation The Mixture released two stunning pop-art singles on Columbia, 'A Love That's Died' and 'Machines'. Publicity pictures distributed at the time portrayed them dressed as old women. McPhee and Cruikshank were reunited in The Groundhogs and McPhee performs with them to this day.

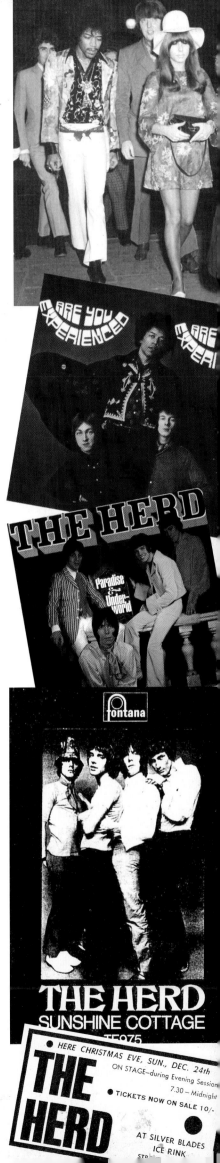

THE HERD

When Alan Howard and Ken Blaikley (the management-songwriting duo responsible for the success of The Honeycombs and Dave Dee, Dozy, Beaky, Mick and Tich) took over The Herd in 1967 it seemed they had lumbered themselves with a group already past its sell-by date. Record label Parlophone and manager Billy Gaff had just dropped them and various line-up changes had left the group leaderless and directionless.

The Herd

Originating from Kent groups The Preachers and Moon's Train (formerly Train), both protégés of Rolling Stone Bill Wyman, The Herd featured Terry Clark – vocals, fifteen year old Peter Frampton (guitar-vocals), Andy Bown (bass), Gary Taylor (guitar) and ex-Preacher Tony Chapman (drums). The group had been together since 1965 and released one flop single after another, including covers of The Velvelettes 'He Was Really Sayin' Something' and the Jagger-Richards comp, 'So Much In Love'. The Stones connection continued with Rolling Stone Bill Wyman being the group's keen supporter, as drummer Chapman had been in Wyman's first band The Cliftons.

Clark and Chapman then left, and drummer Andrew Steele joined. The group were signed to Fontana and as well as taking over songwriting chores, Howard and Blaikley set about re-arranging the group, promoting baby faced guitar player Peter Frampton to leader and Andy Bown switched from bass to organ. Not that this set up was instantly successful. The Herd's first Fontana release 'I Can Fly',

despite being a strong pop single with great harmonies, flopped although it became a hit in Germany. Howard and Blaikley went back to the drawing board and came up with the brainstorm to transform the band into psychedelic teen idols. An adaptation of 'Orpheus In The Underworld' was recorded, retitled 'From The Underworld' and actually reached number six in November '67. This theme continued with another translation 'Paradise Lost', this time from Milton, with its gimmicky striptease horns, made number 15 in January '68.

With teen stardom assured a change of material followed. After Frampton was voted 'the Face of '68' in *Rave* magazine, The Herd felt able to revert back to straightforward pop and dump the literate angle. 'I Don't Want Our Lovin' To Die' naturally charted at their highest position yet in April (number 5) but then the group decided they didn't like that approach after all. Apparently now against their status of pin up pop stars the group blamed Howard and Blaikley and sacked them over accusations of money mishandling. However the pair needn't have worried because everything else The Herd recorded, including Frampton's composition 'Sunshine Cottage' flopped. Steele quit as did Frampton in 1969, to join another disgruntled pop star Steve Marriott in Humble Pie. The rhythm section of Taylor and replacement drummer Henry Spinetti stuck with Bown for one last single 'The Game' before disbanding the same year.

Bown and Spinetti formed Judas Jump with the brass section from Amen Corner; Bown then had a failed solo career before joining Status Quo where he remains today. Taylor was in Seventies one hit wonders Fox. Frampton achieved international success after leaving Humble Pie, forming Frampton's Camel and becoming a solo artist.

HERMAN'S HERMITS

Originally known as The Heartbeats, a nondescript Manchester beat group, the Hermits featured guitarists Derek (Lek) Leckenby and Keith Hopwood, bass player Karl Green, and drummer Barry Whitwam behind frontman Peter Noone, an ex-child actor, who'd appeared in Granada TV's soap opera *Coronation Street*. (He was given his nickname because of a resemblance to the cartoon character Herman Bullwinkle).

Herman's Hermits

Managed by Harvey Lisberg and partner Charley Silverman, an enterprising Mickie Most took the group on in 1964 and pushed Noone forward as Herman's Hermits. The fruits of this fortuitous teaming were instantaneous. Most signed the band to EMI's

Herman's Hermits

The High Numbers

HOLLIES

THE HOLLIES
Jennifer Eccles

Columbia label and succeeded in turning them into an act that for a while actually challenged The Beatles in America. Their first single (released as the abbreviated Herman's Hermits) 'I'm Into Something Good' strolled home to the number one position in September '64 (and 13 in the US).

After a brief misfire with another Goffin-King song 'Show Me Girl' the hits ran almost uninterrupted until 1970. Songs like 'Can't You Hear My Heartbeat?', 'Silhouettes', 'Wonderful World', 'A Must To Avoid', 'No Milk Today' and 'There's A Kind Of Hush' set Herman's Hermits up as household names in America, where Most and EMI concentrated their efforts on grooming Noone as a teen idol. His passing resemblance to a young John F. Kennedy didn't go unnoticed either. In 1965 they sold a staggering 10 million records in under 12 months. A run of corny Vaudevillian music hall compositions like 'Mrs Brown You've Got A Lovely Daughter' (a number one in April '65), 'I'm Henry The VIII, I Am' (number one in July) and 'Leaning On A Lampost' (number nine, April '66) were put out as American-only singles, deliberately intended to extend Herman's amenable English charm. Unfortunately it was all at the expense of the Hermits. As Noone's fame rose so the Hermits glow dimmed and they constantly found themselves unfairly sidelined by Most and used for live duty only; being omitted from actually playing on almost all of their records in favour of session men like Jimmy Page and John Paul Jones. They were nonetheless seen fit enough to appear in two US MGM cash-in movies *When The Boys Meet The Girls* (1964) and *Hold On* (1966), while a third followed with *Mrs. Brown, You've Got A Lovely Daughter* (1968).

As the hits kept coming the divide between Noone and the band got bigger as the move from Columbia to Most's RAK label demonstrated in 1970. The inevitable parting of the ways soon followed and Noone took up the solo option the same year. The Hermits carried on as a live act into the Seventies, signing to RCA with a succession of singers.

Noone continued to record for RAK under his own name, including a cover of David Bowie's 'Oh, You Pretty Things' in 1971 but slowly drifted into acting. He relocated to the US and presented his own TV and radio shows. The original band reformed for a one off show at New York's Madison Square Gardens in 1973 before going their separate ways once again. The Peter Pan-like Noone continues to do media work and in 2001 completed a nationwide tour of the UK. Karl Green and Barry Whitwam still tour the cabaret circuit as The Hermits. Derek Leckenby died of cancer in 1994.

THE HIGH NUMBERS

Peter Meaden, top 'face' during the early days of the original Mod movement, assured his mythic status when he died before he got old in 1978. Widely acknowledged as moulding the early Mod image of The Who, he was hired as the group's publicist by their then manager, local Shepherd's Bush businessman, Helmut Gordon, in

The High Numbers

1964. It was Meaden who first introduced The Who to the clothes-mad world of Mod and carefully planned the group's new identity and name, The High Numbers, by launching them as the country's first performing Mod band.

The group released one single, 'I'm The Face' on Fontana, to virtually no interest. They gamely gigged around for a few months under the increasingly bizarre guidance of Meaden before his pill popping habits rendered him too unreliable and unable to make decisions.

(see also The Who)

THE HIPSTER IMAGE

Mods from Stafford who first appeared on record via a Jimmy Savile-sponsored flexidisc for Keele University Rag Week. They gained a following down south via a residency at legendary Soho Mod hangout the Flamingo during 1965. Late in the year The Image made a fine single for Decca, the moody jazz-tinged 'Can't Let Her Go', produced by ex-Animals' organist Alan Price. Lead singer Colin Cooper later formed The Climax Chicago Blues Band.

(see also Alan Price Set)

The Hipster Image

THE HOLLIES

Because they have never felt a need to apply a sensationalistic veneer to their long career, it has been fashionable in some quarters to demote The Hollies to the second division of the Sixties rock hierarchy. However, in many ways, this Manchester institution should be at the very top of the table because for enduring, high-quality pop, The Hollies have rarely been bettered. Even the most casual music fan will be familiar with hits from the group's remarkable forty-year history as one of the most successful chart acts of all time. Songs like 'I'm Alive', 'I Can't Let Go', 'He Ain't Heavy, He's My Brother' and 'The Air That I Breathe' constitute the fabric of British popular music.

The Hollies

The Hollies history begins in Salford, Manchester in the late-Fifties when schoolfriends Allan Clarke and Graham Nash sang together semi-professionally as The Two Teens. As Ricky and Dane, they had a guest spot with The Flintstones, whose bassist was Eric Haydock, and drummer Don Rathbone. The group's name changed from The Dominators Of Rhythm, to The Deltas, and finally The Hollies, in honour of idol Buddy Holly. In late-1962 local guitar whizz Tony Hicks was poached from local group The Dolphins, in time for an EMI audition.

Producer Ron Richards had seen the group at Liverpool's Cavern Club and was struck by their harmonic abilities. He signed them to record for Parlophone, and after a false start with a cover of The Coasters' '(Ain't That) Just Like Me', released in June 1963, The Hollies found their hitmaking feet with another Coasters cover 'Searchin'', which reached number twelve in October. By then Rathbone had left and Hicks pitched his old Dolphins' bandmate Bobby Elliott (fresh from a stint with Shane Fentone & The Fentones) as a replacement. The group found their follow-up, Maurice Williams & The Zodiacs 'Stay' on tour in Scotland. 'Stay' arguably outshone the original; crashing into the Top 20 where it alighted at eight in January 1964. The group's début album inevitably titled *Stay With The Hollies* was a ready made collection of the band's stage act featuring covers of Chuck Berry, Roy Orbison, Conway Twitty, Arthur Alexander and Bobby Day. Apart from B-sides it also marked the first stirrings of the Clarke-Hicks-Nash songwriting partnership. In a move of non-confidence, similar to Jagger and Richards crediting their earliest Rolling Stones compositions to Nanker-Phelge, the trio used the pseudonym 'L. Ransford' - Nash's grandfather - for songs like 'Little Lover'.

Stay With… also featured a confident handling of Doris Troy's 'Whatcha Gonna Do 'Bout It' and it was another Troy soul classic that provided the group with their fourth single and first Top Five hit. 'Just One Look' shot to number two in March '64 in time for the group's triumphant appearance at the *New Musical Express* Pollwinners Concert the following month. 'Here I Go Again', another high-quality performance showcasing those breathless three-part harmonies, reached four in June. After some persuading Richards agreed to allow a Ransford composition as an A-side. 'We're Through' was admirably inventive for 1964, tied around a shuffle and Hicks' tortuous acoustic Spanish 12-string guitar motif, but its number seven placing wasn't enough to convince Richards to let them have their head in the studio. The tried and trusted outside hit formula was reverted to with 'Yes I Will' (number nine in March '65), a Goffin-King song that the group effortlessly made their own, while group compositions were kept (for the moment) to B-sides and album tracks.

The second album *In The Hollies Style* was a classy collection of covers (Shirley Ellis, Chuck Berry, Jeri Southern) but was actually outnumbered by strong Ransford compositions like 'Come On Home', 'You'll Be Mine' and 'What Kind Of Boy'. Unfortunately the group were pigeonholed as a singles act and the album didn't sell well – a problem that would plague their future long-playing efforts. The Hollies achieved their first number one in June with the Clint Ballard composition, 'I'm Alive', which also made inroads into the American market where the band first toured in April, playing on a multi-artist bill at the Paramount Theatre in New York.

Fellow Manc songsmith Graham Gouldman entered the band's career at this juncture, when they took his 'Look Through Any Window' to number four in September. The song was their most inventive yet, spotlighting the consistently superb performances of Hicks (on 12-string Burns guitar), Haydock on six-string bass and Elliott's snare thundercracks; the latter surely one of the most underrated of British musicians.

A third album *Hollies*, released the same month, was another schizophrenic mix of covers (Peter, Paul & Mary, Lloyd Price, Roy Orbison, The Impressions, The Miracles) and originals such as 'Put Yourself In My Place', I've Been Wrong', 'When I Come Home To You, and 'So Lonely'; the latter receiving double exposure as the B-side to 'Look Through Any Window'.

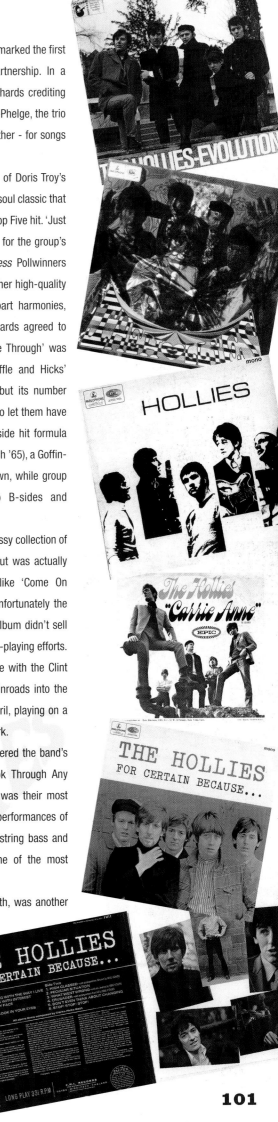

Such were the band's strengths that several quality songs like 'I Can't Get Nowhere With You', 'She Gives Me Everything I Want' and 'Like Every Time Before' lay unreleased (at the time).

The faux-pas that nearly derailed The Hollies' hit machine was an ill-advised cover of George Harrison's *Rubber Soul* contribution, 'If I Needed Someone'. The group put in an admittedly indifferent performance and Harrison slammed the record in an *NME* interview. The record stopped at twenty in January '66. Retreating to lick their wounds the group emerged triumphant with 'I Can't Let Go', a song co-written by US songwriter Chip Taylor (who also penned The Troggs' 'Wild Thing'). The arrangement had been adapted from Evie Sands' US version and restored The Hollies to a more customary number two chart position. The song couldn't fail to miss – from the chugging dramatic intro to the faultless musicianship and harmonies throughout – Paul McCartney actually thought Nash's high note at the end of each chorus was a trumpet! – it remains Hicks' (who chose the song over The Mamas and Papas' 'California Dreaming') favourite Hollies recording.

The song was inevitably included on *Would You Believe?*, (released May '66), another patchwork of covers (Sam & Dave, Otis Redding, Simon & Garfunkel, Buddy Holly) with some experimental Ransford originals that were only partially successful ('Oriental Sadness', the Nash-solo and frankly ludicrous 'Fifi The Flea'). The album also highlighted the group's need for progression. Dashing through a polished but perfunctory 'Sweet Little Sixteen' was all very well, but a fortnight later, The Beatles pushed rock's boundaries with 'Tomorrow Never Knows' in the very same studio.

However there were more immediate things to deal with when Haydock was sacked in June for unreliability. Klaus Voormann (ex-Paddy, Klaus and Gibson) stood in for a Palladium appearance while Jack Bruce (about to join Cream) helped them record the theme to Peter Sellers film *After The Fox*. After considering Pete Quaife (temporarily on leave from The Kinks) the job was given to Hicks and Elliott's ex-Dolphins bandmate, Bernie Calvert, who had replaced Haydock on a European jaunt. Also during this time, a childhood dream was realised when The Everly Brothers recorded several Clarke-Hicks-Nash songs for their *Two Yanks In London* album.

It was business as usual when Gouldman's composition 'Bus Stop' reached number five in July, while the first Clarke-Hicks-Nash A-side 'Stop! Stop! Stop!', inspired by a visit to a New York bellydancing club, reached two in October. The group's confidence at a high, *For Certain Because* was the first album to feature all originals including potential singles 'What's Wrong With The Way I Live?', 'Pay You Back With Interest' and 'Tell Me To My Face'. Tracks like 'Crusader' hinted at the group's willingness to experiment, but 'High Classed' and 'What Went Wrong' were almost MOR pop – an omen of the divisions to come within the group.

1967 was a pivotal year that bore out many group's true colours and The Hollies were no exception. While continuing to play cute on their singles, 'On A Carousel' (number four in March) and Carrie Anne' (three – June), Graham Nash, in particular, craved the serious angle that was afforded contemporaries like The Beatles, Donovan, Eric Burdon, and his new American chum, David Crosby of The Byrds. The Hollies' two albums that year reflected this dichotomy. Ironically the results were best when the group played it straight. *Evolution*, released in June and wrapped in a trendy sleeve designed by Nash's aptly-named designing friends The Fool (for whom he later produced an unlistenable album) included memorable originals like 'Then The Heartaches Begin', 'You Need Love' and 'When Your Light's Turned On' but fell flat on its face with twee nonsense like 'Ye Olde Toffee Shoppe' and 'Lullaby To Tim', a song written for Clarke's son, with Nash's vocal given a vibrato effect. Similarly, *Butterfly* (released in October) was an ambitious attempt to match *Sgt. Pepper* but self-conscious piffle like 'Maker' (featuring Hicks on sitar), 'Elevated Observations' and the overly-lush 'Butterfly', rankled against first class songs like 'Dear Eloise' and 'Would You Believe'. Nash's pride was further dented when the genuinely inventive and advanced 'King Midas In Reverse' failed to reach no higher than eighteen in October.

Throughout 1968 the Hollies recorded several (at the time) unissued songs that were a product of Nash's continued desire to experiment, although ironically 'Wings', a beautiful, delicate song with heartmelting harmonies, was all Clarke's. The group reverted back to the blueprint of uncomplicated pop but the writing was on the wall. Nash gritted his teeth through Clarke's trite 'Jennifer Eccles' (number seven – April '68) and a Tony Hazzard composition, 'Listen To Me' (number eleven – October) but when the group elected to

The Honeybus

record an album of Bob Dylan covers it was the final straw. Nash announced his departure; his final show being in December at the London Palladium with new musical partner David Crosby present.

The Hollies picked themselves up, dusted themselves down with new member, ex-Escorts, Swinging Blue Jeans guitarist Terry Sylvester and the tailor-made Tony Macauley-Geoff Stephens composition 'Sorry Suzanne' was at number three by March '69. The Nash-despised *Hollies Sing Dylan* album was in the shops in May while the sentimental ballad 'He Ain't Heavy, He's My Brother', the song The Hollies remain solely (and unjustly) remembered by, reached three in October. The Hollies success run continued throughout the Seventies, with Clarke temporarily leaving in 1971 to pursue an ill-fated solo career. Ironically a year later the group were at number two in the US (their highest American chart position) with 'Long Cool Woman In A Black Dress' – a song Clarke sang on. His replacement was Swedish vocalist Mikael Rickfors, but 'Clarkey' was back in his old job by 1973.

After Sylvester and Calvert quit in 1981 The Hollies continued into the Eighties with a core trio of Clarke, Hicks and Elliott. Nash, of course, had gone onto superstardom in America with Crosby, Stephen Stills, and when the mood took him, Neil Young. In 1981 the original Hollies line-up was asked to reform to promote 'Holliedaze' – a 'Stars-On-45' treatment of their hits. A new album *What Goes Around* and tour (without the mercurial Haydock) followed in 1983. The Hollies continue to this day, helmed by Hicks and Elliott with ex-Move vocalist Carl Wayne stepping in for the retired Clarke.

(see also Haydock's Rockhouse)

THE HONEYBUS

Formed in London in 1967 by singer-guitarists Pete Dello and Ray Cane with bass player Colin Hare and drummer Peter Kircher, The Honeybus were another Deram signing whose début single 'Delighted To See You' delighted no one and disappeared without trace. The criminally overlooked and inexplicable miss '(Do I Figure) In Your Life?' a song about marital breakdown set to a striking string

The Honeybus

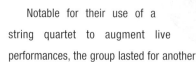

TENDER ARE THE ASHES
(P. Dello)
THE HONEYBUS
Producer: P. Blumsom

arrangement, did equally poor business, but was later revived by Joe Cocker. Third time around and the double-edged blade of a hit 'I Can't Let Maggie Go' turned the group into pop stars (a number eight hit in April '68) but saddled them with the tag of the Nimble bread band for all time after the song was used for a TV advert. Sensing the injustice of what was to come a disillusioned Dello quit to form Lace and was replaced by Jim Kelly.

Notable for their use of a string quartet to augment live performances, the group lasted for another two years but released only a handful of singles, none of which charted. Their 1970 Deram album *Story* (released posthumously) was a fine collection of baroque-pop songs and revealed the group's songwriting strengths.

Dello reformed the band in 1972, recording a one-off single for the Bell label, and again in 1976 only for Decca to re-release 'I Can't Let Maggie Go'. Both Dello and Hare released solo albums in the early Seventies. Kircher resurfaced in The Original Mirrors and an Eighties version of Status Quo.

THE HONEYCOMBS

Like The Applejacks, The Honeycombs were another group that enjoyed the novelty of a woman playing a predominately male role, this time the drummer. Her name was Ann 'Honey' Lantree and she joined her fellow hairdressing friend Martin Murray in a group venture they called The Sherabons in 1963. Honey's brother John came and played bass along with guitarist John Ward and singer Denis D'ell.

Once they changed their name to The Honeycombs (in order to highlight Honey's involvement) the group's rise to fame was instantaneous. They were spotted playing in a north London pub by the team of Alan Howard and Ken Blaikley, who snapped them up and signed them to Pye. Having secured the services of producer Joe Meek the pair wrote The Honeycombs' début single 'Have I The Right'. This was a UK number one in August 1964 and an instant breakthrough hit in the US. The group graced the Top 20 once more in 1965 with the Honey-sung 'That's The Way', but singles like 'Is It Because?', the Ray Davies-composed 'Something Better Beginning', and the dramatic 'Eyes' weren't nearly as popular and failed to make the Top 30. Murray fell offstage breaking his leg and arm, and the group toured Australia in January 1965 with Manfred Mann and The Kinks using an unknown 16-year-old Peter Pye as his replacement. The group lasted another year before Pye let them go and The Honeycombs slipped quietly into obscurity. Denis D'ell attempted a solo career in the Seventies but no one knew about it.

THE HULLABALOOS

An early example of a band cashing in on 'The British Invasion'; gaining recognition and success in the States while remaining almost completely unknown in the UK. This bunch of peroxided blondes originated from Hull and were signed to Columbia in 1964. They released three non-charting singles in England before concentrating on America. Two of these same singles, including a cover of Buddy Holly's 'I'm Gonna Love You Too' made the *Billboard* chart in 1965 as did a third US only release, prompting an inevitable appearance on NBC's hit music show *Hullabaloo* in 1965.

(see also The Bunch Of Fives)

THE HUMAN BEANS

A Cardiff group with a lone 45 to their credit – a creditable cover of the Tim Rose song 'Morning Dew' released on Columbia in 1967. Guitarist Dave Edmunds, bass player John Williams and drummer Tommy Riley then changed their name to Love Sculpture.

(see also Love Sculpture)

THE HUMAN INSTINCT

Before they decided to try their luck in the 'old dart' in 1966, The Human Instinct – in their prior incarnation, The Four Fours – were one of New Zealand's top groups. Once in Britain, however, they found success in the over-populated London scene hard to come by, despite a slew of fabulous pop-psych singles for Mercury and Deram, including 'A Day In My Mind's Mind' (1967) and 'Pink Dawn' (1968).

The Instinct had a great harmony vocal sound and were notable for using microphones attached to their guitars, rather than to the usual microphone stands. Eventually the hard-up combo returned to New Zealand, where a new line-up, featuring only drummer Maurice Greer from the original band, made three sought-after hard rock albums.

The Human Instinct

THE IDLE RACE

Despite releasing a string of fine quasi-psychedelic singles between 1967 and 1971 – the best of which being their first 'The Imposters Of Life's Magazine', this Birmingham band never managed a hit, despite being highly regarded in the business, gaining plugs from DJs John Peel and Kenny Everett.

Formed from the remnants of Roy Wood's old group, Mike Sheridan's Nightriders, The Idle Race are memorable in hindsight for showcasing the first manifestations of singer-guitarist's Jeff Lynne's life-long Beatles obsession.

Lynne left in 1970 following two equally poor selling albums, The Birthday Party and The Idle Race – to join The Move. His replacement was Dave Walker formally of Denny Laine & The Diplomats. This would prove to be the first of numerous personnel changes that revolved around the rhythm section of bass player Greg Masters and drummer Roger Spencer. They eventually evolved out of all recognition into The Steve Gibbons Band.

(see The Move, The Uglys)

THE IN CROWD

Formerly Four Plus One, this London five piece moved from R&B to soul for their second release (and first as The In Crowd); a cover of Otis Redding's 'That's How Strong My Love Is', released May '65. Les Jones was replaced by Steve Howe (ex-Syndicats) in mid–65 in time for their second release 'Stop! Wait A Minute' in August. In November, the group's third and final Parlophone single 'Why Must They Criticise' – a slice of generation gap social commentary – modelled on Sonny Bono's protest singles – was released. In 1966,

'Boots' Alcot left and 'Junior' Woods moved over to bass, drummer Ken Lawrence was replaced by 'Twink' Alder (ex-Fairies) and the group changed their name to Tomorrow in late-66.

(see also The Fairies, Four Plus One, The Syndicats, Tomorrow)

THE IVY LEAGUE

Three session singer-songwriters John Carter, Ken Lewis, and Perry Ford got together as The Ivy League in 1964.

Carter and Lewis had already experienced group life in Carter-Lewis & The Southerners and Ford was already a seasoned session man. These credentials were good enough to secure a deal with Pye subsidiary Piccadilly. The trio's dramatic début single 'What More Do You Want' flopped, and with red faces all round a follow up was hastily recorded. 'Funny How Love Can Be' made it to number eight in February '65, epitomising the trio's high-pitched falsetto vocals, a style that became their trademark, heard on other current hits such as The Who's 'I Can't Explain'. A third single 'That's Why I'm Crying' was a little too similar and stalled at 22 but set the scene for The Ivy League's crowning glory – the number three hit 'Tossin' And Turnin''. This classic pop single deserved to go the extra two places to the top in July. The eagerly awaited début album *This Is The Ivy League* promised much in light of the group's recent chart successes, but when it came out at the end of '65 it was quite disappointing. Over confidence had taken over from good taste as a wide range of musical styles and material were tackled – not all of it suited to the trio's characteristic singing formula; reaching an embarrassing low on 'The Floral Dance'. The album was panned in the music press and unsurprisingly failed to chart. Several more unsuccessful singles followed, including 'Willow Tree' and 'My World Fell Down', covered successfully the following year in the US by Sagittarius. Carter and Lewis quit in '66 and were replaced by Tony Burrows and Neil Landon. This line up went on to masquerade as hippie herberts The Flowerpot Men.

(see also Carter-Lewis & The Southerners, The Flowerpot Men)

PETER JAY & THE JAYWALKERS

The Jaywalkers (Peter Miller – guitar, Tony Webster-guitar, Mac McIntyre – tenor sax/flute, Lloyd Baker – baritone sax/piano, Geoff Moss – acoustic bass, Johnny Larke – electric bass) were lead by drummer Peter Jay. The group spanned the gap from the pre-Beatles days of instrumentals – via the minor hit 'Can Can 62' – to the beat boom. By the time they disbanded in 1967, as Peter Jay & The New Jaywalkers the group had slimmed down to a quintet and were firmly ensconced in the popular soulful mode of the day, thanks largely to the recent addition of vocalist/guitarist Terry Reid.

Indeed, their final single, 'The Hand Don't Fit The Glove', was credited to Terry Reid & The Jaywalkers, rather than drummer Peter Jay. The earlier line-up featured moody, shade wearing Miller as the main driving force on the group's singles for Decca and Piccadilly before quitting The Jaywalkers in 1966 and retreating into songwriting mode. He issued two acclaimed freakbeat singles in 'Baby I Got News For You' (1965, as Miller) and 'Cold Turkey' (1968, under the name Big Boy Pete). An album of unreleased Miller recordings Summerland was issued by Tenth Planet in 1997.

JOHN'S CHILDREN

Another example where a future legend's involvement in a band overshadows any musical merit a band possessed. John's Children were together for little over a year, released only a handful of unsuccessful records, had a US-only album withdrawn and saw their only chance of a hit single banned in the UK. Yet John's Children have become recognised due to Marc Bolan being in the band for a short period in his pre-pixie-glam rock-god incarnation.

But like The Birds, John's Children deserve more than this association. After all they released one of the first out and out mod-psych singles, 'Smashed Blocked', proudly promoted the pre-punk ethic of not being able to play their instruments and by all accounts upstaged The Who on a German tour.

True to form the group started its short but incident-packed lifespan in late 1964, in the ridiculously-monikered Clockwork Onions, featuring Louie Grooner (vocals), Andy Ellison (harmonica), Geoff McClelland (guitar), Chris Dawsett (bass) and Chris Townson (drums) playing in and around the Surrey area. Known by very few as The Few followed by The Silence (due to the combo being the loudest group they knew of!) the group now featured bassist John Hewlett with Ellison as vocalist. The Silence were typical of any one of a dozen similar suburban Mod bands that had sprung up overnight in the wake of The Who and The Small Faces. However, unlike the majority, they were intent on striving beyond the usual R&B covers to forge their own unique sound and identity. The group approached Don Arden, but already flush with a stable of Mod bands he declined. Next on their hit list was ex-Yardbirds manager Simon Napier-Bell, who was harassed into watching the group after Hewlett

Peter Jay & The Jaywalkers

John's Children

MR. GOLDEN TRUMPET PLAYER

JUNIOR'S EYES

BLACK SNAKE

JUNIOR'S EYES

JOHN'S CHILDREN
Fan Club
c/o Gillian Ross
95 Gaysham Hall,
Clayhall, Ilford, Essex.

Also the group's own club
"John's Children's"
22a Bridge St., Leatherhead, Surrey.
Discs Mon - Thur. Groups Fri - Sun.

interrupted his dinner in a St. Tropez night club.

Napier-Bell attended a particularly horrendous performance – held at, of all places, a swimming pool party. As water short circuited the equipment with the group oblivious to the dangers of electrocution – the flamboyant entrepreneur felt he didn't have the heart to desert what he described as positively the worst group he'd ever seen. Seven beers and twelve whiskies later he was managing them. Napier-Bell's first undertaking was to change their name to John's Children (after leader Hewlett), imposing a strict dress code of pure white and forbade the group from entering the studio during the recording of their début single, 'Smashed Blocked' – Mod parlance for being off your head on pills.

Napier-Bell opted for safety and for that matter distance. A bunch of Los Angeles session musicians were roped in to provide the backing track, with Ellison's lead and backing vocals added only once the backing track was safely in the can. Obviously, any similarity between the accomplished recording and the band's live sound was purely coincidental. 'Smashed Blocked' is a noteworthy slice of British eccentricity – equal parts ballad (featuring Ellison's over-the-top spoken intro), psychedelia and pop – and as unorthodox a single as anything gracing the charts in late '66 on

either side of the Atlantic. (Amazingly it charted, albeit fleetingly, at number 98 in the States). A début album, subtly titled *Orgasm*, featured these same session musicians drowned in screams that Napier-Bell had lifted from the *A Hard Day's Night* film! The album was submitted to the group's US label, White Whale whose executives went white-faced at the title and the appalling quality of the music within and promptly shelved it. (It was eventually given a belated release in 1971 and reissued by UK indie label Cherry Red in 1984.)

Some payola nudged the follow up, the aptly titled 'Just What You Want – Just What You'll Get' into the UK Top 50, but Napier-Bell's insistence on using ex-Yardbird Jeff Beck only highlighted the band's shortcomings. First to go was guitarist Geoff McClelland, replaced by Bolan whose inclusion seemed a tad ill-timed since the group had just been dropped by EMI who'd refused to release their third offering 'Not The Sort Of Girl You'd Take To Bed'. Rumours abounded as to whether this deliberately provocative title was nothing more than a clever Napier-Bell ruse in order to force EMI's hand into dropping the band, since an offer from Who manager Kit Lambert to join his Track Records roster was on the table. Whatever the truth, with Bolan on board the group did seem to pick up some momentum and they entered into a more creative and independent period. He also brought to the group his highly original lyrics. 'Desdemona' looked set to give the band their best chance at a bona fide` hit, but the BBC banned it, taking exception to the risque` line 'lift up your skirt and fly'. Another Bolan tune was hurriedly recorded, the psychedelically whimsical 'A Midsummer Night's Scene' but Track withdrew it after a mere 25 copies were pressed. The record is now among the rarest Sixties-related recordings, with copies changing hands for up to £3000.

Not surprisingly it was a deflated group that set off on a consolatory week-long tour of Germany as support to The Who. Buoyed by the challenge of out-feedbacking and out-'autodestructing' Shepherd's Bush's finest, the group rose famously to the occasion. A complete wall of gigantic speaker cabinets, patented by NASA, were erected each night, spanning the entire width of the stage, in order to dwarf The Who's sound system. As a deafening wave of feedback assaulted the crowd head on, bags of feathers exploded, Bolan whipped his guitar with a chain, Ellison and Hewlett indulged in a mock-fight while Townson attempted to hold everything together with relentless tribal drumming. These Who-enraging antics inevitably caused audience riots, and a show in Ludwigshaven was shut down by police using water cannons. Finally the band's equipment was confiscated and the group deported. Ironically, Townson later deputised for an ill Keith Moon on a few Who dates. When Bolan quit that was essentially the end of John's Children, although they carried on for a short while, first as a three-piece and then with roadie Chris Colville drafted in as drummer to allow Townson to switch to guitar. However it was obvious the whole crazy charade was at an end, the last straw being when a Napier-Bell publicity stunt for their record 'Come And Play With Me In The Garden' had the band posing stark naked with strategically placed flowers. John's Children ceremoniously burned their white stage outfits and finally called it a day in 1968.

Ellison released a Track solo single 'It's Been A Long Time' (as featured in the film *Here We Go Round The Mulberry Bush*) in early-68. Its B-side, the Who-like 'Arthur Green', performed and credited to John's Children was, ironically, the group's finest hour. Further solo singles (including a cover of The Beatles 'You Can't Do That') followed before Ellison formed glamsters Jet in 1974 and later, Radio Stars. Townson and Hewlett formed proto-punkers The Jook until Hewlett managed Sparks and found religion while Townson joined Ellison in Jet. Ellison and Townson reform John's Children periodically with ex-Sparks, Jet and Radio Stars bassist, Martin Gordon along for the ride with Morrissey guitarist (and mega-John's Children fan) 'Boz' Boorer. Ironically, John's Children now enjoy a considerably higher profile than in their chaotic non-career with reissues of priceless singles and unreleased material, and a slim volume on their misadventures. *(see also Marc Bolan)*

PAUL JONES

When Paul Jones left Manfred Mann in July 1966 his solo career looked assured. However, it certainly wasn't the stuff of legend. It started off well enough with his first single 'High Time', written and produced by Mike Leander, making an impressionable number four in October 1966. In 1967 he made his big screen début playing opposite Jean Shrimpton, the supermodel of her day, in Peter Watkins' cult classic *Privilege*. A Leander song from the film 'I've Been A Bad Boy', beat a path to number five in February. The soundtrack EP also topped the EP charts in May, but his patchy first album *My Way* failed to make any impression. Things went decidedly down hill from there with a third single, 'Thinkin' Ain't For Me', stopping short of the Top 30 in September, while 'Sons And Lovers' missed completely.

'And The Sun Will Shine', a strong cover of a Bee Gees song featured Paul McCartney on drums, while its B-side, 'The Dog Presides' featured Jeff Beck on guitar. The downhill slide continued with 'When I Was Six Years Old', 'Aquarius' (a song from the hit musical *Hair*) and a cover of a minor Mama Cass US hit, 'It's Getting Better'. Jones decided to concentrate on acting instead and appeared in several West End productions, including *Joseph And The Amazing Technicolor Dream Coat* and *Hamlet*. Since 1979 he's divided his time between various presenting roles on both TV and radio while fronting The Blues Band with fellow Manfred Tom McGuinness. He continues to host a successful BBC Radio 2 show devoted to his love of the blues and gospel.

(see also Manfred Mann)

HARLEM JONNS RESHUFFLE

A play on Bob and Earl's soul classic 'Harlem Shuffle' this Lancashire blue-eyed soul collective relocated to Watford after scoring a deal with Fontana in 1968. The result was two singles, including a cover of Adam Apples' northern soul classic 'You Are The One I Love', and a self-titled R&B cover-filled album.

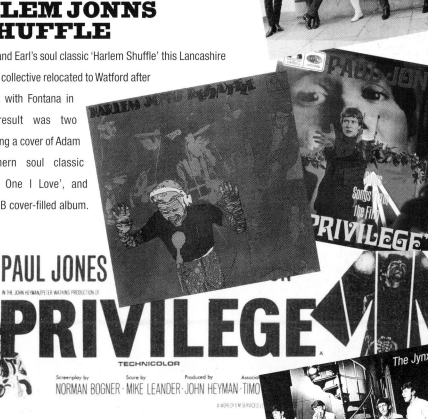

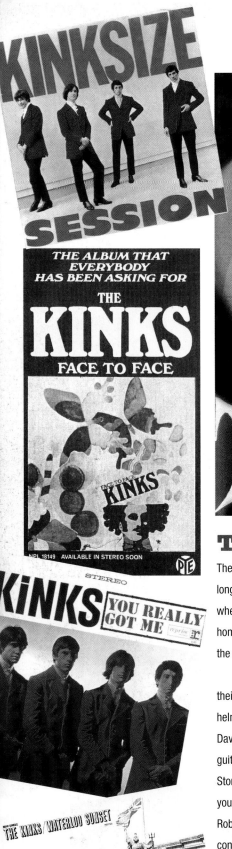

THE KINKS

The Kinks rank among the most distinguished, idiosyncratic and longest-running of the Sixties English beat groups. Paradoxically, when some of their greatest work was being ignored in their homeland, the group drew a devout American following attracted by the very Englishness of Ray Davies' highly original compositions.

Hailing from Muswell Hill in north London, the group started their musical life as The Ravens with 16-year-old Dave Davies at the helm, Ray's schoolfriend Pete Quaife (bass) and John Start (drums). Dave's older brother Ray attended Hornsey School of Art and played guitar with The Dave Hunt R&B Band. After catching the early Rolling Stones at the Marquee, Ray quit Hunt's band and joined up with his younger sibling in The Ravens. The group backed a singer called Robert Wace at various debutante balls but when Wace lost his confidence one night Ray stepped in to sing, proving he had natural singing abilities coupled with a blossoming gift as a song writer. Wace retreated to the role of co-manager with his friend Grenville

Collins. The pair brought in manager and agent Larry Page to help them successfully secure a record deal with Pye, teaming them with American expat producer Shel Talmy, and the group auditioned for leading impresario Arthur Howes on New Year's Eve 1963 who was impressed enough to book The Kinks on several important tours. The older Start was fired and auditions brought in South Londoner Mick Avory in early '64.

The Ravens were then rechristened The Kinks, a name inspired by the early Sixties slang trend of describing things as kinky (Honor Blackman from TV's *The Avengers* wore 'kinky boots') and one which causes dispute to this day as to who suggested it (an ominous portent of the bitter disagreements that surround The Kinks early career). The Kinks logo, a kinky booted foot at the bottom of each letter, was designed by Avory's father. For publicity pictures Page kitted them out in black leather jackets, capes, and caps while controversially, Dave brandished a whip. This image was eventually subsumed by visually distinctive matching pink hunting jackets.

Howes suggested The Kinks record a song he'd seen go down well in The Beatles act – a cover of Little Richard's 'Long Tall Sally'. The Kinks' tepid version failed miserably, as did the follow-up, the Mersey-influenced Ray Davies original 'You Still Want Me'. The third and crucial decider, 'You Really Got Me' was recorded twice – the original version was rejected by Ray for being slow and swamped with echo. A young, untried Davies was taking a gamble in demanding it be re-recorded but he got his way. The master, captured in two takes, the first simply to get the balance right, was a triumph in every way – a sterling performance conceived in difficult circumstances. It raced to number one in September 1964; its metallic riff inadvertently giving birth to the 'heavy metal' genre. It's worth noting that newboy Avory didn't play on these first singles, nor on the group's first album, as producer Shel Talmy initially didn't trust his abilities over session drummer Bobbie Graham. Additionally Talmy brought in session guitarists like Big Jim Sullivan and a young Jimmy Page, who was rumoured to have been responsible for the wild solos in the Kinks early work (not so, they were all Dave's work). Page & co. did augment the group on their début album *Kinks* – a spirited collection of covers and some promising Davies originals like 'So Mystifying', 'I Just Can't Go To Sleep' and 'Stop Your Sobbing' – later covered to great effect in 1979 by The Pretenders –

The Kinks

DAVE DAVIES
NEW HIT SINGLE
7N 17429
SUSANNAH'S STILL ALIVE

released in October. 'All Day And All Of The Night' used the same tested riff formula to great effect (number two in November), while 'Tired Of Waiting For You', rewarded the group with their second UK number one in February '65. A second album *Kinda Kinks* was cut on the run and was less effective but pointed toward the increasing maturity of Ray's writing with 'Nothing In This World Can Stop Me Worrying About That Girl' and 'So Long'.

The pressure cooker atmosphere of sudden acceptance was taking its toll and at a gig in Cardiff in April, Dave turned around and spat at Avory while kicking part of his kit over. The normally imperturbable drummer rose to his feet and hit Dave over the head with his crash cymbal and beat a swift exit. The incident was smoothed over as a gimmicky stage device but behind the scenes The Kinks were all but over. Page rallied them together for a disastrous American tour in June, during which they managed to fall

foul of the US Federation of Musicians, a dispute that resulted in a four-year ban from that country. Singles success continued throughout '65 with 'Everybody's Gonna Be Happy' (17 – April), 'Set Me Free' (nine – June) and the revolutionary 'See My Friend' – the first pop song to make use of the Indian drone and to have an ambiguous gay theme (10 – August). By now, The Kinks sound had toned down from the metallic edge of 'You Really Got Me' and 'All Day And All Of The Night' to more subtle Ray Davies compositions like 'Well Respected Man' (off the September '65 *Kwyet Kinks* EP), the first of his third person character studies that marked him down as a quirky English observer. The volume was turned up again for the great double-sider 'Till The End Of The Day'/'Where Have All The Good Times Gone' (eight – December), and for the group's third album *The Kink Kontroversy* (December 1965). As well as an exciting version of Sleepy John Estes 'Milk Cow Blues', it featured such

The Kinks

reflective Davies songs like 'Ring The Bells', 'The World Keeps Going Round', 'I Am Free' (sung by Dave) and 'You Can't Win' mixed with upbeat fare like 'I Gotta Get the First Plane Home' and 'When I See That Girl Of Mine'.

1966 proved to be a successful year for The Kinks with 'Dedicated Follower Of Fashion' (four -March), 'Sunny Afternoon (the group's third number one in July – featuring a killer 'declaration of intent' B-side, 'I'm Not Like Everybody Else') and 'Dead End Street' (five – December), while *Face To Face*, the group's first cohesive LP, released in November, featured such acute and witty Davies' observations as 'Rosie, Won't You Please Come Home' (written to his sister Rose), 'Dandy', 'Too Much On My Mind', 'Holiday In Waikiki', and 'Fancy', again utilising the drone effect used on 'See My Friends'. Unfortunately, like many of their contemporaries, The Kinks were perceived by their conservative record company as a singles act and the album failed to sell; a problem that was to blight the group's progress for the remainder of their term with Pye. That June, Quaife was involved in a serious road accident and retired from the band to recuperate. His place was taken by ex-Mark Four bassist John Dalton who stayed with the group until November when Quaife was readmitted.

The Kinks were massively popular in Europe and a Continental-only single, 'Mr. Pleasant' was the first piece of Kinks product in 1967, but perhaps Ray's finest moment came with 'Waterloo Sunset'; sharp observation, with a guitar riff laden with tape echo melded to a memorable melody, smothered in heartmelting harmonies. The Terry

and Julie characters were based on Terence Stamp and Julie Christie. The single reached number two (in May) while 'Autumn Almanac', another finely observed slice of English custom – Saturday football, Sunday roast, Blackpool holiday – got to three in November.

Concurrently, brother Dave had an unexpected hit with the delightfully Dylanesque 'Death Of A Clown' (which reached number three in August). With Ray's encouragement he released three further singles ('Susannah's Still Alive', 'Lincoln County' and 'Hold My Hand', featuring The Kinks backing him) over the next two years, but none was as successful and plans for a solo album were put on hold.

The Kinks' 1967 album *Something Else…* was a continuation of the themes explored on *Face To Face* with 'David Watts' (later covered by The Jam in 1978), 'Two Sisters' (a clever female mirror of the Davies siblings lifestyles), 'Situation Vacant', 'Afternoon Tea' and 'End Of The Season'. Again it sold disappointingly in proportion to its quality as did a live document of a scream-drenched Glasgow concert *Live At Kelvin Hall*.

Undaunted Ray's writing throughout 1968 stayed admirably on the same course with the child-like 'Wonderboy', the poignant 'Days' and the piece de resistance *The Kinks Are The Village Green Preservation Society*. The album was an artistic triumph with some of the group's strongest songs – including the title track, 'Do You Remember Walter?', 'Big Sky', 'Village Green', 'Animal Farm' – each loosely tied to a concept of loss of innocence in the face of increasing modernity. The album, released in October, received glowing reviews which unforgivably failed to translate into sales, although paradoxically its quintessentially English nature created a devout American Kinks kult. By the end of '68 a disillusioned Quaife had left, to be replaced again by Dalton. A filler single, 'Plastic Man' was issued in April but failed to rise any higher than 31. *Arthur Or The Decline And Fall Of The British Empire*, inspired by a Granada television play Ray was commissioned to write, continued Ray's look back at how his beloved England had changed, with such jaunty ditties as 'Victoria', 'Drivin', 'Shangri-La' (all released as singles), anti-war indictments ('Yes Sir, No Sir', 'Some Mother's Son'), resigned ennui ('Brainwashed', 'Nothing To Say') and wistful melancholia ('Young And Innocent Days'). Again the album wasn't pushed but became a cult favourite in America where the relaxation of The Kinks touring ban meant the group could finally recover vital lost ground.

The Kinks continued into the Seventies augmented by keyboard player John 'the Baptist' Gosling and switched from Pye to RCA in 1971. Further albums followed – including two voluminous attempts to expand the *Preservation* format in the mid-Seventies. The Kinks signed to Arista in 1977 the same year that Dalton and Gosling left the group to be replaced by various auxiliary members including ex-Mike Cotton Sound, and Argent bassist Jim Rodford. The Kinks became a hugely popular 'arena rock' group in the US in the late Seventies-early Eighties, where their record sales far outstripped their English returns, although 'Come Dancing' returned the Kinks to the Top 20 in 1983. In 1984 Avory was replaced by Bob Henrit (ex-Roulettes, Unit Four Plus Two, Argent) and The Kinks carried on sporadically touring and releasing albums to 1995.

In 1994, Ray's highly-rated semi-fictional autobiography *X-Ray* was published, followed by brother Dave's no-holds-barred *Kink* in 1996. To promote *X-Ray* Ray took a successful 'Storyteller' tour around the globe and is currently planning a musical titled *Come Dancing*. With the mid-Nineties advent of Britpop, he was universally hailed as being the most archetypal of British songwriters.

Dave plays club dates with his American band and works on the occasional film score. Quaife retired from music and after a spell living in Denmark emigrated to Canada where he became a graphic designer. Avory helps maintain The Kinks' office Konk while keeping his hand in playing with various musicians including ex-Jimi Hendrix Experience bassist Noel Redding and ex-Animals keyboardist Dave Rowberry in Shut Up Frank and his erstwhile bandmates Dalton and Gosling in the Kast-Off Kinks. In 2002 there is talk in the Davies camp of reactivating The Kinks for a future project.

(see also The Mark Four)

The Kinks

THE KIRKBYS

The Kirkbys left just one fine RCA single in the stomping 'It's A Crime', an acerbic beat number from 1966 that surprisingly didn't make any chart impression. Their lead singer was Jimmy Campbell, who next showed up in the 23rd Turnoff for one exquisite single, before pursuing a solo career in the early Seventies. He later collaborated with fellow Scouser Billy Kinsley in Rockin' Horse.

(see also The Merseybeats, The Merseys, 23rd Turnoff)

The Kirkbys

The Knack

THE KNACK

A fine beat group from Ilford, responsible for two great 1965 singles on Decca: 'She Ain't No Good' and 'Time, Time, Time' (both recorded as a single by The Clique on Pye) and the latter's A-side 'It's Love Baby (24 Hours a Day)'.

Four not-so-great 1966-67 singles on Piccadilly followed, including covers of The Lovin' Spoonful's 'Did You Ever Have To Make Your Mind?' and 'Younger Girl'. Most of the group, including the Gurvitz brothers Adrian and Paul went on to the considerably heavier Gun and Three Man Army.

THE KOOBAS

Possibly the least well-known of Brian Epstein's post-Beatles charges from the Mersey era, The Koobas – Stu Leatherwood and Roy Morris (guitars), Keith Ellis (bass), and Tony O' Riley (drums) formed in 1962 and broke up in 1968.

As for the band's history, you could read a biography of any period Liverpool beat group, omit the name, and it would still read fairly accurately – four young guys growing up in post war Liverpool, leaving school to play in various local groups, before getting together and forming their own band.

Leatherwood and Morris had been in The Thunderbeats, while Morris and Ellis had come from The Midnighters. The group originally called themselves The Kubas but changed the spelling to The Koobas in 1965. Inevitably, due to mutual connections the group signed with Brian Epstein's NEMS company, and appeared in the Mersey celluloid package *Ferry Cross The Mersey*. The group secured a deal with Pye and a support slot on the Beatles final UK tour in December 1965. The Koobas' début single was a cover of Kim Weston's 'Take Me For A Little While', while the follow-up 'You'd Better Make Up Your Mind' (released May '66) was equally unsuccessful. The group were popular in Germany and spent a great

The Koobas

deal of there time there, gigging and appearing on TV shows like Bremen's *Beat!Beat!Beat!* In 1966, the group were offered a deal with Columbia/ EMI but their three-year stint with the label was an equally damp squib, despite some fine output including a cover of Cat Stevens 'The First Cut Is The Deepest' going head-to-head with P.P Arnold's more successful version. A quaintly English, faux-psych, self-titled album was released in 1969 (which is now a considerable collector's item) but by then, The Koobas had thrown in the towel. Ellis went on to Van der Graaf Generator, while Leatherwood joined March Hare featuring Pete Dello (ex-Honeybus).

ALEXIS KORNER'S BLUES INCORPORATED

The US have their Godfathers and their Boss, but Britain has only managed the Daddy or in Korner's case 'the Daddy of them all'. It's a title openly acknowledged and respected with good reason by the scores of R&B musicians and latterday rock gods who owe their start to Korner.

Born in Paris, the multi-lingual Korner was passionate about black American folk and blues music and his crusading zealousness brought him into contact with a like-minded soul, Cyril Davies. The two transformed the London Skiffle Club into the London Blues and Barrelhouse Club, where they not only performed together but backed visiting US bluesmen. As well as this, the duo had a regular gig, performing an R&B set during an interval in noted jazzman Chris Barber's set.

Although the purist jazzers looked down their noses Korner and Davies were encouraged and broke away to form their own group, Blues Incorporated. The two founded the Ealing Club, below the ABC teashop opposite Ealing Broadway station in early 1962 as a platform for this exotic, little-known music. The original line-up of Blues Incorporated additionally featured Art Wood (vocals), Keith Scott (piano), Andy Hoogenboom (bass) and Charlie Watts (drums). Word of the club spread and soon the likes of Long John Baldry, Paul Jones, Mick Jagger, and Eric Clapton had singing spots while Blues Incorporated later featured the future members of the Graham Bond Organisation – Bond, Jack Bruce, Ginger Baker and Dick Heckstall-Smith in its fluid line-up. Jagger, Keith Richards and Dick Taylor saw Brian Jones playing breathtaking Elmore James slide runs, while sitting in (as Elmo Lewis) with Korner & Co., and the seeds of The Rolling Stones were sown. *R&B From The Marquee*, featuring Long John Baldry on vocals, is an accurate encapsulation of Blues Inc's influences but also exposes their limitations as pioneers rather than innovators. Little wonder that Korner's younger pupils were able to take his example and run with it. That same year (1962) Korner and Davies disagreed over billing and Davies quit to form his own Cyril Davies R&B All-Stars.

Korner continued in a jazzier direction with future Pentangle rhythm section Danny Thompson (bass) and Terry Cox (drums) and coloured American vocalist Herbie Goins. The group gained a weekly residency on the early evening children's television show *Five O'Clock Club*. Korner dropped the Blues Incorporated appellation for such temporary ventures as Free At Last (a duo with future Led Zeppelin vocalist Robert Plant), New Church, and CCS, whose 1970 big-band instrumental hit version of 'Whole Lotta Love' was used as the theme to *Top Of The Pops*. Korner's old pupils didn't forget their debt and Korner's 1972 album *Bootleg Him!* featured highlights from his illustrious career. Korner successfully pursued a concurrent career in broadcasting with the BBC and in the late Seventies he formed Rocket 88, an informal gathering of Bruce, Watts, Heckstall-Smith and Stones pianist Ian Stewart. His death from cancer on New Year's Day 1984 robbed the world of British blues and jazz of one of its founding fathers.

(see also The Artwoods, Long John Baldry, Graham Bond Organisation, Cream, Cyril Davies R&B All-Stars, Herbie Goins & The Nightimers, Manfred Mann, The Rolling Stones)

BILLY J. KRAMER & THE DAKOTAS

Kramer's real name was William Howard Ashton, while The Dakotas were a Manchester band (Tony Mansfield – drums, Ray Jones – bass, Mike Maxfield and Robin MacDonald – guitars) formed in 1962. In 1963 Brian Epstein played matchmaker and teamed them up.

A deal with EMI and Parlophone predictably followed and Epstein fashioned the group with a batch of Lennon and McCartney giveaways. 'Do You Want To Know A Secret' (featuring producer George Martin on piano), recorded by The Beatles on their début album *Please Please Me* as a vocal vehicle for George Harrison, with B-side 'I'll Be On My Way' gave Billy J. a début hit at number two in May, while 'Bad To Me' went one better; topping the charts for two weeks in August. Even the Dakotas scored an instrumental hit in their own right with 'The Cruel Sea' in July. Billy J. passed on 'I'm In Love' which instead was donated to The Fourmost; plumbing for 'I'll Keep You Satisfied' (their third straight hit, number four – December 1963).

Billy J. and co. appeared with The Beatles on the bill of the Fabs' 1963 Xmas season at the Finsbury Park Astoria and a year-end all-Liverpool edition of the popular networked variety show *Thank Your Lucky Stars*.

Kramer dispensed with Beatle assistance for his fourth single and opted for 'Little Children' – a number written by Mort Shuman and John McFarland. The decision was seen to be correct as it provided him with another number one in March '64 and also broke the band in America where it reached number seven in May.

A line up change in July and a quick reshuffle saw bass player Ray Jones leave and Robin MacDonald trade six strings for four. Ex-Pirates guitarist Mick Green joined and another Lennon-McCartney donation 'From A Window' took them back to the Top 10 the same month.

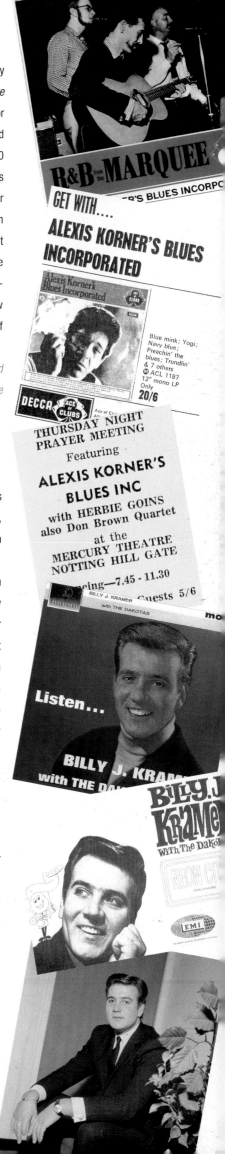

Denny Laine

The group then made the mistake of easing off the momentum by touring overseas and didn't release a single for several months. When the Fab-free 'It's Gotta Last Forever' was finally issued it flopped miserably. Over the ensuing months it became clear that Kramer's popularity was waning. Underestimating the fickleness of the record buying public coupled with the passing of Merseybeat had rendered him yesterday's man. His final hit came in May 1965 with Burt Bacharach's 'Trains And Boats And Planes' which made it to number 12. A further two singles, 'Neon City' and 'We're Doing Fine' (the latter ironically probably Kramer's best single) failed to chart and the group were forced to scrape a living on the Northern club scene.

Kramer decided to go it alone in late 1966, releasing a string of flop singles on Parlophone, Reaction and NEMS, while the Dakotas carried on with another ex-Pirate Frank Farley replacing Mansfield; recording for Page One and Fontana, including a surprisingly tough B-side 'The Spider And The Fly' in 1968. Kramer reverted to his real name in the Seventies in a failed attempt to catch the public off guard. Kramer continues to ply his trade on the nostalgia circuit.

DENNY LAINE

Denny Laine (real name Brian Hines) has had more than one bite of the rock cherry. An important player in the Sixties Birmingham beat scene Laine joined his first group Johnny & The Dominators after acquiring an electric guitar. While holding down a job as an electrical goods trainee he formed his first group Denny Laine & The Diplomats in 1962 featuring Phil Ackrill (guitar), Steve Horton (bass), Bev Bevan (drums), vocalist Nicky James, and Robert Davis (now known as comedian Jasper Carrott). The group were notorious around the Birmingham scene for having matching suits, peroxided hair while trying to pass themselves off as two sets of brothers. Laine became part of the Birmingham beat amalgamation that was The Moody Blues. He was an excellent guitar player and vocalist, as demonstrated by the group's huge international hit 'Go Now' which topped the charts in 1965. Unfortunately none of the group's subsequent output was anywhere near as successful and Laine finally abandoned the Moodies in September 1966.

After spending time in Spain Laine formed Denny Laine's Electric String Band, a short-lived experimental affair notable for the pioneering use of a Royal Academy quartet using amplified classical string instruments – an idea later filched by his Brummie brethren, Roy Wood and Jeff Lynne. Joining him in the venture was the unreliable ex-Pretty Things drummer Viv Prince, and Spooky Tooth bassist Andy Leigh. As a soloist Laine was signed to Deram and became a frequent feature on John Peel's *Top Gear* radio show. He seemed about to achieve single success with his wonderfully baroque 'Say You Don't Mind' (with an arrangement scored by John Paul Jones) but incredibly it did nothing, When the follow up 'Too Much In Love' fell on equally deaf ears the band prematurely split in August 67.

The Limeys

Loose Ends

Loose Ends

Loose Ends

Love Affair

Laine drifted though the rest of the Sixties. His next Secunda-guided venture Balls with fellow Brummies Trevor Burton and Steve Gibbons folded after only one single – the Burton-penned 'Fight For My Country'. An equally unsatisfactory stint with Ginger Baker's Airforce followed (Laine's version of Bob Dylan's 'Man Of Constant Sorrow' becoming a single in 1970) before Laine got the call to join Paul McCartney's new group Wings in August 1971. 'Say You Don't Mind' finally became the hit it so rightly deserved to be when revived in 1972 by Colin Blunstone. Laine stayed with Wings until his official departure in April 1981. Always a restless spirit, he filed for bankruptcy in the mid-Eighties (he had sold his lucrative co-publishing rights to the million-selling hit 'Mull Of Kintyre' to co-author Paul McCartney) and sporadically continues to record and perform.

THE LIMEYS

Not much is known about the above group outside of the fact that they were from north London and had four singles on Pye and Decca, the most notable of which was a strong cover of The Strangeloves' 'Cara-Lin' (1965), produced by Mike Berry.

LOS BRAVOS

Los Bravos hold the distinction of being the only Spanish act to have a Top Five hit in Britain and America, with the classic 'Black Is Black', a song composed by two Englishmen Tony Hayes and Steve Wadey. The group, originally known as Los Sonor, were voted Spain's top beat group following two domestic Top 10 hits. Following heavy rotation on the pirate stations, 'Black Is Black' reached number two in Britain in July '66 and four in the US in September. Unfortunately, follow-ups like 'I Don't Care' and a fine cover of a Vanda-Young song, 'Bring A Little Lovin' (1968) failed to repeat the process, and the group returned to El Spanola. Hasta la vista.

THE LOOSE ENDS

A moody-looking bunch of Brummies who were responsible for two solid singles on Decca in 1966, both covers – The Young Rascals' 'I Ain't Gonna Eat My Heart Out Anymore' (with it's soul-beat flip 'Send The People Away') and a gutsy version of George Harrison's 'Taxman', aimed squarely at the discotheque floor, and its equally moddy flip, 'That's It'.

LOVE AFFAIR

The Love Affair were originally known as The Soul Survivors, fronted by sixteen-year-old apple-pie faced mod Steve Ellis, with an early line-up of Morgan Fisher (keyboards), Ian Miller (guitar), Warwick Rose (bass), and Maurice Bacon (drums).

Miller was replaced by Michael George, who in turn made way for Rex Brayley, while Rose was replaced by Mick Jackson. The group were actually built around Bacon whose wealthy father Sidney managed them, along with Decca Records' marketing director John Cokell and in-house photographer, David Wedgbury. The group's name was changed to The Love Affair and a Mike Vernon-produced cover of The Rolling Stones' *Between The Buttons* track, 'She Smiled Sweetly', with a Small Faces-style Morgan/Ellis original, 'Satisfaction Guaranteed' on the flip, became the group's début single.

The record did nothing, the group were dropped by Decca and Fisher left to complete his exams and was replaced by Lynton Guest. A change to CBS and the group were offered US soulman's Robert Knight's 'Everlasting Love' by Cokell. The song had already been turned down by The Tremeloes but was a certified smash in the hands of producer Mike Smith and musical arranger Keith Mansfield. The Love Affair took it all the way to number one in February 1968. However the fresh-faced group suffered a Monkees-style backlash when it was discovered that Ellis was the only member of the group who appeared on the record (the rest of the band's sound being supplied by session men).

Ignoring allegations of conning the public the group released a string of identical singles; another Robert Knight cover 'Rainbow Valley' (number five in April), and the Philip Goodhand-Tait composed 'A Day Without Love' (number six in September), 'One Road' (number 16, February '69) and 'Bringing On Back The Good Times' (number nine in July). However the group were still smarting over their image as pop puppets – their début album *The Everlasting Love Affair* was largely the work of the dreaded sessionmen. Fisher returned to replace Guest in the summer of '68 and a parting of the ways occured when Ellis quit in December 1969 to pursue a solo career while the rest of the group pursued a more progressive direction as L.A with singer Gus Eadon from the Elastic Band (who also featured future Sweet guitarist Andy Scott among their ranks). Ellis formed Ellis Group with Zoot Money and later, Widowmaker with ex-Mott The Hoople guitarist Luther Grosvenor (alias Ariel Bender) before temporarily retiring from the music business. Fisher joined the Third Ear Band and the mid-Seventies version of Mott The Hoople. He now lives in Japan. Ellis has recently returned to performing and recording under his own name.

Love Sculpture

LOVE SCULPTURE

Famous for first introducing guitar hero and roots rocker Dave Edmunds to the world, Love Sculpture evolved in 1967 from an earlier Cardiff combo, The Human Beans, and débuted with the great 'River To Another Day'. They are best remembered on a chart level for a revved-up version of Khachaturian's 'Sabre Dance' that smashed into the Top 10 in December 1968. The rest of the power trio's output had a strong blues flavour, as evidenced on their two albums *Blues Helping* and *Forms And Feelings*. However, Love Sculpture's swan song was probably their finest moment, a splendid psychedelic pop nugget entitled 'In The Land Of The Few', released a few scant months before Edmunds solo début 'I Hear You Knocking' hit the top of the charts in 1970.

(see also The Human Beans)

LULU

Born Marie MacDonald McLaughlin Lawrie in Glasgow, Scotland, in 1948, Lulu first found fame when her best remembered song, 'Shout!', crashed into the British charts in May 1964. This lead to her being dubbed the 'British Brenda Lee'.

Lulu was reportedly singing by the time she could walk and, at the age of six, had won a talent contest in Blackpool. In 1963, she was discovered by London impresario Marian Massey singing with the group, The Gleneagles (Ross Nelson & Jim Dewar – guitars, Alec Bell – keyboards, Jimmy Smith – sax, Tony Tierney – bass and David Miller – drums). A recording contract was arranged with Decca and Massey renamed them Lulu & The Luvvers. Their début single, 'Shout!', a hit for The Isley Brothers in 1960, reached number seven in the singles charts, and a resilient British entertainment figure had arrived.

Lulu and her group were in constant demand, appearing regularly on the BBC

Lulu & The Luvvers

television pop music shows *Gadzooks!* and *Stramash*. However there was some consternation from the Luvvers when Decca's production people replaced the group members with sessionmen like Jimmy Page and Big Jim Sullivan on their records. Page's playing can be heard on a cover of Betty Everett's 'Can't Hear You No More' – the follow-up to 'Shout' which flopped completely. A rival cover (to Them) of 'Here Comes The Night' and The Rolling Stones throwaway 'Surprise, Surprise' fared equally poorly but the ballad 'Leave A Little Love' restored her to the British Top 10 in 1965. The following year Lulu became the first British female pop singer to sing behind the Iron Curtain, but her home achievements had paled and when the Decca contract expired, Lulu & The Luvvers parted company.

In 1967 she signed with Columbia and producer Mickie Most. A sprightly cover of Neil Diamond's 'The Boat That I Row' reached number six in April and she made her screen début, co-starring opposite Sidney Poitier in the classroom drama *To Sir With Love* for which she also sang the theme tune. Although relegated to the B-side of the inferior 'Let's Pretend' in the UK, the song went to number one in America, resulting in high profile appearances such as *The Ed Sullivan Show*. Rumours flourished at this time of her alleged romances with Eric Clapton and Monkee Davy Jones. However, it was Bee Gee Maurice Gibb who won the lady's heart and the two were married in Chalfont-St-Peters, Buckinghamshire, in February 1969.

Success followed success for Lulu. She was chosen to co-host the first colour BBC2 music related programme, *Two Of A Kind*, and in 1968, like Dusty, Cilla and Sandie she was given her own BBC show, *Lulu's Back In Town*. A piece of nonsense composed by Marty Wilde, 'I'm A Tiger' reached number nine in November '68 while a second series *Happening For Lulu* followed in '69. That same year she tied for first place in the Eurovision Song Contest with the execrable 'Boom Bang-A-Bang'. Following Dusty's example Lulu decamped to Alabama to record *New Routes* with producer Jerry Wexler at Muscle Shoals.

In the Seventies her marriage to Gibb ended and she continued to record on a regular basis. A cover of David Bowie's 'The Man Who Sold The World', produced by Bowie who played sax on the record, reached number three in February 1974. Today, Lulu still appears regularly on television and radio and was at number one again with 'boy band' Take That on their 1993 hit collaboration 'Relight My Fire'.

Lulu & The Luvvers

Lulu & The Luvvers

THE MAGIC LANTERNS

The Magic Lanterns, from Lancashire (Jimmy Pillsbury – vocals, Peter 'Coco' Smith and Alistair 'Les' Beverage – guitars, Ian Moncur – bass and Alan Watson – drums) had a minor hit in 1966 with 'Excuse Me Baby' on CBS. To give them their due they weren't easily disheartened; carrying on for another five years with no further chart action. It wasn't for want of trying though, recording 'Rumplestiltskin' (written by Graham Gouldman), 'Knight In Rusty Armour' (successfully recorded by Peter and Gordon), 'Auntie Grizelda' (a Monkees novelty) and even 'We'll Meet Again'.

THE MAGIC MIXTURE

An obscure group that recorded an enjoyable – if typical – psychedelic pop album *This Is The Magic Mixture*, for the budget Saga label in 1968. Creating music if not quite magic were singer guitarist Jim Thomas, Melvyn Hacker (bass), Stan Curtis (keyboards), and Jack Collins (drums).

MANFRED MANN

Strictly speaking Manfred Mann shouldn't actually qualify for this book because the group's namesake was born in Johannesburg, South Africa, but the group were predominantly British and managed to score an impressive 22 chart hits with two different line-ups.

Mann (nee Manfred Lubowitz) moved to England in 1961 as a personal protest against apartheid. He and drummer Mike Hugg formed the Mann-Hugg Blues Brothers the following year and their first inductees were sax and guitar player Mike Vickers, and bass player Dave Richmond. When the tide turned on instrumental modern jazz in London's clubs the group switched over to R&B, adding harp player and vocalist Paul Jones in mid-63, an Oxford undergraduate who under the name Paul Pond had played with Brian Jones as Elmo Lewis and sat in with Alexis Korner's Blues Incorporated at the Ealing Club.

The group were signed up by EMI producer John Burgess, who shortened their name to the communal Manfred Mann; recording for the HMV label. For a man hired to create hits, Burgess's decision to release a jazzy instrumental shuffle, 'Why Should We Not', as an opening gambit was most bizarre.

'Cock-A-Hoop', while more representative of their onstage sound, was another flop. Richmond left in late 1963, and was replaced by ex-Roosters guitarist Tom McGuinness, who bluffed his way into the job by saying he played bass. His joining was fortuitous, as the band's hit streak began with the instant, infectious '5-4-3-2-1', which the pioneering weekly pop show *Ready, Steady, Go!* adopted as their signature tune for a spell. (The show would go on to use several 'Manfreds' songs in this way.) The result was a number five hit in March 1964.

Their next release, 'Hubble Bubble (Toil And Trouble)' narrowly missed the Top 10, perhaps due to a simultaneously-released EP featuring '5-4-3-2-1' harming sales. There would be no such oversight when it came to their next 45. 'Do Wah Diddy Diddy' was Manfred Mann's major breakthrough and their first number one in July (topping the charts in America in September). The group's début album *The Five Faces Of Manfred Mann* appeared in September and was a strong seller, accurately reflecting the diversity of their set from ballads to R&B to jazz touches.

A two-year stretch of continuous hits, all cover versions ensued, including 'Sha La La' (originally by The Shirelles – three in the UK; 12 in the US – October '64), 'Come Tomorrow' (Marie Knight, 4 in January 1965) 'Oh No Not My Baby' (Maxine Brown, 11 – April '65) and a cover of Bob Dylan's 'If You Gotta Go, Go Now' (number two – September '65). The same year the band also delivered a strong cover of Dylan's controversial anti-war missive 'With God On Our Side' on their best-selling EP *The One In The Middle*. Dylan went on to rank Manfred Mann among the best interpreters of his material.

All of this made Manfred Mann one of the top 10 recording groups in the UK. However Mike Vickers wanted to pursue a career in production and left in November '65. Tom McGuinness switched to his natural instrument of guitar and ex-Graham Bond Organisation and John Mayall's Bluesbreakers bassist, Jack Bruce was drafted in. Taking advantage of the first personnel upheaval in the group, bandleader Mann extended the line-up to include trumpeter Henry Lowther and saxophonist Lyn Dobson. This line-up was showcased superbly on the *Machines* and *Instrumental Asylum* EPs (both 1966), and tracks on the *Soul Of Mann* compilation (1967).

The group seamlessly returned to the number one spot with 'Pretty Flamingo' in May 1966, but more line-up shenanigans followed, only now, they were more serious. Singer and visual frontman Paul Jones and Bruce both left while the single was still in the charts; Jones to go solo and Bruce to join Cream. Rod Stewart and Long John Baldry were among the applicants auditioned as replacements for Jones. The successful choice turned out to be Mike D'Abo from the little known A Band Of Angels. While the fact that he was a physical ringer for Jones worked in his favour the more crucial factor for his acceptance in the group was that their wives got along! German-born Klaus Voormann (ex-Paddy, Klaus & Gibson) was recruited on bass.

In mid-66 the Manfreds jumped ship to Fontana. HMV reacted to Jones's departure and the group's defection by releasing an EP *As Was* and single, 'You Gave Me Somebody To Love'. D'Abo's vocal début put the Manfred Mann hit machine back on line with another Dylan cover, 'Just Like A Woman', which reached number ten in August, while the follow up, 'Semi-Detached Suburban Mr Jones', did even better at two in November. Although the group weren't successful in the album format, *As Is* was a brave albeit partially successful attempt to establish their own identity with the help of songs written by D'Abo and Hugg.

Manfred Mann

The group's first single of 1967 maintained the formulae with yet another effortless hit in the classic Manfreds tradition. 'Ha Ha Said The Clown' (written by songwriting hack Tony Hazzard) reached number four in April. Two bizarre releases followed – an instrumental version of Tommy Roe's US hit, 'Sweet Pea', which was lucky to reach 36, and at a time when the likes of Alan Price were tackling his material, the group covered Randy Newman's 'So Long Dad', released in September, which failed to chart at all. The group withdrew to lick their wounds and to consider their next move. A song selected from the publishing acetates of Bob Dylan's 'basement tapes' restored their standing, when an excellent version of 'Mighty Quinn' clocked up the Manfreds' third number one in February '68.

It certainly looked like the band's chart reign was unstoppable with a further run of hits including 'My Name Is Jack' (June '68, from the Barry Feinstein film *You Are What You Eat*), and 'Fox On The Run' (December '68). However, come May of 1969, the group found themselves with a record they hated, 'Ragamuffin Man', in the charts, and by mutual agreement, decided to pack it in. D'Abo had been moonlighting with the Immediate label, writing and producing for Chris Farlowe and Rod Stewart, as well as appearing in a pantomime production of *Gulliver's Travels*. Upon the dissolution of the Manfreds, he continued along this path, as well as collaborating with ex-Dave Clark Five organist, Mike Smith. He received an unexpected windfall when Welsh group The Stereophonics successfully covered his composition 'Handbags And Gladrags' in 2001.

With the onset of the serious Seventies Mann and Hugg played together briefly as Emanon (no name spelt backwards) but as soon as the dust settled they reactivated the far more lucrative and marketable Manfred Mann mantle – changed slightly to Manfred Mann Chapter Three – and signed to Vertigo for a year. Hugg quit to pursue a lucrative career writing commercial jingles while Mann went for the long haul as Manfred Mann's Earth Band, scoring hits with covers of Bruce Springsteen's 'Blinded By The Light' and Dylan's 'You Angel You'. Tom McGuinness formed the highly respected McGuinness Flint with ex-John Mayall's Bluesbreakers drummer, Hughie Flint and songwriters Benny Gallagher and Graham Lyle; scoring Top Five hits with 'When I'm Dead And Gone' and 'Malt And Barley Blues' in 1970-71. In 1991, to mark McGuiness's fiftieth birthday, a unique line-up of Jones, D'Abo, Hugg, Vickers, McGuiness and ex-Family/Blues Band drummer Rob Townsend reunited as The Manfreds for a one-off show at the Town And Country Club, North London. The gig went down so well that the group tour annually under the collective banner The Manfreds. Manfred himself doesn't join in, forbidding the group to use his name (despite the fact that it was a collective!)

Having operated a studio on the Old Kent Road for some years, Mann moved back to his native South Africa in the Nineties and continues to tour with a new version of his Earth Band.
(see also A Band Of Angels, Graham Bond Organisation, Cream, Paul Jones, Alexis Korner's Blues Incorporated, Paddy, Klaus & Gibson)

THE MARAUDERS

This Stoke On Trent R&B group hopped on the Merseybeat bandwagon and had a minor hit in 1963, with their début Carter-Lewis written single, 'That's What I Want'. The song reached number 43 but three subsequent releases on Decca and Fontana failed to make a mark.

The group were included on the Decca compilation albums *Saturday Club* and *Live At The Cavern*. Singer and guitar player Byan Martin, guitarist Danny Davis (who had released five Pye and Parlophone singles in 1960-62), Kenny Sherratt (bass) and Barry Sargent (drums) were the marauding Merseybeaters in question.

THE MARK FOUR

This Hertfordshire four piece – Kenny Pickett (vocals), Eddie Phillips (guitar), John Dalton (bass), and Jack Jones (drums) – evolved from Jimmy Virgo & The Blue Jacks, featuring Jones and Dalton. When they split Dalton and Jones formed The Mark Four in 1963 with Pickett on vocals, along with Mick 'Spud' Thompson on rhythm, and Norman 'Miff' Mitham, the original guitarist with Cliff Richard & The Drifters. The latter was dispensed with and replaced by Phillips, a guitar whizz from Leytonstone, East London. The group's true influences – rock'n'roll and country – were in complete contrast to the prevailing R&B leanings of most groups at the time. On the ill-advice of their manager Ian Swan, the group's début single for Mercury in May 1964 was a cover of Bill Haley's 'Rock Around The Clock', backed by Larry Williams 'Slow Down'. Mercury made the band record Marvin Gaye's 'Try It Baby' as the follow-up over the group's original choice of Chuck Berry's 'Around and Around'. The B-side was Johnny Otis's 'Crazy Country Hop',

The Mark Four did eventually redress their sound and image imbalance after witnessing groups like The Four Plus One and The Dave Davani Four, and a stint in Germany as Kenny Lee & The Mark Four. The group dropped their set and made a conscious shift into R&B. Phillips began experimenting with feedback, which he put to good use on the band's single for Decca in August 1965.

'Hurt Me If You Will ' and it's B-side 'I'm Leaving' were superb examples of freakbeat at its finest, particularly 'I'm Leaving' with its feedback passages and insistent drumming. For all its innovative nature the single slipped by unnoticed, as did its follow-up, the Animals-sounding 'Work All Day (Sleep All Night)' B/W 'Goin' Down Fast', released February 1966 on Fontana. In late-65 Dalton and Thompson quit and bassist Tony Cooke joined, who in turn was succeeded by ex-Merseybeat and Tony Sheridan bass player, Bob Garner. By then however The Mark Four were going under the name The Creation. In 1966 Dalton temporarily and then permanently replaced Pete Quaife in The Kinks. *(see also The Creation, The Kinks)*

The Marmalade

THE MARK FIVE

For a short period four became five, with the addition of a second guitar player of a second guitar player Mick Thompson, they recorded just one single for Fontana, 'Baby What's Wrong', before changing their name back to Mark Four when Thompson left. Makes sense.

THE MARMALADE

Previously Scottish showband Dean Ford & The Gaylords, a name change to The Marmalade coincided with a move to London and a switch from Decca to CBS in 1967. Their first singles for the label, 'It's All Leading Up To Saturday Night' and 'Can't Stop Now' went nowhere while their third single, the Graham Nash-produced 'I See The Rain' – a glorious mix of Move harmonies with Hendrix-style guitar deserved to be a smash but despite receiving plaudits from Jimi himself as his favourite single of 1967, it bombed. Slowly, the group fortunes changed by getting more prestigous gigs, including a support slot on an October – November '67 package tour featuring The Who, Traffic and The Herd.

When another psych gem, 'Man In A Shop' flopped, CBS

producer Mike Smith decreed that a more mainstream pop direction was called for, which the group somewhat reluctantly adhered to. After shooting themselves in the foot by passing on covering Robert Knight's 'Everlasting Love' the chart breakthrough came when 'Lovin' Things', an almost note-for note cover of The Grass Roots US hit, reached number six in June, but the follow-up – a Howard-Blaikley song 'Wait For Me Mary-Anne', a blatantly trite commercial song if ever there was one, stiffed at number thirty in October. With a canny eye on the Xmas market a cover of The Beatles 'Ob-La-Di, Ob-La-Da' from the recently-released 'White Album', went to number one, fending off a rival version by The Bedrocks.

A further extremely commercial hit, 'Baby Make It Soon' (nine, June 1969) followed but 'Butterfly' failed to flutter and the band absconded to Decca with the promise of complete artistic control and a third lease of life. It also enabled them to get a foothold in the States with 'Reflections Of My Life', a self-penned ballad by Junior Campbell, which reached number ten on the *Billboard* charts in April 1970. It did even better in England; getting to three as did its equally plaintive follow-up, 'Rainbow'. Unfortunately this success gave Campbell the idea to go solo. He left in 1970 to be replaced by ex Poets' guitarist Hughie Nicholson, who joined just as the group shifted from Decca to EMI. Alan Whitehead also upped sticks (selling his stories of the group's groupie escapades to *The News Of The World*) and was replaced by another ex-Poet Dougie Henderson. The hits carried on regardless until more personnel problems literally tore the band apart. Pat Fairley was next to call it a day followed by Hughie Nicholson. This left Dean Ford and Graham Knight to revert to their old soul showband days and form a new six-piece line-up that signed to EMI in 1974. Another line up (featuring Knight, Whitehead, and eventually, Campbell) regrouped in '76 and had one last hit with the prophetically-titled 'Falling Apart At The Seams'. Dean Ford carried on as a solo artist without much success while drummer Alan Whitehead opened a successful glamour agency and video company Electric Blue.

(see also The Attack, Dean Ford & The Gaylords, The Poets)

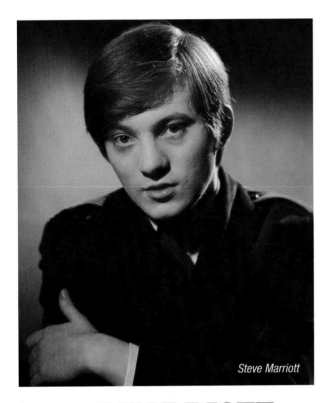

Steve Marriott

STEVE MARRIOTT

Prior to major fame with The Small Faces, Steve Marriott was a child actor who made his stage début at 14 playing the Artful Dodger in Lionel Bart's *Oliver!* He went on to study for two years at the Italia Conti drama school in London's Islington and landed many film and TV roles. These included *Mr. Pastry's Progress*, *Night Cargoes*, *Dixon Of Dock Green* and the Peter Sellers classic *Heaven's Above*. He also starred with David Hemmings and Heinz in the quickie beat group movie knock-offs *Live It Up* and *Be My Guest*. His musical début was actually on the stagecast World Record Club album of *Oliver!*, singing 'Consider Yourself', 'Be Back Soon' and 'I'd Do Anything'. Decca signed him to a one-off single deal in 1963, which produced the Buddy Holly-ish 'Give Her My Regards'. Inevitably it did nothing, but from little acorns . . .

(see also Steve Marriott's Moments, The Small Faces)

STEVE MARRIOTT'S MOMENTS

A pre-Small Faces musical pursuit for Marriott, The Moments were an East London five-piece, who were managed by the legendary Pete Meaden. Originally known as Steve Marriott & The Frantic Ones (shortened to just The Frantics) and The Moonlighters, alongside a harp-playing Marriott were guitar players Sean Buckley and John Weider, bass player Jimmy Winston and drummer Kenny Rowe.

They recorded one solitary single for the US market, a cover of The Kinks 'You Really Got Me' while the original was still in the charts. The Kinks took it to number one; the Moments didn't. Marriott moonlighted playing harmonica with the Andrew Oldham Orchestra until a fateful meeting with Ronnie Lane in the J60, an East Ham musical instrument shop got The Small Faces rolling. John Weider later joined Eric Burdon & The New Animals and Family, while Kenny Rowe popped up in Capability Brown. Jimmy Winston joined Marriott in The Small Faces.

(see also Eric Burdon & The Animals, Family, Steve Marriott, The Small Faces, Jimmy Winston's Reflections)

JOHN MAYALL'S BLUESBREAKERS

Like Alexis Korner John Mayall deserves special kudos as the 'father of British blues' by discovering and providing a platform for a host of legendary British blues musicians who benefited from his patronage. Hailing from Cheshire, Mayall formed his first group in 1955 as The Powerhouse Four. After completing his National Service he moved south to London as a commercial artist, forming Blues Syndicate who evolved into the Bluesbreakers. The line-up in 1963 consisted of Mayall (vocals/keyboards/guitar), Roger Dean (guitar), John McVie (bass) and Hughie Flint (drums). The quartet came to the attention of Decca producer Mike Vernon and the group were signed to the label. The group's infectious début, the Mayall-composed 'Crawling Up A Hill' was more jazzy in a Georgie Fame vein, but like so many artists working in a similar vein (Fame, Farlowe, Money) enthusiastic club audiences didn't translate into sales. A second single, 'Crocodile Walk' and a verite` live recording *John Mayall Plays John Mayall – Live At Klook's Kleek* sold little beyond the faithful to chart. In the first of many personnel changes Mayall's iron rule came into play when Dean was sacked for unprofessionalism. Mayall's reputation as a hard taskmaster preceded him, unsurprising when the Bluesbreakers performed up to two gigs a night, seven days a week. He was also known for his eccentricity, at one point living in a treehouse, where his priceless pornography collection was lovingly tended. Dean's replacement was a 20-year old Surrey guitarist, formerly of The Yardbirds, who could replicate the solos of Chicago blues masters like Albert King and Buddy Guy with almost effortless ease. Eric Clapton's brief liaison with John Mayall's Bluesbreakers

John Mayall

Beryl Marsden

John Mayall's Bluesbreakers

John Mayall

remains for many white blues and R&B enthusiasts both musicians' most magical period. It was arguably Mayall's greatest line-up, showcasing the band's skills in their best light. Clapton's presence ensured a faithful legion followed the Bluesbreakers from gig to gig and cries of 'Give God a solo' were not uncommon. The reticent Clapton was to find this holy status a burden (graffiti claiming 'Clapton is God' appeared on London walls) but it certainly didn't affect his or the Bluesbreakers' profile. In August '65 Clapton suddenly absconded on a disastrous Grecian working holiday and Mayall temporarily had to work with guitarists Jeff Kribbett and a young Clapton acolyte Mick Taylor.

With Clapton back in the ranks by November the group went on to record an album that immortalised his groundbreaking playing. Such was his role that Mayall broke with protocol and gave Clapton special billing. The recording of *Bluesbreakers With Eric Clapton* occurred quickly with the impact of Clapton's biting solos achieved by the effect of turning his Marshall stack up to concert levels in the studio. The sleeve, with Clapton's face buried in the *Beano* (a popular English children's comic), is as famous an image as any from the era and, according to photographer David Wedgbury, happened completely spontaneously. "Eric just started reading the comic while he waited for me to set up the shot, I looked up from my viewfinder and there he was immersed in it. Straight away I knew I had my picture."

Despite the album's massive success upon its release in July 1966 the guitarist left the same month to form Cream. Unbowed, Mayall replaced him with Green and sacked Flint, replacing him briefly with Aynsley Dunbar for another groundbreaking album *A Hard Road* (proving as influential as its predecessor) and a series of singles, 'Looking Back', 'Sitting In The Rain', 'Curly' (credited to The Bluesbreakers) and 'Double Trouble', featuring Green's Peter B's and Shotgun Express ex-bandmate, Mick Fleetwood. However in '67 the line-up was turned on it's head when Green and Fleetwood quit to form Peter Green's Fleetwood Mac, closely followed by McVie. The new guitarist was Mick Taylor who had nervously depped for a missing Clapton at a Mayall gig in his native Welyn Garden City. This line-up stayed fairly constant for the albums *Crusade*, *The Diary Of A Band (Vols. 1 and 2)*, *Bare Wires*, and *Blues From Laurel Canyon* until Taylor replaced the late Brian Jones in The Rolling Stones in June '69. Mayall continues to tour the world with various bands from his base in Los Angeles, while continuing his policy of promoting the talents of young blues musicians.

(see also The Peter B's, Cream, Fleetwood Mac, The Gods, The Rolling Stones, Shotgun Express, The Yardbirds)

THE MERSEYBEATS

Not a lot of people know this but The Merseybeats settled on their name long before it was used by the media to describe the form of music they came to represent. The band originally formed in Liverpool in 1961 as The Mavericks with Tony Crane (guitar), Billy Kinsley (bass), David Ellis (rhythm) and Frank Sloan (drums). Shortly therafter Aaron Williams and John Banks (ex-Pacifics) replaced Ellis and Sloan. The group also made the usual Hamburg trip where, oddly enough, they developed a rather effeminate stage uniform of tailored Spanish bolero jackets, frilly shirts and jewellery, and specialised in romantic ballads as opposed to black leather and wild rockers.

The image attracted a large female following and in the stampede to sign anything remotely Liverpudlian The Merseybeats were spotted by A&R man Chris Parmeinter who signed them to Fontana. The group also caught the eye of Brian Epstein who in 1963 signed them to his management company NEMS. However the two soon parted company over image. Their début single, an uptempo cover of Dionne Warwick's 'It's Love That Really Counts', was a minor hit, reaching number 24 but its follow up was the slower and more suitable 'I Think Of You' which got to number five. Founding member Billy Kinsley quit for a short spell in early '64 complaining of personal pressure and was replaced by future Creation bass player Bob Garner. Garner himself was in turn relieved by ex-Big Three bassman Johnny Gustafson before Kinsley finally returned to the fold, arriving back in time for the group's third big hit, an early cover of Bacharach and David's 'Wishin' And Hopin' that sailed into the Top 20 and peaked at number 13. Unfortunately the group finished the year on a disappointing note, stuck at number 40 with 'Last Night (I Made A Little Girl Cry)'.

Things started to go into a slow decline in 1965. Merseybeat may have inadvertently been named after them but it was fast becoming a millstone around their necks. The whole scene had become incredibly passé and was even derided by John Lennon. Despite this the group did manage to keep up a fairly healthy profile for a while, thanks chiefly to their hordes of female followers. They were still packing out the band's live performances and awarded them two more minor hits that saw them through to 1966. A change of management looked promising and could have breathed new life into the band when Kit Lambert and Chris Stamp took over the reins in August 1965.

Aaron Williams decided he'd had his fifteen minutes of fame and retired gracefully from the music scene, but is occasionally coaxed out to perform with Kinsley in his Merseycats. John Banks formed a duo with Johnny Gustafson in 1966 called imaginatively John and Johnny. Gustafson went on to Quatermass and session work alongside short stints with Roxy Music and Gillan. Banks died in 1990.

(see also The Big Three, The Creation, The Merseys)

THE MERSEYS

When The Merseybeats split, manager Kit Lambert paired vocalists Tony Crane and Billy Kinsley off as The Merseys. For live work the pair used a backing band from Liverpool called The Fruit Eating Bears but for studio chores they utilised the talents of Jimmy Page, Jack Bruce and Clem Cattini. This arrangement got off to a flying start with their first single, a cover of The McCoys' 'Sorrow' which reached number four in May '66. Unfortunately it wasn't a lasting relationship and proved to be their only chart entry. A subsequent cover of Pete Townshend's composition, 'So Sad About Us' (recorded and released prior to The Who's version) failed to chart, and further follow-ups, 'Rhythm Of Life' and 'The Cat' missed completely, despite high profile TV slots and tours organised by agent Robert Stigwood.

The duo drifted into cabaret work under their old name The Merseybeats. Crane eventually went solo, releasing singles under his own name, while Kinsley formed Liverpool Express. In 1973, The Merseys were suddenly contemporary again when David Bowie covered 'Sorrow' and released it as a single from his *Pin-Ups* album; reaching number three. Crane can still be found fronting a version of The Merseybeats on the cabaret circuit today.

(see also The Merseybeats)

THE MICKEY FINN

From the East End of London, The Mickey Finn (Alan Marks – vocals, Micky Waller – guitar, 'Fluff' – organ, Mick Stannard – bass, Richard Brand – drums) issued six singles on five labels over four years. Stannard was replaced by John Burkitt for the group's first three singles, credited to Mickey Finn And The Blue Men.

'Tom Hark' was released in January '64 on the specialist Blue Beat label, and the calypso/ska trend followed for the group's next release on Oriole, 'Pills' (released March '64). Both releases featured the harmonica talents of one Jimmy Page – who'd obviously forgotten to bring his guitar to the sessions. The controversial 'Pills' was followed three months later by a cover of Chuck Berry's 'Reelin' And Rockin' – later covered with more success by the Dave Clark 5.

Stannard rejoined and the band changed their name to The Mickey Finn and signed to Columbia for a cover of the old standard (and a hit for Brit Ian Whitcomb in the US) 'This Sporting Life' (re-titled 'The Sporting Life'), produced by Shel Talmy and released in March '65. The band released two further flops 'I Do Love You' (Polydor, 1966) and 'Garden Of My Mind' (produced by Richard Gottehrer, Direction, 1967) before splitting. As well as being fixtures of the R&B scene, the group were regularly featured at May Balls and deb parties, and even opened George Harrison's Mayfair nightclub Sybilla's in 1966.

(see also Jimmy Page)

THE MIGHTY AVENGERS

These not so mighty Rugby-based mortals (Tony Campbell – vocals/guitar, Teddy Mahon – guitar/harmonica, Mike Linnell – bass, and Biffo Beech – drums) thought they'd found their niche in pop by covering Jagger-Richard cast-offs, after the group's first Decca

single 'Hide Your Pride' flopped. Produced by Andrew Loog Oldham The Avengers bashed out three in a row – 'So Much In Love', 'Blue Turns To Grey' and '(Walkin' Thru The) Sleepy City' between 1964 and '65. Only 'So Much In Love' dented the chart at number 46 in November '64 before Oldham looked for another group to play with.

THE MINDBENDERS

Following the parting of the ways between Wayne Fontana & The Mindbenders in late-1965 the boys in the backing band, who were actually quite a competent beat group with a fine drummer in Ric Rothwell, decided to carry on with guitarist Eric Stewart handling the vocal chores, ably assisted by bassist Bob Lang. Their début single 'Groovy Kind Of Love' became a huge international hit in February and reached number two on both sides of the Atlantic. Subsequent releases such as 'Can't Live With You, Can't Live Without You' and 'Ashes To Ashes' were not so huge, despite being strong songs. The group also recorded Rod Argent's 'I Want Her She Wants Me' a year before Argent's own Zombies recorded it for their classic 1967 album, *Odessey And Oracle*.

The Mindbenders had a cameo role in the film *To Sir With Love* and a last chart entry with the Graham Gouldman-produced 'The Letter' (a rather weak cover of The Box Tops' US hit) in 1967. When Lang and Rothwell announced they were leaving to open up shops in 1968 it finished the band.

Nonetheless remaining Mindbender Eric Stewart struggled on for a while, bringing in a succession of replacements including Gouldman but eventually accepted the group's struggling status and disbanded The Mindbenders in 1969. Stewart followed Gouldman into production and session work before they formed Hotlegs and eventually became half of 10CC.

(see also Wayne Fontana & The Mindbenders, The Mockingbirds)

THE MINISTRY OF SOUND

There is a persistent rumour that this group, who released one single on Decca in 1966 ('White Collar Worker'), is the first recorded evidence of future Sweet bassist Steve Priest.

THE MOCKINGBIRDS

One of the great ironies of his pre-10CC career is the fact that, while able to write a multitude of successes for The Yardbirds, Herman's Hermits, The Hollies and others, Graham Gouldman was unable to attain a hit – either on his own, or with his excellent mid-Sixties combo The Mockingbirds.

Formed in Manchester in 1964, the group evolved from The Whirlwinds and also featured Bernard Basso, Steve Jacobson, and ex-Sabres Kevin Godley (drums). Within a two-year period the group's small but perfectly formed five 1964–66 singles shared between Columbia, Immediate and Decca included 'That's How Its

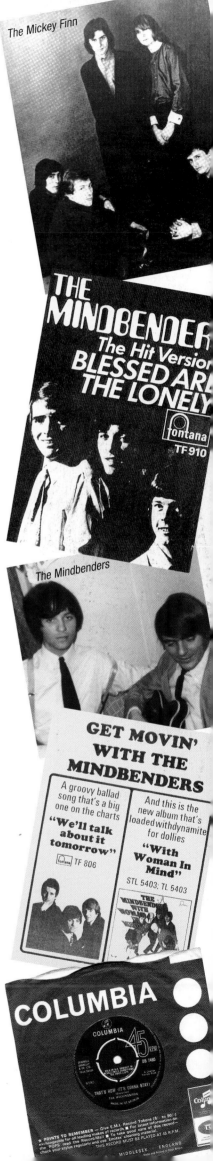

Gonna Stay', 'How To Find A Lover' and the jangly riff and harmonies of 'You Stole My Love'; all superb beat/pop penned by Gouldman.

Gouldman left in 1968 to join the fast-crumbling Mindbenders. He and guitarist Eric Stewart then formed Hotlegs who turned into 10CC with Gouldman's Mockingbird mate, Godley and guitarist Lol Creme.

(see also Wayne Fontana & The Mindbenders, The Mindbenders)

The Ministry Of Sound

The Mockingbirds

The Mods

THE MODS

An extremely obscure outfit that most definitely were not Mods, but hoped the 1964 association would rub off on them. Their only stab at the singles market with 'Something On My Mind' on RCA went nowhere.

THE MOJOS

Liverpool beat merchants originally known as The Nomads who changed their name (didn't any one keep their first name?) to The Mojos in 1963. After winning a song writing contest sponsored by Carlin Music, they landed a licensing deal with Decca Records. The band at the time was singer Stu James, Adrian Wilkinson – guitar, Keith Karlson – bass, Terry O' Toole – piano and John Konrad – drums.

They had already played a residency at Hamburg's Star Club and were vying with The Merseybeats for the most popular band (girl wise) on Merseyside. Their first single, 'Forever', went wide of the mark and prompted an impatient Wilkinson to leave in 1964. He joined an aimless band called The Mastersounds and was replaced by Nicky Crouch (ex-Faron's Flamingos), who signed up in time to record The Mojos seminal classic 'Everything's Alright'. This brilliant slice of pop deserved to go all the way but stalled at number nine,

and marked the last time that The Mojos came anywhere near the top spot. The group's next two releases, 'Why Not Tonight' and 'Seven Daffodils' made the lower reaches of the Top 30 but they disintegrated at the end of the year. James and Crouch reformed with the arguably stronger line-up of bass player Lewis Collins and drummer Aynsley Dunbar, renaming themselves Stu James & The Mojos but broke up anyway in 1966.

James quit performing and went into music publishing while Dunbar joined up with John Mayall's Bluesbreakers and The Aynsley Dunbar Retaliation. Following their demise in 1970 Dunbar concentrated on session work, including David Bowie's tribute to the Sixties *Pin-Ups* which featured a cover of the Mojos' 'Everything's Alright'. He then relocated to America, playing with Frank Zappa, Jefferson Starship and Journey. Late arrival Lewis Collins turned to acting and is best known as Bodie from TV's *The Professionals*.

(see also Faron's Flamingos, John Mayall's Bluesbreakers)

ZOOT MONEY'S BIG ROLL BAND

Bournemouth's George Bruno (or as he preferred to be called Zoot Money) had already gone through one line-up of his Big Roll Band by the time he settled in London in 1964. Once there he quickly established himself and his band as one of the capital's top live acts on the R&B club scene. He moonlighted for a while with Alexis Korner's Blues Incorporated before securing his own residency at the all-night Flamingo Club. Here he became a firm favourite with London's Mod fraternity, playing a sophisticated mix of R&B, jazz and soul. They signed a one off single deal with Decca Records and released 'Uncle Willie' which bombed completely, then moved to Columbia in 1965 for a second attempt. This proved to be far more productive, resulting in the albums *It Should've Been Me* and *Zoot*, recorded live at the Mod stronghold Klook's Kleek in 1966.

Both albums enhanced the bands growing reputation and even rewarded them with a bit of chart action in 1966 when Zoot made it to number 23. Success followed singleswise too, with 'Big Time Operator' making number 25 and things seemed to be literally on a roll for them. However, Zoot, a carefree character who was just as interested in being a showman as he was a musician, didn't seize the opportunity or build on it. He was notorious for dressing up in outlandish costumes, ad libbing and dropping his trousers on stage, all of which greatly undermined the band's potential and made them look decidedly cabaret. The band was also unusually unstable, with changing line-ups never staying together long enough to really gel. Unsurprisingly it was all over by 1967. With the onset of flower power Zoot saw an opportunity to dress up even more, so he formed Dantalian's Chariot, an unashamedly psychedelic outfit which lasted little under a year. In 1968 he put together the album *Transition* but it was pretty poor and did nothing. He saw the decade out as a member of Eric Burdon's American based New Animals.

*Zoot Money's
Big Roll Band*

The musicians that passed through the ranks of The Big Roll Band are too numerous to list here, but the core of the group revolved around guitar player Andy Summers, bass player/vocalist Paul Williams, drummer Colin Allen, and sax player Nick Newell. Both Summers and Allen expanded their minds with Zoot in Dantalian's Chariot, and Summers was also in Eric Burdon's New Animals. Williams recorded a couple of solo singles before joining John Mayall and then Juicy Lucy. Summers eventually found success with The Police.

Zoot still does roaring business on the pub and club circuit today. He also put his dressing up to good use by turning to acting in the Eighties and now he often pops up in various TV dramas, comedies, and children's programmes.

(see also Eric Burdon & The (New) Animals, Dantalian's Chariot, Alexis Korner's Blues Incorporated, John Mayall's Bluesbreakers)

THE MOODY BLUES

Moody Blues fans have four very different phases from which to choose when it comes to deciding which part of the group's long and distinguished career best sums up these 'Brummie Beatles'. There's the R&B Denny Laine-led era of 1963 to 1966, followed by the quasi-classical pomp rock period, helmed by Justin Hayward and John Lodge, between 1966 and the group's temporary split in 1974. Then there's the serious stockbroker rock years that followed the reformation in 1978 and lasted until the mid-Eighties, and finally the Elvis-styled Las Vegas casino version that is with us today.

The Moody Blues resulted from an amalgamation of players from several Birmingham beat bands. Leader and guitarist Denny Laine (nee' Brian Hines) had fronted Denny & The Diplomats, drummer Graeme Edge was previously with Gerry Levene & The Avengers (also featuring a young Roy Wood), keyboard player Mike Pinder had served with The Crewcats, flautist Ray Thomas fronted El

OPERATION BIG BEAT

135

The Moody Blues

Riot & The Rebels, while bass player Clint Warwick had played with Butlins band, The Rainbows.

The band moved to London in 1964 after their manager Tony Secunda secured them a Monday night residency at the Marquee Club, as well as a recording deal at Decca with his partner Denny Cordell producing. A lucky break came when TV's *Ready, Steady, Go!*, featured the group performing their début single 'Lose Your Money' (penned by Laine and Pinder) in September 1964. Next came a Bessie Banks cover 'Go Now' which went straight to number one in the UK in January 1965 and made the US Top 10 in March. Unfortunately, they were unable to sustain this meteoric rise and failed with ill-chosen follow-ups 'I Don't Want To Go On Without You' (a Drifters cover – number 33), 'From The Bottom Of My Heart' (22) and 'Everyday' (a disappointing 44). The band's 1965 album *The Magnificent Moodies* was a typical hasty début of the day – the big hit single ('Go Now') mingling with the group's stage act including covers of James Brown ('I'll Go Crazy', 'I Don't Mind') and a Ray Thomas vocal on a version of Gershwin's 'It Ain't Necessarily So'.

Despite still being popular in Germany the group were flailing in Britain. Their last single with the original line-up 'Boulevard De La Madelaine' was a slice of pseudo French nonsense that unsurprisingly failed to chart, and Warwick quit in May '66 followed by Laine in September, thus triggering phase two. Both were respectively replaced by another ex-El Riot member, John Lodge, and the group's only non-Brummie, guitarist Justin Hayward, from Swindon, who had previously played with Marty Wilde's Wilde Three, and had two flop singles on Pye and Parlophone behind him. The new Moodies got off to a bad start by releasing three singles, 'Life's Not Life', 'Fly Me High', and 'Love And Beauty' which all sold miserably.

A new direction was needed, and fast. Thus their next release in 1967 was an experimental, pseudo-classical concept album called *Days Of Future Past* – an ambitious orchestral project recorded with conductor Peter Knight and the London Festival Orchestra which slotted a classical score between each Moodies track. It also spawned the group's biggest hit to date 'Nights In White Satin'. The group stuck with their new, winning formula and released a further five orchestral albums on similar lines, all of which were phenomenally successful. They also inadvertently invented the concept album, attracting plenty of critical flak for their trouble. In 1969, the group formed their own record label Threshold which released the band's output as well as solo projects and material by other artists.

The Moodies split at the peak of their powers in 1974 to allow each member the opportunity to pursue individual solo projects, most of which were equally and annoyingly successful. They reformed in 1978 with Swiss whiz Patrick Moraz replacing Pinder on keyboards and took up exactly where they'd left off.

(see also Denny Laine)

137

The Move

THE MOVE

Birmingham's finest The Move were the result of three separate groups disintegration. Singer Carl Wayne and the rhythm section of bass player Ace (Chris) Kefford and drummer Bev Bevan, had all been in Carl Wayne & The Vikings. Guitarist Roy Wood was with Mike Sheridan's Nightriders and second guitarist Trevor Burton, in Danny King and the Mayfair Set. They came together as The Move in January 1966 and were a regular attraction at the city's Cedar Club throughout the year. Manager Tony Secunda signed the band and took them to London, setting them up with a Marquee Club residency which attracted enough publicity through Secunda-perpetrated antics (smashing up TV sets on stage, decapitating mannequins of leading politicians and even destroying a car with an axe) to secure a record deal.

The group signed to Decca's new progressive label Deram and set about releasing a string of impeccable pop classics, written by Wood and produced by Denny Cordell. These commenced with 'Night Of Fear', a startlingly original song with razor sharp harmonies and a memorable arrangement incorporating Tchaikovsky's *1815 Overture*. The record peaked at number two in January 1967, while follow-up 'I Can Hear The Grass Grow' confirmed the bands psychedelic credentials, even though composer Wood protested he liked nothing stronger than a pint of bitter! It reached number five in May.

Despite their ever-changing trendy image changes; Al Capone gangsters one minute, psychedelic dandies, the next, London's hip cognoscenti decried them when they attempted to play underground venues like UFO or the 14-Hour Technicolour Dream hippie happening at Alexandra Palace, in April. This made no difference to their chart positions or the quality of Wood's songwriting as demonstrated with 'Flowers In The Rain'. To promote the record Secunda scammed a mock postcard depicting then Prime Minister Harold Wilson in a supposedly compromising situation with his secretary. When one fluttered through the mail hatch of 10 Downing Street the Premier was unamused and successfully sued the band through the High Court, resulting in all the record's royalties being donated to charity (an order that continues to this day). The single hardly suffered from such publicity; instead it received the distinction of being the first song ever played on BBC's new commercial station Radio 1 on 30 September, and eventually reached number two in October. The Move's next 45 'Cherry Blossom Clinic', a song about a mental hospital patient became an exercise in damage limitation. It was withdrawn for fear of causing more adverse and (expensive) publicity and replaced with the Eddie Cochran-inspired 'Fire Brigade', a number three hit in February '68. Both songs eventually appeared on the bands self-titled début album, released in April, which peaked at 15. It was late in coming as an album had supposedly been completed as early as spring '67 but the master tapes were stolen. Duffers like the Bevan-sung 'Zing!

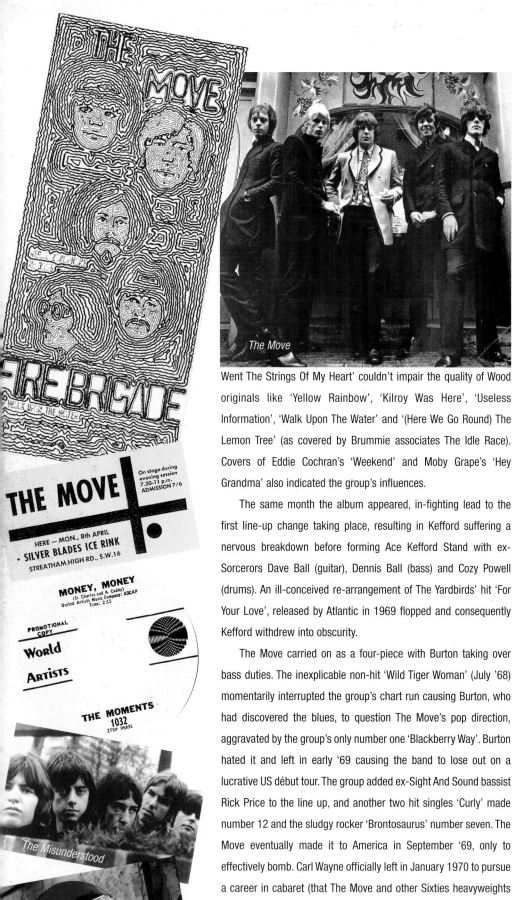

The Move

The Misunderstood

The Ministry Of Sound

Went The Strings Of My Heart' couldn't impair the quality of Wood originals like 'Yellow Rainbow', 'Kilroy Was Here', 'Useless Information', 'Walk Upon The Water' and '(Here We Go Round) The Lemon Tree' (as covered by Brummie associates The Idle Race). Covers of Eddie Cochran's 'Weekend' and Moby Grape's 'Hey Grandma' also indicated the group's influences.

The same month the album appeared, in-fighting lead to the first line-up change taking place, resulting in Kefford suffering a nervous breakdown before forming Ace Kefford Stand with ex-Sorcerors Dave Ball (guitar), Dennis Ball (bass) and Cozy Powell (drums). An ill-conceived re-arrangement of The Yardbirds' hit 'For Your Love', released by Atlantic in 1969 flopped and consequently Kefford withdrew into obscurity.

The Move carried on as a four-piece with Burton taking over bass duties. The inexplicable non-hit 'Wild Tiger Woman' (July '68) momentarily interrupted the group's chart run causing Burton, who had discovered the blues, to question The Move's pop direction, aggravated by the group's only number one 'Blackberry Way'. Burton hated it and left in early '69 causing the band to lose out on a lucrative US début tour. The group added ex-Sight And Sound bassist Rick Price to the line up, and another two hit singles 'Curly' made number 12 and the sludgy rocker 'Brontosaurus' number seven. The Move eventually made it to America in September '69, only to effectively bomb. Carl Wayne officially left in January 1970 to pursue a career in cabaret (that The Move and other Sixties heavyweights like The Kinks and The Hollies had perilously dabbled in). Wayne was replaced by ex-Idle Race guitarist Jeff Lynne. The second album *Shazam* although now considered a classic sold poorly at the time and the group found themselves looking for a new record label. They signed to EMI's Deram equivalent, Harvest (yet again down to three men following the departure of Price) and released their swansong album *Message To The Country*. Two final singles 'China Town' (1971) and 'California Man' (1972) arrived posthumously and managed to chart despite the fact The Move had since metamorphosed into The Electric Light Orchestra.

Trevor Burton formed Balls with ex-Moody Blues leader Denny Laine and ex-Uglys Steve Gibbons. He and Gibbons then formed The Steve Gibbons Band, and despite several high-profile tours supporting The Who, the band never quite made the grade. Burton continues to gig with local Birmingham bands. Kefford effectively became a casualty of the rock and roll lifestyle and his own paranoia though he is still alive and planning a comeback. Roy Wood left ELO in 1972 and formed Wizzard with Price and had a comfortable run of hits including two number ones. He continues to gig as Roy Wood's Wizzo and other various names. Wayne's solo career never took off and he was reduced to appearing in the long-running Midlands soap opera *Crossroads*. After a long stint in the musical *Starlight Express* on London's West End, he accepted an offer to replace Allan Clarke in the modern-day Hollies. Lynne and Bevan achieved multi-platinum success with ELO into the Eighties. When Lynne left Bevan carried on as ELO 2. Lynne eventually went solo and with a little help from George Harrison became a successful producer and a member of The Travelling Wilburys. In 2002 he wrestled back control of ELO from Bevan and now uses the name as a solo vehicle.

(see also The Idle Race, The Uglys)

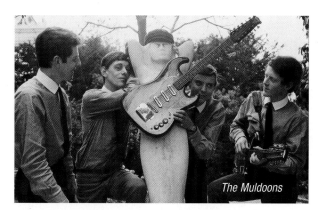

The Muldoons

THE MULDOONS

An extremely obscure combo, clad in matching shirts and Burns guitars, who had just one Decca release in 1965. The record 'I'm Lost Without You' featuring a jazzy groove with some cool organ lines, was produced at the famed Jacksons Studio in Rickmansworth, which indicates a southern origin.

THE MULESKINNERS

A fairly typical R&B outfit formed at Twickenham's School of Art, they backed visiting blues giant Howlin Wolf in 1964 and released a couple of singles on Fontana, including a cover of Wolf's 'Back Door Man'. Their singer, Terry Brennan, had previously played with Eric Clapton and Manfred Mann's Tom McGuinness in The Roosters. Keyboard player Ian McLagan went on to The Small Faces via a short stint in the Boz People, fronted by future King Crimson-Bad Company bassist, Ray 'Boz' Burrell. The other 'Skinners were Nick Tweddell, Dave Pether, Pete Brown and Mick 'Chippy' Carpenter.

(see also The Small Faces)

RE·ADMISSIONS BY PASS OUT) AFTER 9·30

The Marauders

The N' Betweens

THE N' BETWEENS

Formed in Wolverhampton in 1966, The N' Betweens – Johnny Howells (vocals), Noddy Holder (b. Neville Holder) – guitar, Dave Hill – guitar, Jimmy Lea – bass, and Don Powell (b. 10 September 1950 – drums) – built up a loyal following in the Midlands after the instrumentalists decided to ditch Howells and Holder took over on vocals. They were discovered by Californian scenester Kim Fowley, who arranged a one-off recording for Columbia in 1966, thanks to Holder's involvement with the label during his time with Steve Brett & The Mavericks. A cover of The Young Rascals 'You Better Run' promptly went nowhere. The group recorded other tracks for Fowley during this time, including 'I'm Just What You Need' – a blatant rewrite of Sam and Dave's 'I Take What I Want'.

Another period of obscurity beckoned before the group's agent arranged an audition with Fontana A&R man, Jack Baverstock. Baverstock changed their name to Ambrose Slade; recording a single, 'Genesis', and an album *Beginnings* (reissued as *Beginnings Of Ambrose Slade* in 1975) for Fontana in 1969.

The band then came to the attention of ex-Animal and Jimi Hendrix manager, Chas Chandler, who shortened their name to simply Slade. An experienced pub and club covers band, whose early image was a cross between suedehead and skinhead, they released a swansong single for Fontana, 'Wild Winds Are Blowing' credited as The Slade. As the Seventies dawned the group evolved from skin to glam, becoming one of the biggest singles bands of the era, spawning no less than 23 Top 30 hits. Holder is now a DJ on Piccadilly Radio in Manchester, Lea has effectively retired, and Hill and Powell front a Slade II band.

THE NASHVILLE TEENS

Proving that the Merseysiders didn't have the field to themselves in early Sixties Hamburg was Surrey septet The Nashville Teens. Formed in Weybridge during 1962 by singers Art Sharp and Ray Phillips the first line-up comprised Michael Dunford (guitar), John Hawken (piano), Pete Shannon (bass) and Roger Groom (drums).

Dunford and Groom left the following year, to be respectively replaced by John Allen and Barry Jenkins, for an extended period in Germany. While learning their trade there (with additional vocalist Terry Crow) the band played residencies at the famed Star Club and backed visiting US giant Jerry Lee Lewis. On their return to England in 1964 they repeated the experience with Chuck Berry and earned themselves a management contract with Don Arden and a recording deal with Decca. A début single – a cover of John D Loudermilk's 'Tobacco Road' – was produced by Mickie Most and shot them to number six in August '64. It also gave The Nashville Teens a foothold in America where it made the US Top 20 in October (they were assumed to be American because of the name). Another Loudermilk song 'Google Eye' (an ode to a fish) was chosen as a follow up and

The great sound of
THE NASHVILLE TEENS
THE LITTLE BIRD F 12143
Producer · Andrew Loog Oldham

DECCA The Decca Record Company Limited Decca House Albert Embankment London S E 1

gave them a second top-tenner in November but it was to be their last with Most.

In 1965 a chance to broaden their American popularity was botched when a visa mix-up forced the band to abandon a US tour with The Zombies. A third single appropriately entitled 'Find My Way Back Home' was recorded while the band were stuck in New York but stalled at 34 in March. Decca were blamed for not supporting the group and neglecting them promotions-wise. Once home again they made an impressive appearance alongside The Animals in the beat movie *Pop Gear* and released a critically acclaimed (but poor selling) self-titled EP. 'This Little Bird' (produced by Andrew Loog Oldham, which ironically lost out in chart honours to Marianne Faithfull), 'I Know How It Feels To Be Loved' and 'The Hard Way' (produced by Shel Talmy) were only minor hits. Groom rejoined the group in February '66 when Jenkins jumped at the opportunity to replace John Steel in The Animals. The Teens' chart profile began to ebb away from then on but luckily they could still fall back on their in-demand live reputation backing visiting American artists like Carl Perkins and Bo Diddley. In 1969 Hawken left to form Renaissance with ex-Yardbirds Keith Relf and Jim McCarty.

The occasional single continued to slip out unnoticed, including the Roy Wood song 'Ella James', produced by its composer, and line-ups came and went right through into the Seventies and even the Eighties. Art Sharp left in 1972 and went to work for Don Arden while Ray Phillips still fronts a version of the band (despite the teen tag) today. *(see also The Animals, Eric Burdon & The New Animals)*

BIG BEAT

The Nashville Teens

Neat Change

NEAT CHANGE

Discovered by Spencer Davis, the fresh-faced Neat Change released just one single on Decca in 1968, the string-dominated 'I Lied To Auntie May', composed by Herd members Peter Frampton and Andy Bown. Ex-Syn guitarist Peter Banks was briefly involved with the band before joining Yes. *(see also The Herd, The Syn)*

THE NERVE

Reg Presley protégés The Nerve (Ian Day, Robb Duffy, Steve Taylor, Barry Satchelle, and Robin Hirst) came from Troggs country i.e Andover, in Hampshire. They were also signed to manager Larry Page's Page One label and Reg produced their four non charting singles, 'No. 10 Downing Street' (1967), 'Magic Spectacles', 'It Is' and 'Piece By Piece' (1968). *(see also The Troggs)*

THE NEW BREED

A moody trio of East Enders, two of Greek descent, who dressed like The Ivy League but sounded classically mod on their sole, menacing 1965 Decca outing, 'Unto Us'. It's an intriguing record that is a unique example of 'freakbeat gospel', sharing lyrical similarities with other religious beat records from the likes of The Joystrings and The Crossbeats.

THE NEW FORMULA

Hailing from Northamptonshire, The New Formula were an unabashedly commercial outfit who made some enjoyable but unsuccessful 1967-68 records for Pye/Piccadilly, including 'Burning In The Background Of My Mind' and a cover of Chris Clark's 'I Want To Go Back There Again'. They also released a version of the mantra 'Harekrishna' in August 1969 at the same time George Harrison produced a version for the Radha Krishna Temple. However there's no evidence to suggest the mystic Fab was at all influenced by this. Those chanting were Ricky Dodd, Martin Fallon, Mike Harper, Bruce Carey and Tommy Guthrie.

THE NICE

Keith Emerson and Lee Jackson had been the keyboard virtuoso and bass player respectively with Gary Farr and The T-Bones. Emerson had also spent time as a VIP before teaming up with David O' List and Brian Davison in early-67 to form The Nice, who were originally set up as a backing band for ex-Ikette singer and dancer (Pat) P.P. Arnold. Pat had signed to Immediate Records and wanted a group set-up along the lines of The Small Faces.

The idea was to play review-style shows where The Nice would play a set of their own material prior to backing the singer. However things backfired when their popularity threatened to outshine Arnold. Andrew Oldham stepped in as manager, providing the group with an Immediate record contract. The Nice hit the London club scene as an act in their own right, and quickly established themselves as a vital part of the capital's psychedelic nightlife with a sound dominated by Emerson's keyboard skill and a set of reworked classical compositions. Their début album *The Thoughts Of Emerlist Davjack* (a play on the group's surnames) released in 1967 was basically a studio version of the live show and featured overlong versions of 'War And Peace' and 'Rondo' which didn't help it to sell.

O' List left directly after and the group carried on as a three piece; recording a track that would become totally synonymous with The Nice, a rock interpretation of the *West Side Story* classic 'America'. The ambitious seven minute single was released in July '68 and reached number 21. Unfortunately its composer Leonard Bernstein hated it and consequently had it banned in the States. The band retaliated by burning the Stars And Stripes live on stage at the Royal Albert Hall but all that achieved was to get them barred there as well! The Nice continued to pursue their classical niche throughout 1969 and clocked up some impressive album sales with their last self-titled Immediate release; a half-live, half-studio album that reached number three. A change of label to Charisma in 1970 brought further albums *The Five Bridges Suite* and *Elegy* but by 1972 the group were in disarray. Jackson and Davison begrudgingly accepted that Emerson's flamboyant role would overshadow and dominate their input. However the scant acknowledgement of their efforts unsurprisingly gave rise to resentment. So of course they split up.

Emerson bought enough keyboards to open a shop but formed Emerson, Lake, and Palmer instead. O'List joined up with ex-John's Children's front man Andy Ellison in Jet. Jackson formed the band Jackson Heights, while Davison went Every Which Way. There was a Nice reunion of sorts in 1974 when O'List and Davison got together with Swiss keyboard player Patrick Moraz as Refugee until Moraz upped sticks to join Yes. *(see also P.P Arnold, The Attack, Gary Farr & The T-Bones, The VIPs)*

LONG PLAY 33⅓ R.P.

The Overlanders

The Outer Limits

THE OUTER LIMITS

Originally from Leeds, The Outer Limits (Jeff Christie – vocals/guitar, Stan Drogie, Gerry Smith and Gerry Layton) debuted on Deram in 1967 with the Northern soul-styled 'Just One More Chance' and its punkier B-side, 'Help Me Please'. Their later 1968 single on Immediate subsidiary Instant, 'The Great Train Robbery', was less impressive.

Through a circuitous route, Christie later formed his own self-named combo and had a hit with the wretched bubblegum holiday camp favorite 'Yellow River' (featuring The Tremeloes on backing vocals and instruments) and 'San Bernadino' in 1970. His former cohorts meanwhile returned home to Leeds and released an anachronistic cover of '(I'm Not Your) Steppin' Stone' on their own label.

Paddy,
Klaus & Gibson

PADDY, KLAUS & GIBSON

Paddy Chambers had been in Faron's Flamingos, German-born Klaus Voorman had been an artist friend of The Beatles during their earliest days in Hamburg, while Gibson Kemp was guitarist in Rory Storm & The Hurricanes.

The three got together in London in 1965 and signed a management contract with Tony Stratton-Smith and a recording deal with Pye. Stratton-Smith booked the band into the Pickwick Club, Piccadilly where they were seen by Klaus's pals The Beatles. At the Fabs' suggestion Brian Epstein bought out their contract. The trio released three singles including 'No Good Without You Baby' (also covered by The Birds) but called it a day in 1966 when none of them charted. There was talk circulating in the music press that the group would link forces with members of The Who when that group came close to splitting but these proved unfounded.

Chambers joined a late formation of The Escorts. Voorman designed album sleeves for The Beatles' *Revolver* (1966) and *The Bee Gees First* (1967), and replaced Jack Bruce in Manfred Mann in mid-66. In '69 he became part of John Lennon's Plastic Ono Band and in the Seventies became an in-demand session musician, playing on Lennon's mid-Seventies albums among others.

Voorman is still a successful designer in his native Germany and is still a part of The Beatles' inner circle; being commissioned to design the three *Anthology* sleeves. *(see also The Beatles, The Big Three, Faron's Flamingos, Manfred Mann)*

JIMMY PAGE

Like the other pair (Eric Clapton & Jeff Beck) in the triumvirate of Yardbirds rock guitar heroes, Jimmy Page hailed from Surrey. Having learnt guitar from the age of 12, Jimmy joined his first group, Neil Christian & The Crusaders. As an art student, Jimmy would travel into London to pursue his new passion for blues music, sitting in with harpmaster Cyril Davies. After a brief stint with Carter Lewis & The Southerners, in 1964, Jimmy moved into the studio and at the age of 20 became the hottest young studio guitarslinger in town; playing on countless sessions by the likes of Lulu, Petula Clark, Val Doonican, Tom Jones, Dave Berry, Them, The Kinks, The Who, The Pretty Things, et al.

In 1965, Page moved into production, working for Andrew Loog Oldham's Immediate label (a collection of electric blues arrangements featuring Clapton and Page were released as *Blues Anytime*) and got to release his own single on Fontana, 'She Just

Satisfies' – based around the same R&B riff that Page co-wrote with Ray Davies for 'Revenge' – an instrumental on The Kinks' début album (on which he played).

Needless to say, the record vanished into obscurity and now changes hands for considerable sums. That same year, Page had been offered the vacant guitarist's position in The Yardbirds when Eric Clapton departed but because of illness and his lucrative session work, Page declined. However, when an opening arose with the same band in June '66 when bassist Paul Samwell-Smith quit, he accepted. In July 1968, The Yardbirds finally disbanded. After approaching Chris Dreja to continue (who politely declined the offer), Page enlisted his old session associate John Paul Jones, plus two young musicians from the Midlands singer Robert Plant and drummer John Bonham. Led Zeppelin were born.

(see also Carter-Lewis & The Southerners, Joe Cocker, Cyril Davies R&B All-Stars, The Mickey Finn, Terry Reid, The Yardbirds)

THE PARAMOUNTS

The Paramounts, from Southend, were a typical secondary school covers band formed in 1959 to play local youth clubs and dance halls featuring Gary Brooker (vocals, keyboards), Robin Trower (guitar), Chris Copping (bass), and Mick Brownlee (drums). Copping and Brownlee were replaced by Diz Derrick and B.J Wilson respectively.

The group were unusually accomplished musicians and a shining future was predicted from the various musicians they supported. Sensing their potential EMI signed The Paramounts in 1963 and their début single 'Poison Ivy', released in December, cracked the Top 40 the following month at number 35.

The Paramounts finest moment came shortly after when they were name checked by The Rolling Stones on the TV show *Thank Your Lucky Stars* as 'the finest R&B band in England'. Unfortunately that wasn't enough to ensure career longevity and five further 1964-65 singles (all US cover versions) and an ultra-rare EP failed to sell. The group fell back on their musicianly abilities, backing fellow Essex natives Chris Andrews and Sandie Shaw, before folding in 1966.

The following year Brooker formed Procol Harum in which all of The Paramounts members ended up at one time or another.

(see also Procol Harum)

PETER & GORDON

Doctor's sons Peter Asher and Gordon Waller shunned a career in medicine for a career of clean-cut unassuming pop pleasantry, aided by a few coveted giveaways from Paul McCartney, who was famously dating Asher's actress sister Jane.

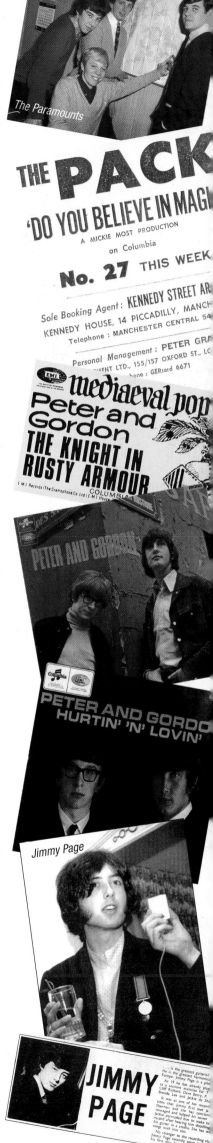

Peter & Gordon

The duo's début Lennon-McCartney single 'A World Without Love' went straight to number one in March 1964, as well as reaching the peak position in the Fabs-obsessed States in May. The formula was repeated for the follow up 'Nobody I Know' which peaked at number 10 in June (US #12). However the magic Macca touch couldn't make it three in a row because 'I Don't Want To See You Again' inexplicably flopped in Britain but entered the US Top 20 in October, as did a fine cover of Del Shannon's 'I Go To Pieces' (US #9 in January '65). They were soon back to strength with covers of Buddy Holly's 'True Love Ways' which sent them to number two and number 14 in the States, and The Teddy Bears' 'To Know You Is To Love You' (number five in June; US #24).

America loved slightly nerdy-looking English singing duos more than the British did in the Sixties and Peter & Gordon were no exception. The group were permanent fixtures on US pop shows like *Shindig!*, *Hullabaloo*, and made a cameo on *The Dick Van Dyke Show*. Such was their toothsome appeal, the lads even made a radio jingle for Macleans toothpaste. The hits continued from '65 into '66 with a cover of Barbara Lewis's 'Baby I'm Yours' (number 19, October) and another McCartney donation 'Woman' (an experiment under the pseudonym 'Bernard Webb' to see if the public would buy an uncredited Lennon-McCartney composition). The results spoke for themselves – UK number 28, US # 14 in March '66. Gimmicky 'ye olde English' ditties 'Lady Godiva', 'Knight In Rusty Armour' and 'Sunday For Tea' were inevitably more successful with the Anglo-obsessed Yanks. Unfortunately Peter & Gordon's run of chart success came to an end on both sides of the Atlantic with the changing climate of 1967 and the two split up the following year.

Thanks to the McCartney connection Asher went on to work as a producer for Apple Records before moving to Los Angeles where he found even greater success as a manager and producer for soft-rockers like James Taylor and Linda Ronstadt.

Waller didn't fare so well and had several aborted attempts at a solo career that reached the not-so-dizzy heights of playing Judas dressed as Elvis in Tim Rice's and Andrew Lloyd Webber's *Joseph And The Amazing Technicolour Dream Coat*. He occasionally pops up as a guest at Beatles conventions in his adopted America.

(see also The Beatles)

THE PETER B's

An interesting, but ultimately aimless, period in the early careers of Mick Fleetwood and Peter Bardens. The band sometimes billed, as Peter B's Looners were an instrumental unit that played the usual round of London's clubs. After a short acrimonious spell in Them, organist Bardens, who had been in The Cheynes with former Bo Street Runner Fleetwood, formed the band in 1966. Their lone Columbia 45 'If You Wanna Be Happy' featured the recording début of a young apprentice butcher from Bethnal Green, Peter Green, who replaced guitarist Mick Parker. Following the single's failure, the

group carried on as a backing unit to singers Rod Stewart and Beryl Marsden in Shotgun Express. Bass player Dave Ambrose went on to Brian Auger's Trinity. Bardens formed the short-lived Village, released two Transatlantic label solo albums, The Answer (1970) and a self-titled follow-up (1971), before cracking it with his next outfit, Camel. He died of lung cancer, aged 56, at his relocated base of Los Angeles on January 22, 2002.

(see also Brian Auger Trinity, The Bo Street Runners, The Cheynes, Shotgun Express, Rod Stewart, Them)

Pinkerton's Assorted Colours

PINKERTON'S ASSORTED COLOURS

The public school pride of Rugby, Pinkerton's Assorted Colours (Samuel 'Pinkerton' Kemp – vocals/autoharp, Tom Long and Tony Newman – guitars, Barrie Bernard – bass and Dave Holland on drums) were maligned at the time for their somewhat desperate visual presentation devised by Fortunes' manager Reg Calvert.

Yet behind the bright 'clobber' lay pop magic in the form of some wonderful singles for Decca, commencing with the hit 'Mirror Mirror' (number nine in February 1966), followed by 'Don't Stop Loving Me Baby' and 'Magic Rocking Horse'. Kemp's autoharp gave the band an interesting sound and in 1967 the band moved to Pye and renamed themselves Pinkertons Colours, and then Pinkertons, though these later singles are less interesting.

PINK FLOYD

Imagine The Who or The Kinks becoming massively successful after their creative lynchpins (Pete Townshend and Ray Davies respectively) departed early in proceedings as victims of hallucinogenic drugs. Unimaginable, is it not? But this is exactly what happened with Pink Floyd. The group's early appeal lay almost entirely in the charismatic, eccentric genius of Roger 'Syd' Barrett who, after a combination of psychological and chemical meltdown, withdrew from the band within two years of their formation. When Barrett became a recluse, the remaining members replaced him with his childhood friend and went on to become one of the biggest bands in the world.

Plastic Penny

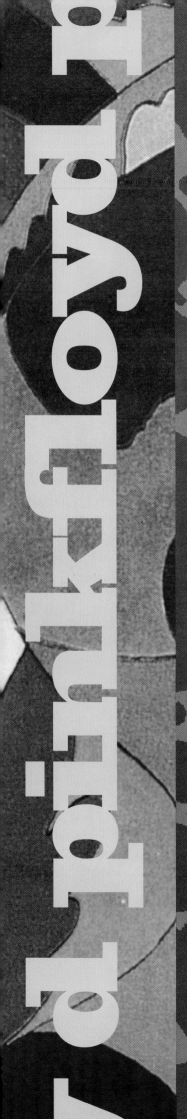

Pink Floyd's roots began with Barrett, Roger Waters and Dave Gilmour attending Cambridge High School. Barrett and Gilmour embarked on a hitchhiking, busking tour around Europe before 'Syd' as he was nicknamed, began a course at Camberwell Art College, London, while Waters studied architecture at the city's Regent Street Polytechnic. There Waters formed an R&B/Jazz group Sigma 6 with fellow students Rick Wright (keyboards), Nick Mason (drums), Clive Metcalfe (bass) and Wright's future wife Juliette Gale (vocals). Guitarist Bob Close replaced Metcalfe, Gale dropped out while Waters became bassist. With Waters' friend Barrett and vocalist Chris Dennis joining, the group toyed with names including The T Set, The Screaming Abdabs and The Abdabs before eventually becoming The Pink Floyd Sound – a name derived from a record in Barrett's collection by blues musicians Pink Anderson and Floyd Council.

Dennis left, Barrett took over vocals and sometime in late '65 the group ventured into a demo studio to cut raw versions of Slim Harpo's 'I'm a King Bee' and a Barrett original 'Lucy Leave'. Although rough, the demo indicated the group's idiosyncratic approach and Barrett's distinctive touch. By early '66 Close had departed and the group became simply The Pink Floyd. A series of gigs at the Marquee and the broadminded London Free School in the west London suburb of Notting Hill Gate brought them to the attention of Peter Jenner and Andrew King, who became their managers. The group were now pushing the envelope with extended improvisations of 'Louie, Louie' and Barrett originals like 'Interstellar Overdrive' which became launchpads for various unorthodox ideas such as Barrett playing through a Binson echo unit and rolling a ball-bearing down the neck of his guitar, while a primitive lightshow devised by the group's mentor (and landlord) Mike Leonard flashed behind them. Pink Floyd became the house band at UFO, usually known as The Blarney Cub, on Tottenham Court Road. While Irish jigs occupied the week Friday night played host to the capital's freaks who talked, smoked, danced or plotted revolution while the Floyd assaulted the senses. Elektra Records representative Joe Boyd had tried to cajole record company people down to see the group and eventually took matters into his own hands by recording them at Sound Techniques Studio, Chelsea. The band cut a lengthy 16-minute version of 'Interstellar Overdrive', filmed for Peter Whitehead's Swinging London study, *Tonite Let's Make Love In London* and two Barrett originals, 'Candy And A Currant Bun' (originally under its more controversial title 'Let's Roll Another One') and 'Arnold Layne', a startlingly non-conformist but quirkily commercial ditty about a transvestite who goes around pinching womens' underwear from clothes lines.

Boyd leased the tapes to EMI who eventually woke up to the group's potential and signed them in March. However the hapless Boyd was elbowed out of the arrangement due to the company only using in-house producers. After King slipped an undisclosed sum to

pirate radio the record reached the lowest rung of the Top 20 in May '67 despite a blanket ban by the BBC. The Floyd began recording their début album with ex-Beatles engineer turned producer Norman Smith at Abbey Road, while The Beatles completed *Sgt. Pepper* in the adjoining studio. The Floyd became the underground's darlings with high profile appearances at the 14-Hour Technicolour Dream event at Alexandra Palace in April and Games For May (featuring a prototype quad sound system) at the Queen Elizabeth Hall. However the strain and constant hallucinogen use was starting to tell on Barrett whose behaviour became increasingly erratic. Turning up to *Top Of The Pops* in his Kings Road finery the group were alarmed to find him scruffy and unshaven, dressed in exactly the same clothes for the following week's appearance. The third week he arrived in new clothes which he then discarded for scruffy rags quite unbefitting a pop star. Such eccentric behaviour couldn't deter 'See Emily Play' reaching number six in July.

The Pink Floyd's startling début album *The Piper At The Gates Of Dawn* followed a month later and remains a glowing testament to the group's early musical inventiveness, studio experimentation and, above all, Barrett's highly original, childlike songwriting; 'Lucifer Sam', 'Matilda Mother', 'Flaming', 'Gnome', 'Chapter 26', and the completely off-the-wall 'Bike' were unkike anything else in the English songwriting canon. The spaced out numbers like otherworldy opener 'Astronomy Domine', 'Pow R Toc H', and 'Interstellar Overdrive' were more controlled than in a live setting though none the less impressive for that. The album reached six in the chart and after a European sojourn the Floyd departed on an American jaunt in October. The visit to the acid-drenched West Coast should have been the jewel in the group's crown but instead it brought them to their knees thanks to Barrett's unreasonable behaviour. Matters didn't improve on an English package tour with Jimi Hendrix, The Move and The Nice, with the latter's Davey O'List having to frequently sub for the errant guitarist. In the studio Barrett's songwriting and ideas had become totally surreal and abstract but in many ways they bordered on demented genius with 'Jugband Blues', 'Apples And Oranges', Scream Thy Last Scream' and 'Vegetable Man' – the latter two tracks so deranged they remain locked away.

The observational 'Apples And Oranges' was far too unorthodox to be successful as a single (and promptly flopped when released in October) while the poignantly autobiographical 'Jugband Blues' (complete with Salvation Army band told to 'play what they like') ended up on the Floyd's second 1968 album *A Saucerful Of Secrets* by which time Barrett was no longer a member of the group.

In a bind Waters called on Gilmour in January '68 to act as auxiliary guitarist to cover Barrett's unpredictable or practically non-existent contributions. The original idea of Barrett to retire from the road but to continue functioning in the studio as a composer was quietly abandoned and Syd was let go in April '68.

Pink Floyd

The Poets

THE POE

THAT'S THE WA
IT'S GOT TO BE

DECCA

At first the group struggled to find their way without Barrett but Waters eventually emerged as the driving force. Through pioneering visual and sound presentations at their concerts and albums like *Meddle*, *Dark Side Of The Moon*, *Wish You Were Here*, *Animals* and *The Wall*, Pink Floyd Mark II became one of the biggest supergroups of the Seventies. Barrett released two albums of deranged madness, *The Madcap Laughs* (1969) and *Barrett* (1970), while apochryphal tales of his bizarre behaviour entered rock folklore. Having effictively retired from the outside world he now lives a quiet life in his native Cambridge.

The Plague

THE PLAGUE

A shame that The Plague are so obscure because both sides of their 1968 Decca single are superb – the topside, 'Here Today, Gone Tomorrow' in particular being a fierce power-pop mover with a backwards guitar fade-out.

THE POETS

The Poets have often been described as 'the Scottish Zombies', but that comparison only goes part of the way to describing their haunting and quite unique sound. Formed in 1963 – George Gallagher (vocals), Tony Myles (guitar), Hume Paton (guitar), John Dawson (bass), and Alan Weir (drums) – were discovered on the cover of *Beat News* in mid-1964 by Andrew Loog Oldham, who had eloped to Scotland to marry his underage girlfriend, Sheila Klein. The Poets' Beau Brummel image attracted the attention of the flamboyant Stones manager who contacted the group's manager to arrange an audition. Within weeks The Poets were signed to a Decca recording contract with 'Now We're Thru' as their début release in October '64.

The song's mysterious wall-of-sound marked by minor key acoustic 12-string, reverberating piano and drums, and singer Gallacher's emotive voice – a sort of Glaswegian folk rock was out-of-sorts with typical beat fare and only just made it to the Top 30. While 'Now We're Thru' had been plaintive, 'That's The Way It's Got To Be' (released February '65) was urgent, demanding freakbeat, with a seductive 12-string riff. However with minimal promotion, it disappeared – the shape of things to come for all Poets singles. The group returned to the formula of 'Now We're Thru' for the Zombies-like 'I Am So Blue' but when it too failed, it seemed that Decca and Oldham were more preoccupied with cash cows The Rolling Stones. Myles left and was replaced by Fraser Watson, and the group were shunted over to Oldham's newly formed Immediate. 'Call Again'

(October '65) and an echo-laden cover of Marvin Gaye's 'Baby, Don't You Do It' (January '66) gave contemporary versions by The Who and The Small Faces a run for their money.

With general apathy displayed toward them, The Poets virtually split at the end of '66 and Gallagher formed a new line-up with Watson, Ian McMillan (guitar), Norrie McClean (bass) and Jim Breakey (drums) plus second vocalist Andi Mulvey. However Gallagher and Breakey suddenly left. Mulvey and Watson remained determined and the group released what many aficionados regard as their best release 'Wooden Spoon'/'In Your Tower'. The A-side featured West Coast-style harmonies and a propulsive, piano-driven bass riff while the B-side nodded to psychedelia with an Indian-style flute. The record flopped and songwriters Mulvey and Watson departed; the later joining The Pathfinders who turned into Apple Records band White Trash. The Poets hobbled on until 1971 with various members going off to form Blue. Despite receiving universal apathy during their existence The Poets are still cherished in their native Scotland and have since become one of the era's most revered acts amongst the Sixties beat cognoscenti.

BRIAN POOLE & THE TREMELOES

Given the weight of hindsight, it must seem crazy that Decca Records elected to sign Brian Poole & The Tremeloes in favour of The Beatles for no better reason than they came from Essex which was closer to London than Liverpool – but distance was a factor in those pre-motorway days and Decca's A&R department simply felt convenience was the overriding factor. For all we know they might have performed better at their audition too, since Brian Poole and his Tremeloes had been together since 1960, initially imitating Buddy Holly, and thus had the same weight of gigging experience behind them as did the not quite yet fabs.

Their first hit for Decca was a cover of 'Twist And Shout' which reached number 4 in July, 1963, and this was followed two months later by their only number one 'Do You Love Me' which, as any guitarist knows, is based on the same chord sequence as 'Twist And Shout'. After two more top tenners, 'Candy Man' (originally by Roy Orbison) and 'Someone Someone' (The Crickets), things went pear shaped as both group and singer were unable to compete with the emerging hi-energy R&B bands. Poole elected to go solo, taking the MOR route into cabaret and eventually wound up in the family butcher's business. The Tremeloes, meanwhile, struck out on their own and found enormous success as a lightweight pop outfit.

Poole and some original Trems resurfaced on the nostalgia circuit in the Nineties, while Poole's daughters Karen and Shellie had five top twenty hits as Alisha's Attic in the late Nineties.

(see also The Tremeloes)

Brian Poole & The Tremeloes

The Powerhouse

JIMMY POWELL

Powell is significant in that he is responsible for one of the earliest and toughest British R&B releases of the Sixties. 'Sugar Babe (Parts 1 & 2)'. His début Decca single has a power unknown to most British records in 1962. As the beat boom took off he formed the Five Dimensions, who gained a residency at Ken Colyer's Studio 51 club in Great Newport Street, London. At one time the line-up included none other than Rod Stewart on harmonica. Consistently soulful, Powell was never able to penetrate beyond clubland, though he continued to record into the Seventies. *(see also Rod Stewart)*

THE POWERHOUSE

Not to be confused with the short-lived supergroup featuring Eric Clapton, Paul Jones, Jack Bruce and Steve Winwood, assembled by Jac Holzman for the 1966 Elektra sampler *What's Shakin'*, this Manchester big band had a stomping version of Sam Cooke's 'Chain Gang' among their two Decca releases.

THE PRETTY THINGS

In 1964 The Pretty Things threatened to topple The Rolling Stones from their 'kings of R&B' perch. This didn't eventuate but for a while things looked promising for this wild, untamed five-piece who ironically hailed from the same area of Kent.

Guitarist Dick Taylor had played in a school band called Little Boy Blue & The Blue Boys with Mick Jagger and attended Sidcup Art School with Keith Richards. All three witnessed Brian Jones playing with Alexis Korner's Blues Incorporated at the Ealing Club in early 1962 and by the middle of the year, the four were playing together as The Rollin' Stones. When the Stones turned professional Taylor chose to remain at art school to complete his studies.

He was soon making music again, however, teaming up with fellow Sidcup student and Stones' acquaintance Phil May on vocals, guitarist Brian Pendleton and bass player John Stax. Naming themselves The Pretty Things (in homage to Bo Diddley but a perfect name in retrospect with their hairy, unkempt image suggesting they

The Pretty Things

were anything but pretty), the group went through a succession of drummers as their reputation spread, thanks to a residency at the 100 Club, which lead to a contract with Fontana.

Soon after, the group found their missing link in Vivian ('Viv') Prince, who had played in Carter Lewis & The Southerners amongst others, and had a unique jazzy drumming style. On top of that he was a complete madman. From their very conception the Pretties were considered wilder, scruffier, rougher, and downright more outrageous than the Stones, so much so that it actually hindered their career. The group certainly never achieved anything near their true potential despite releasing some of the finest records of the era. The group's first single, the raving 'Rosalyn', written by songwriter Jimmy Duncan, was released in June '64, straying just outside the Top 40. For a follow-up the group considered another Duncan original 'Get Yourself Home' (later handed to fellow reprobates The Fairies) before settling on the similar-sounding 'Don't Bring Me Down'. Set to Prince's seductive stop-start rhythm and May's sneering vocal, the single rose to ten in November and the Pretties had arrived. Newspaper stories appeared about the group's appearance and hair-length (May arguably had the longest hair of any beat group member at the time) and suddenly the Stones had competition for the mantle 'the group that parents love to hate.' Shows often

ended in riots, particularly on the Continent, and one classic advertisement byline stated 'last month in Liverpool they made tough men cry'!

The Pretties' were causing ripples elsewhere. In America, the 'Don't Bring Me Down' lyric 'and then I led her underground' was construed as 'and then I laid her on the ground', resulting in an outright ban, which although good for publicity, seriously hampered their progress. A May-Taylor composition 'Honey I Need' with its echoey production got to 13 in March '65 but it was the end of their chart challenge to the Stones. The band's classic self-titled début album appeared the same month making number six and remains a vital document of their raw untamed approach. A sultry cover of Solomon Burke's 'Cry To Me' (also covered at the same time by those damned Stones!) was released in July but instead of directing their attention to America, manager Bryan Morrison packed the group off on a disastrous two-week tour of New Zealand with Sandie Shaw, where Prince came into his own; being openly drunk, setting fire to stage curtains, chopping up stages with an axe, and staging live crayfish races in hotel lobbies. The New Zealand tabloid press bayed for blood and the group were thrown out of the country. Prince's manic behaviour got him sacked shortly after their return. He briefly depped for The Honeycombs and The Who (being the perfect substitute for Keith Moon), recorded an obscure 1966 Columbia single 'Light Of The Charge Brigade' before drifting in and out of various bands. One of rock's great lunatics he was last heard of terrorising the locals in Portugal.

The Pretty Things second album *Get The Picture* (released December '65), featured Prince on some tracks, while Mitch Mitchell, Bobby Graham and John 'Twink' Alder played on the rest. Prince's official replacement was Skip Alan (nee' Alan Skipper) who played on the group's next single, 'Midnight To Six Man' (December '65)– a garage tour de force, with Nicky Hopkins on piano – which peaked at a disappointing 46. Another searing single – the grungy 'Come See Me' and B-side 'LSD' (not a reference to pounds, shilling and pence!) – could only manage three rungs higher. Two unrepresentative singles – 'A House In The Country' (a Ray Davies song recorded by The Kinks) and the poppy, brassy 'Progress'- followed before Pendleton and then Stax quit. May's pals Wally Allen and John Povey (ex-Bern Elliot and The Fenmen) were recruited, bringing a new vocal harmony style to the group.

In a valiant effort to keep abreast of shifting times the album *Emotions* appeared. Granted there were some worthwhile songs but it completely lacked the level of creativity expected of groups by the mid-Sixties. The group protested at the smothering horn arrangements added without their knowledge and disowned it. Having fulfilled their commitments with Fontana, the new line-up eagerly signed to EMI, recording for Columbia with ex-Beatles engineer and Pink Floyd producer Norman 'Hurricane' Smith. The group recorded two British psychedelic genre' defining 1967/68 singles, 'Defecting Grey' and 'Talkin' About The Good Times' while working on their magnum opus and what is widely acknowledged as the first-ever 'concept album' *S.F. Sorrow*.

The album was a remarkable and idiosyncratic work and an artistic triumph which took months to record. However when it was released in December 1968 it fell on deaf ears, despite being lauded by contemporaries like Pete Townshend, who admitted the record's inspiration helped him finish his still-developing *Tommy*.

Halfway through the sessions Alan quit and was replaced by the group's old friend Twink. Parts of the album were performed at underground grottoes such as the Roundhouse accompanied by a Twink mime routine. In 1969 Taylor decided to leave, joining Liberty Records as a producer of Hawkwind's early records. Twink followed suit to join The Pink Fairies. Taylor was replaced by Peter Tolson and Alan returned for The Pretty Thing's 1970 album (their first for EMI's progressive subsidiary Harvest) *Parachute*, which received no less an accolade than 'Album Of The Year' in *Rolling Stone*; not reflected by its number 43 chart position and disappointing sales.

The Pretty Things disbanded but reformed in 1972 with May, Alan, Povey, Tolson, keyboardist/guitarist Gordon Edwards and bassist Stu Brooks. This line up recorded three albums – one for Warners *Freeway Madness* and two for Led Zeppelin's Swan Song label – *Silk Torpedo* and *Savage Eye*. Long-time fan David Bowie covered 'Rosalyn' and 'Don't Bring Me Down' on his 1973 *Pin-Ups* album, creating interest in the original band.

This second lease of life saw the group through to another dissolution in 1977. Of course that wasn't the end of the Pretties. Taylor eventually returned to the fold when they reformed once again in 1979. The Pretty Things have been with us in one shape or form ever since and their thirtieth anniversary was marked by the group winning back the rights to their back catalogue. A double CD anthology *Bloodied But Unbowed* appeared in 1995 followed by the re-release of the band's original albums. To mark its twentieth anniversary The Pretty Things (with Dave Gilmour) performed the entire *S.F. Sorrow* album where it was originally recorded at Abbey Road Studios, and repeated the performance (with Gilmour and guest narrator Arthur Brown) at the Royal Festival Hall in 2001.

(see also The Fairies, The In Crowd, Tomorrow)

ALAN PRICE SET

When Alan Price left The Animals in May 1965 (seen downing a bottle of Newcastle Brown ale, days later, with Bob Dylan in the film *Don't Look Back*) Price put together his self-named quintet, featuring a rhythm section of Ray Slade and Ray Walters, plus brass section John Walters, Clive Burrows, and Steve Gregory.

After a flop with Chuck Jackson's 'Any Day Now', Price reached number nine in April '66 with a stirring cover of Screaming Jay Hawkin's 'I Put a Spell On You'. Covers of standards, 'Hi-Lili, Hi-Lo' and 'Willow Weep For Me' were less successful until his discovery of

the Randy Newman songbook made 'Simon Smith And His Amazing Dancing Bear' reach four in March '67. Price prided himself on his song writing abilities, so it comes as surprising that he composed only one hit 'The House That Jack Built' – a song about a mental institution that reached four in August. His next attempt, 'Shame' wasn't as successful and so an outside source was returned to in Sonny Rollins' 'Don't Stop The Carnival', which reached 13 in February '68.

Price disbanded the Set in 1968 to go solo, teaming up in a creatively unfulfilling collaboration with Georgie Fame. Price successes continued into the Seventies with a number 11 hit 'Rosetta' (1971) and the score for the film *O Lucky Man* (1973) in which he also appeared, as well as *Alfie Darling* (1975). 'Jarrow Song' notched up another hit in 1974 but after that Price's career was less eventful. He twice rejoined the original Animals line-up, first in 1977 for an unsuccessful album *Before We Were Rudely Interrupted* and later, a US tour in 1983. Like his ex-compadre' Fame, Price continues to tour worldwide with his own band.

The Set's John Walters went on to be a successful BBC Radio One producer, responsible for the long running *John Peel Show* among others. He died in 2001.

(see also The Animals, Georgie Fame)

THE PRIMITIVES

Oxford's finest The Primitives (Jay Roberts –vocals, Geoff Eaton – guitar, John E Soul – guitar/harmonica, Roger James – bass, and Mike Wilding – drums), previously known as The Cornflakes, were long-haired Pretty Things-styled R&B ravers signed to Pye in 1964. The group recorded two of the most regarded examples of British R&B, a rough reading of Sonny Boy Williamson's 'Help Me' (released November '64) and an original 'You Said' (released January 65) featuring Jimmy Page on guitar. Both are frantic and frankly dangerous pieces of plastic that proved a little too ferocious for the charts. The group subsequently added a lead singer, Mal Ryder (aka Paul Couling), and the line-up changed to Ryder – vocals, Roberts – bass/organ, Stuart Linnell – guitar and Mick Charleton – drums for 'Every Minute Of Every Day' (August '65) as Mal & The Primitives. Linnell and Charleton were replaced by Dave Sumner and David 'Pick' Withers respectively in 1966. Deserting the over-crowded beat scene in England, The Primitives went to Italy, along with The Sorrows, and became a successful nightclub act at The Piper Club, Rome. While there the group made Italian-only recordings including the punky singles 'Yeeeeeeh!' (a cover of The Young Rascals 'I Ain't Gonna Eat My Heart Out Anymore', 'Johnny No' and an album Blow-Up. (In '66 they also recorded a French only EP). Ryder became an Italian heartthrob while Withers later found success with Man, Rockpile and Dire Straits.

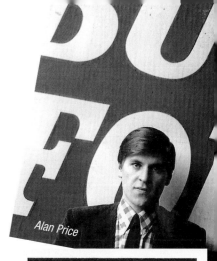

Alan Price

THE PRICE to play

a truly great first LP from the

ALAN PRICE SET

THE PRICE to play

DECCA

© LK 4839   12″ mono record

DECCA

ALAN PRICE SET
I PUT A SPELL ON YOU
TECHYO-DA

Procol Harum

P.J. PROBY

Texas born P.J.Proby was among the more charismatic contenders in the UK Pop Olympics. He arrived in Britain in 1963, having already made a few records in the US under the same of Jett Powers, though his real name was James Smith. He scored two top tenners for Decca in 'Hold Me' (May '64) and 'Together' (September '64) but his most memorable record was a dramatic reading of 'Somewhere' from the musical *West Side Story* which Liberty released in December '64. His deep throated, epic delivery thrilled fans and he followed this up with equally dramatic versions of 'I Apologise' (originally recorded by Billy Eckstein) and another *West Side Story* tune 'Maria'. Proby appeared on stage in a flowing white shirt and tight black trousers, his long black hair tied back in a ribbon, and the girls loved him but the gravy train became unhitched when he split his trousers on stage at the ABC Cinema in Croydon and was accused by our moral guardians of obscenity. A long and spectacular fall from grace followed, Proby's increasingly straightened circumstances exacerbated by alcoholism, disputes with the Inland Revenue and confrontations with anyone and everyone whenever a comeback was attempted. At one stage he was working as the caretaker in a block of flat in Shepherds Bush in West London. At other times he's been an Elvis impersonator.

(see also The Walker Brothers)

PROCOL HARUM

Procol Harum (loosely translated: beyond these things) formed in 1967 as a platform for the songs of ex-Paramount pianist Gary Brooker and songwriter Keith Reid. (The group took their name from DJ and mentor Guy Steven's cat!) Brooker assembled a band comprising keyboard player Matthew Fisher, guitarist Roy Royer, bassist Dave Knights, and drummer Bobby Harrison. The group's début single 'A Whiter Shade Of Pale' (based on Bach's *Cantata No.3 In D*) was one of the biggest things to happen chartwise during the 1967 Summer of Love. It effortlessly made number one in June but caused the band to almost implode because of it.

Within weeks a round of hiring and firing ensued due to the group's inability to recreate the song live. Royer and Harrison were unceremoniously sacked to make way for ex-Paramounts Robin Trower and Bernie ('B.J') Wilson. The pair later won a court battle over unfair dismissal and formed Freedom in 1968.

Producer Denny Cordell shifted Procol Harum from Deram over to Regal Zonophone and the band recorded a follow-up 'Homburg', arguably a pale imitation of their début. Their self-titled début album was a curiously unsatisfying affair and consequently failed to chart in the UK. The US version tacked on 'A Whiter Shade Of Pale' and reached number 34 on the *Billboard* charts. When 'Quite Rightly So' and a second album *Shine On Brightly* (1968) struggled to make an impression at home the group decided to concentrate on the US albums market where *Shine On Brightly* had reached number 24.

After this the band concentrated on consolidating their US success, where their third album *A Salty Dog* (1969) reached number 27. Fisher and Knights were next to go replaced by the last of the Paramounts, Chris Copping.

Procol Harum continued to produce several well received albums and the odd minor hit single in the States for much of the Seventies before making a discreet exit in 1977. Brooker continued with a solo career, including a cover of Murray Head's 'Say It Ain't So, Joe' while becoming a member of Eric Clapton's touring band. As well as periodically reactivating Procol Harum with Fisher he was last seen as part of Bill Wyman's band The Rhythm Kings. Robin Trower became a solo guitar hero in his own right.

(see also The Paramounts)

THE PUDDING

Great name, but sadly that is all The Pudding are notable for – that and the fact that their lone 1967 Decca release, 'The Magic Bus' failed to rise, despite pre-empting The Who's recording by a year.

The Pussyfoot

THE PUSSYFOOT

Originally known as The Rare Breed who recorded a 1966 single 'Beg, Borrow And Steal' for Strike this London group (Terry 'Barnyard' Barfield, Terry 'Goodmayes' Goodman, David 'Turnip' Townend, John 'Fingers' William and guitarist David Osborne) specialised in daft nicknames and a vocal harmony style not unlike The Association, as heard on their 1966 Decca début, 'Freeloader'.

The Pudding

Procol Harum

The Quik

Art Wood's Quiet Melon

The Red Squares

Terry Reid

THE QUIK

Although little is known about the group, one of The Quik's three overlooked Deram singles from the time is now a sought-after Sixties nightclub record. Despite its brevity, the finger-clicking 'Bert's Apple Crumble' (1967) is the ultimate mod raver; two minutes of piano, bass, sax and handclaps, a marshalled drum roll and a pumping B-3 that packs the dancefloor whenever it's played. It was even used as background music for a BBC Radio television trailer in 2001. The Quik's final single, the spooky 'I Can't Sleep' is also notable for that same Hammond creating a quasi-psychedelic air.

THE RED SQUARES

Though they only had a couple of releases in the Motherland, The Red Squares (singer David 'George' Garriock, Ronnie Martin and Dave Bell – guitars, Pete Mason – bass and Andy Bell – drums) were a well-known commodity on the Continent, in particular Denmark, where they made a comfortable living. Their Danish releases boast an album as well as assorted singles most of which reveal the group's diversity and their predilection for harmonies. However, their classic moment is a 1967 single 'You Can Be My Baby', a caustic Who-fuelled rocker with slashing chords and a furious rhythm. For that moment alone, The Red Squares deserve their place in the freakbeat history book.

TERRY REID

If this was an American high school yearbook Terry Reid's entry might read 'the guy most likely to'. He didn't of course; in fact Reid's entire career was a spectacular lesson in underachievement, but for a while it looked promising,

Originally singer with Peter Jay & The Jaywalkers, Reid was picked out for solo stardom in 1966 by producer Mickie Most. He signed to Columbia and released two singles, 'The Hand Don't Fit The Glove' and 'Better By Far', both of which flopped miserably. They did, however, bring him to the attention of Jimmy Page who was sufficiently impressed to offer Reid a role in his new group venture Led Zeppelin. Unfortunately Most had the young guitarist/singer on a tight rein and contractual obligations prevented the merger. Reid charitably recommended Robert Plant instead.

In 1969 he formed a power trio with drummer Keith Webb and keyboard player Pete Solley and set out to conquer the States where he recorded the American only albums *Bang Bang, You're Terry Reid* and *Superlungs*. He remained in America throughout the Seventies, making a name for himself as a phenomenal live guitarist, and even hovered on the periphery of The Rolling Stones around the time of Mick Taylor's departure. Another three albums kept up his profile and the threat of greatness, but somehow the break never came and his career slowly petered out. He was never the most prolific of performers to begin with and his last album, *The Driver*, was released in 1991. *(see also Peter Jay & The Jaywalkers, Jimmy Page)*

REMO FOUR

Having played in Liverpool skiffle groups since the late Fifties, The Remo Four's original line-up featured Colin Manley (lead guitar), Don Andrews (bass), Keith Stokes (rhythm guitar), and Harry Prytcherch (drums). The latter two were replaced by Phil Rogers and Roy Dyke respectively. The Remo Four replaced The Searchers behind singer Johnny Sandon, backing him on a tour of US army bases in France. When returning to Liverpool Brian Epstein offered the Four a gig backing Billy J. Kramer but they elected to stay loyal to Sandon. Epstein signed them to NEMS regardless and a deal with Pye was procured. Two singles with Sandon, 'Lies' and 'Magic Potion' went nowhere and singer and group parted company.

The Remo Four then backed Epstein protégé Tommy Quickly on record and stage, while releasing two instrumentals – ''I Wish I Could Shimmy Like My Sister Kate' and 'Sally Go Round The Roses' – on Piccadilly, as well as a one-off backing Gregory Phillips on his 1964 Pye single, 'Everybody Knows'. In 1964, Andrews was replaced by Blackpool-born keyboardist Tony Ashton and the Four's music pursued a more jazzy-R&B direction. From 1965 until their demise in 67, the group spent most of their time in Germany where they were enormously popular, releasing many recordings there, collected together as the *Smile* album on the Star Club label. On returning to England, the group were contacted by old pal George Harrison to contribute the backing to the Western-flavoured tunes for his *Wonderwall* soundtrack. During the sessions, a track produced by Harrison, 'In The First Place', was recorded but never used for the film. It was belatedly released as a single in 1998 to mark the film's thirtieth anniversary.

Ashton and Dyke formed Ashton, Gardner & Dyke with ex-Birds, and Creation bassist Kim Gardner. Following their demise Ashton joined Family, followed by an equally brief collaboration with Deep Purple's Jon Lord and Ian Paice. He continued in production work while occasionally surfacing here and there for the odd jam, until his

death from cancer on May 28, 2001. Dyke formed Budgie, where he was later joined by Gardner, and is married to the buxom ex-Hawkwind dancer Stacia.

THE RIOT SQUAD

Chiefly remembered for being an early home of drummer John 'Mitch' Mitchell and for a fleeting visit by Jon Lord, The Riot Squad were a group of session musicians featuring Mitchell, Graham Bonney (vocals), Ron Ryan (guitar), Bob Evans (sax), Mark Stevens (organ) and Mike Martin (bass). Managed by Larry Page, who hustled them a Kinks tour support slot in 1965, the group released seven unsuccessful singles for Pye between 1965 and '67. The group's production was later taken over by Joe Meek by which time Mitchell had joined Georgie Fame's Blue Flames and in October '66 successfully auditioned for The Jimi Hendrix Experience

(see also Georgie Fame, Jimi Hendrix Experience)

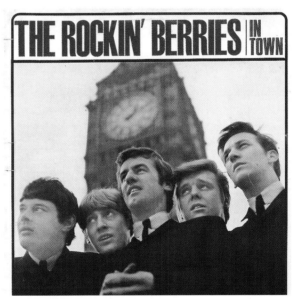

THE ROCKIN' BERRIES

Birmingham beat merchants The Rockin' Berries (Clive Lea – vocals, Geoff Turton and Chuck Botfield – guitars, Roy Austin – bass and Terry Bond – drums) were yet another band that spent most of their early existence playing in Germany.

They signed to Decca in 1963 and released two flop singles before moving to Pye. After yet another flop 'I Didn't Mean To Hurt You' American scenemaker Kim Fowley suggested they record a song by US vocal group The Tokens. The Berries version of 'He's In Town' made it to number three in November '64. The group missed

out on a sure-fire hit as a follow up when Pye made the Berries record 'What In The World's Come Over You' instead of 'Funny How Love Can Be' – written and recorded by labelmates The Ivy League, who took it into the Top 10 while The Berries limped to number 23. A cover of The Reflections 'Poor Man's Son' returned the Berries to the Top Five in June before they concentrated on their natural home in cabaret and pantomime. (The group's second album *Life's A Bowl Of Berries* contained a version of 'The Laughing Policeman'. Enough said!) Turton went on to release some truly awful records as the truly awful Jefferson.

THE ROCKIN' VICKERS

This Blackpool beat band are best remembered for being home to Ian Kilminster, better known as Lemmy from Motorhead. The group, formed in 1963 with a line-up of Harry Feeny (vocals), Ian Holdbrook (guitar/harmonica), Steven 'Vickers' Morris (bass) and Ciggy Shaw (drums), were originally billed as The Reverend Black & The Rocking Vicars. The group were signed to Decca in '64 for a cover of Neil Sedaka's 'I Go Ape'. When this was unsuccessful Decca relieved them from their oversubscribed roster and Holdbrook quit. Enter Kilminster, actually a clergyman's son! After a time Shel Talmy spotted them and produced their two '66 CBS singles – 'Its Alright' (blatantly modeled on The Who's 'The Kids Are Alright' earning a 'Townshend' songwriting credit) and a cover of The Kinks 'Dandy' (a successful hit for Herman's Hermits in the US). The group split shortly thereafter with Kilminster going on to Sam Gopal, Hawkwind and Motorhead as Lemmy.

THE ROLLING STONES

While The Beatles bestraddled the Sixties like a colossus, the only group to offer a serious challenge to their supremacy was an R&B five piece from London. The Beatles appeal crossed barriers of age, sex and creed, and The Rolling Stones were shrewdly marketed as the Fab Four's rough antithesis. In the Sixties you were either a Beatles' fan or a Rolling Stones' fan, with fence sitting frowned upon. Lurid headlines like 'Would you let your daughter go with a Rolling Stone?' became grist to the Fleet Street mill, enhancing their bad boy image, and sustaining a career that has spanned four decades.

The Rolling Stones were formed by teenagers with a love of electrified Chicago R&B popularised by such greats as Muddy Waters, Jimmy Reed, Elmore James, Little Walter and Willie Dixon. In 1960/'61 Mick Jagger and his recently reunited schoolfriend Keith Richards got together with mutual friend Dick Taylor in the London commuter belt suburbs of Dartford and Sidcup to share their passion for a mysterious and earthy music that in the early Sixties was still largely unknown in Britain. Originally called Little Boy Blue & The

The Rolling Stones

Blue Boys, word reached the trio of a new R&B club opened over the other side of London in Ealing.

It was run by like-minded blues zealots Alexis Korner and Cyril Davies, and one night sitting in as a special guest 'all the way from Cheltenham' was a blond kid calling himself Elmo Lewis (aka Brian Jones, paying homage to his idol Elmore James). Jagger, Richards, Jones and Taylor teamed up with the musicians that Brian had recently been rehearsing with, guitarists Geoff Bradford and Brian Knight and pianist Ian 'Stu' Stewart. The group rehearsed at The Bricklayers Arms in Soho but Richards' Chuck Berry obsession was anathema to a purist like Bradford who quit, as did Knight.

On July 12, 1962 The Rollin' (sic) Stones (a name taken from a line in the Muddy Waters song, 'Mannish Boy'), made their début at the Marquee Club in Oxford Street, featuring Jagger, Richards, Jones, Taylor, Stewart and future Kink, Mick Avory on drums. Avory was replaced after the one gig by Tony Chapman. When Taylor quit to pursue his art studies Chapman recommended his old bandmate William Perks (aka Bill Wyman). At 26 Wyman was seven years older and married with a child, but these shortcomings were overlooked because Wyman had a spare Vox AC30 amp. The group persuaded

FUTURIST · SCARBOROUGH

6.15 MONDAY, MARCH 8 8.40

ON THE STAGE   ONE NIGHT ONLY

ERIC EASTON presents

THE ROLLING STONES

DAVE BERRY AND THE CRUISERS

THE KONRADS THE CHECKMATES

YOUR COMPERE JOHNNY BALL

GOLDIE AND THE GINGERBREADS

SPECIAL GUEST STARS **THE HOLLIES**

PRICES: 12/6 10/- 7/6 5/-   All seats may be booked in advance

Brian

Bill

Keith

Charlie

Mick

163

ex-Blues Incorporated drummer Charlie Watts to leave his current band Blues By Six to join the Stones, replacing the sacked Chapman in January '63.

From here on in things moved fast. Jones persuaded club promoter Giorgio Gomelsky to let the Stones take over the Sunday afternoon residency at the Crawdaddy Club, in the basement of the Station Hotel in Richmond, Surrey. Soon the kids were queing to get in and word started spreading. Journalist Peter Jones of *Record Mirror* witnessed the crowd reaction and tipped off publicist colleague Andrew 'Loog' Oldham. A week later Oldham witnessed the Stones' sexy panache for himself and became their manager at the expense of the hapless Gomelsky. He got the group signed to Decca but insisted that five was better than six and 'Stu' was relegated to roadie and occasional keyboard player on the group's records, a role he accepted with admirable grace.

In June, the Stones' tentative début – a cover of Chuck Berry's 'Come On' (which the group had re-cut twice) was released. Oldham had the group wearing matching houndstooth jackets to promote the record (which stalled at 21), including their début television appearance on Thank Your Lucky Stars. The uniforms were jettisoned during the group's first theatre tour of Britain with Little Richard, Bo Diddley and The Everly Brothers in September.

Ironically, it was the patronage of their supposed rivals The Beatles that provided the Stones with their much-needed chart breakthrough. 'I Wanna Be Your Man' was dashed off at a rehearsal and reached number twelve in December. The song was notable for Jones' stinging slide solo, unusual on a British pop record of the time. In the middle of their second nationwide tour with The Ronettes and Marty Wilde, the group's third single – a Bo Diddley take on Buddy Holly's 'Not Fade Away' – went all the way to three in March, followed a month later by the Stones' classic début album, a raw yet confident document that projects all the Stones' early swagger in covers like 'Route 66', 'I Just Want To Make Love To You', 'Mona', 'I'm A King Bee' and 'Walking The Dog'. The band may have been behind

the establishment endorsed Beatles in terms of sales but their image and sound was winning enough converts to put them ahead of the Fabs in a Best Group poll in *Melody Maker*. In June the group realised a cherished dream and embarked on their first visit to America. The trip was full of ups – a riotous opening show in San Bernadino – and downs – playing to empty audiences in middle America, being publicly insulted by Dean Martin on the networked *Hollywood Palace* TV programme. However these were overshadowed by a visit to the sacred Chess studios in Chicago where most of their favourite blues sides had been cut.

It was at Chess that the group cut the material for their next single ('It's All Over Now') and EP (*Five By Five*), both number ones on their respective charts in mid-64. Following riotous Continental visits the group returned to America in October to find their fan base swelling, but Jones missed some dates due to illness – an early clue to his frailty. A cover of Willie Dixon's 'Little Red Rooster' went straight to number one. For a down home slide blues to be voted top by unfamiliar ears was another first the Stones could chalk up. The song was rumoured to be Jones' (whose slide playing excels throughout) most favoured Stones performance.

A second album, imaginatively titled *Rolling Stones No.2*, followed in January, while 'The Last Time' – the first of the group's three classic '65 number one singles – was issued in February. The song was also the first to feature the Jagger-Richards appellation, as the group had previously composed under the in-joke pseudonym Nanker-Phelge. '(I Can't Get No) Satisfaction' was a worldwide chart topper in the halcyon summer of '65 and cemented the Stones' status as anti-social dissenters, a bad boy role further enhanced when Jagger, Jones and Wyman were hauled before the law for urinating on a garage station wall. *Out Of Our Heads* and 'Get Off Of My Cloud' were further sucesses in October while a year-end American tour was the first to pay dividends, thanks to notorious business manager Allen Klein, who favourably renegotiated the Stones' Decca deal.

The following year passed in much the same fashion with riotous Australian, European and American tours, singles '19th Nervous Breakdown'/'As Tears Go By' – number two in February, 'Paint It Black' (number one – May) and 'Have You Seen Your Mother, Baby, Standing In The Shadow?' (number five – October) and a ground-breaking album *Aftermath*, released in April, composed entirely of Jagger-Richard songs of the calibre of 'Mother's Little Helper', 'Lady Jane' and misogynist anthems like 'Under My Thumb', and 'Out Of Time'. 'Goin Home' stretched out over the ten-minute mark while the colourful touches of sitar, marimba, and dulcimer were contributed by multi-instrumentalist Jones. By the end of the year the Stones could ease back on their breakneck schedule, their position in the top echelon of groupdom safely assured. Touring was put on hold while the group recorded the holding operation that was *Between The Buttons*, released in January '67.

1967's Summer of Love came to represent anything but for the Stones. There was controversy surrounding the permissiveness of their single, 'Let's Spend The Night Together', a double A-side with 'Ruby Tuesday' (number three in February). That same month Jagger and Richards were infamously busted for drugs in a suspected *News Of The World* set-up. The unholy alliance between Jagger, Richards and Jones reached breaking point when Richards relieved Jones of his paramour Anita Pallenburg during an eventful Moroccan holiday. On May 10, the day that Jagger and Richards were committed to trial Jones was busted in suspicious circumstances. Jagger, Richards and associate Robert Fraser were tried, convicted and imprisoned in June at West Sussex Quarter Sessions, Chichester. Jagger and Richards were released (and eventually cleared) on appeal. Jones' trial was heard in October and likewise he was convicted and sentenced before being released on appeal. However the law had found the Stones' achilles heel and Jones was busted again the following May but narrowly escaped with a fine in September.

In August '67, the darkly sardonic 'We Love You' was released, followed by *Their Satanic Majesties Request* in December. However the album was savaged at the time as being the Stones knee-jerk reaction to psychedelia. Time has subsequently revealed its strengths.

In '68 the Stones bounced back with 'Jumpin' Jack Flash' and *Beggar's Banquet*, whose proposed sleeve of a graffitied toilet was the subject of a stand-off between group and record company for several months before finally being released in December. Tracks like 'Sympathy For The Devil', 'No Expectations', 'Street Fighting Man (inspired by Jagger's participation in the Grosvenor Square anti-Vietnam demonstrations), and 'Stray Cat Blues' were testaments to the Stones rejuvenated creativity and the underrated songwriting partnership of Jagger-Richards. The pair had rediscovered their love of old blues 78s (Rev. Fred McDowell's 'Prodigal Son') and Richards' introduction to country and gospel produced 'Dear Doctor' and 'Salt Of The Earth' respectively. 'Jumping Jack Flash' and *Beggar's Banquet* also began a fruitful five year association with ex-Spencer Davis Group/Traffic producer Jimmy Miller.

The group were eager to return to the road but Jones condition was a cause for concern. He had barely contributed anything to *Beggars Banquet* due to his rampant drug use and paranoia, confirmed by his cadaverous appearance in the shelved *Rolling Stones Rock And Roll Circus* television special. Despite being the Stones' founder and the soul of the group the creative axis had swung firmly towards the powerbase of Jagger and Richards. In June, it was announced that Jones was leaving to pursue a solo career; his place being taken by 20-year old guitarist Mick Taylor. A new single 'Honky Tonk Woman' appeared (number one in July) and a massive free concert at Hyde Park was announced when the shock news broke of Jones being found dead in the swimming pool at his home at Cotchford Farm, East Sussex on July 3. He was 27. A verdict of misadventure was recorded but the events surrounding that evening are shrouded in mystery.

As the decade closed the Stones returned to America as 'The Greatest Rock 'n' Roll Band In The World' with another seminal set, *Let It Bleed*, in the stores. However the tour was marred by the farce

The Roving Kind

that was Altamont, with an audience member being fatally stabbed as the Stones performed. The event signified an ominous welcome to the Seventies. The Stones continued to release further important and influential albums in *Sticky Fingers* (1971) and *Exile On Main Street* (1972) – but subsequent records and performances raised the ugly sceptre of self-parody. As the group themselves summed it up 'It's only rock 'n' roll but I like it'.

A dissatisfied Taylor quit in 1974 to pursue an erratic solo career. Ex Birds/Jeff Beck and Faces guitarist Ron Wood replaced him in 1975 and the Stones continued to trade off their legend, pioneering stadium rock while releasing the occasional great record. Wyman retired in 1994 and the bass-for-hire position went to Miles Davis sessionman, Daryl Jones. Forty years on from their formation, 'The Greatest Rock 'n' Roll Band In The World' have just announced an anniversary tour. *(see also Jeff Beck Group, The Birds, The Creation, Cyril Davies R&B All-Stars, The Gods, Alexis Korner's Blues Incorporated, John Mayall's Bluesbreakers)*

THE ROULETTES

Formed in London in 1962 The Roulettes featured singer, guitar player Russ Ballard, guitarist Peter Thorpe, bass player John Rodgers, and drummer Bob Henrit. Originally on Pye the group signed to Parlophone in 1963 as Adam Faith's backing band, while releasing singles in their own right.

The Roulettes achieved a spectacular four-year run of uninterrupted chart failures, including two singles on Fontana, before splitting in 1967. Of these, the unusual 'The Long Cigarette' was particularly memorable while a rare but undistinguished 1965 album, Stakes And Chips now commands a three figure sum.

Russ Ballard and Bobby Henrit went on to be the Two, in Unit Four Plus Two, before forming Argent with ex-Zombie Rod Argent. Rodgers was killed in a car crash in 1964 and was replaced by John 'the Mod' Rogan. Henrit replaced Mick Avory in the latter day Kinks and now plays once again with Rod Argent and another ex Zombie, Colin Blunstone.

(see also The Kinks, Unit Four Plus Two, The Zombies)

THE ROVING KIND

Vocalist Gary James led this group from Plymouth, who issued two obscure but average singles, 'Ain't It True' and the title-contrasting 'Lies A Million' on Decca in 1965-66.

RUPERT'S PEOPLE

Rupert's People were a late Sixties psych band that actually didn't exist when their first single 'Reflections Of Charles Brown' was released in 1967. The most stable line-up – Rod Lynton (guitar, vocals), Ray Beverley (bass), Steve Brendell (drums), John Tout (organ), and for a short spell, Dai Jenkins (guitar) – were brought in to replace a short-lived group of musicians who in turn had replaced the Fleur de Lys. Confused? You will be!

Lynton, Beverley and Brendell were originally The Sweet Feeling whose 1967 Columbia single 'All So Long Ago' featured a backwards-tape extravaganza 'Charles Brown' on the B-side. Manager Howard Conder saw the song's potential, asked Lynton to put the lyrics to the tune of Bach's 'Air On A G String' and roped in the Fleur de Lys to help record it (with Lynton and organist Peter Solley) while Lynton and the Fleur de Lys co-wrote 'Hold On'. Both songs were released as a Columbia single in July '67 but Conder had a slight problem in the fact that neither Lynton or the Fleur de Lys (apart from singer Chris Andrews) were interested in promoting it – possibly due to the song's similarity to Procol Harum's current hit 'A Whiter Shade Of Pale'.

Condor hastily cobbled a version of Rupert's People together featuring Andrews, ex-Merseybeats drummer John Banks, ex-Knack guitarist Adrian Curtis (nee Gurvitz) and ex-Screaming Lord Sutch & The Savages drummer Tony Dangerfield. Andrews shortly split to pursue an uneventful career as Tim Andrews (see entry) and was replaced by Gurvitz's brother Paul, with the addition of organist John Tout. It seemed this was much ado about nothing as 'Reflections Of Charles Brown' failed to chart, despite Conder buying plugs on Radio Caroline. With the band slipping out of his control the ever-persistent manager fired the whole band and asked The Sweet Feeling to reconsider becoming Rupert's People. They agreed; Tout was retained as organist, with ex-Iveys guitarist Jenkins for two more non-charting Columbia singles, 'A Prologue To A Magic World' and 'I Can Show You'.

Of the varied personnel the Gurvitz brothers went on to form Gun while Tout replaced John Hawken in Renaissance and was later in Wishbone Ash. Lynton played on John Lennon's *Imagine* album and various other Apple records, before moving into the other side of the business as a record company PR. Brendell also worked for Apple, assisting wth what would eventually become The Beatles *Anthology* series, and worked with John and Yoko's film company, Joko Productions.

The Sweet Feeling line up of Rupert's People reformed for the first time in 1999 and have since played a selection of shows for the Mod promoters New Untouchables. Their recordings before, during and after Rupert's People were released by Circle Records as The Magic World Of Rupert's People in 2001. *(see also Tim Andrews, (Les) Fleur De Lys, The Knack, The Merseybeats)*

PAUL & BARRY RYAN

Fifties singer-actress Marion Ryan and her promoter-impresario husband Harold Davison were the driving force behind the careers of their twin sons. Launched in 1965 Paul & Barry Ryan were the epitome of manipulated mother's boys.

Everything about them, from their carefully styled hair to their tailored mod suits, was totally contrived. They were given a catalogue of songs to record and were put on the bill on every high profile tour their dad took on the road. For two years the brothers enjoyed the sort

BIG NEW HIT FROM
PAUL & BARRY RYAN
KEEP IT OUT OF SIGHT

WRITTEN BY HIT COMPOSER CAT STEVENS

ON DECCA F12567

PAUL AND BARRY RYAN

Sing Les Reed's latest hit

DON'T BRING ME YOUR HEART-ACHES

DECCA

F12260

Paul & Barry Ryan

of exposure groups three times more popular than themselves received; scoring a respectable amount of chart hits, including 'Don't Bring Me Your Heartaches' (December 1965), 'Have Pity On The Boy' (February 1966), 'I Love Her' (June 1966), the Hollies-penned 'Have You Ever Loved Somebody' and a Cat Stevens' song 'Keep It Out Of Sight' (April 1967). Then in 1968 the boys decided to pack it in.

Barry embarked on a solo career and Paul opted to be songwriter, writing the million-selling 'Eloise' (number two in November 1968). Nothing else did anywhere near as good except 'I Will Drink The Wine' which, while not a big seller, was covered by none other than Frank Sinatra. Neither brother managed to sustain their respective careers. During 1969 Barry had an accident, receiving major burns to his face. In the Seventies Paul moved to America and eventually opened a chain of hairdressing salons. He died on 29 November 1992.

WHO ARE THE WAY OUT ONES?

The Score

THE SCORE

The obscure Score took The Beatles 'Please Please Me' and audaciously slowed it down with a soulful backbeat, aggressive fuzz guitars and musical references to both 'Satisfaction' and 'Shapes Of Things'. For such an ambitious approach, both band and record promptly sank upon its release in November '66.

THE SEARCHERS

The Searchers were always more than just another Merseybeat group. While not posing any real threat to The Beatles, from the very beginning, the group established a sound all of their own which saw off any serious competition from their Scouse rivals. Another reason the group looked and sounded more assured than the likes of Gerry & The Pacemakers or Billy J Kramer & The Dakotas, was that they appeared to have no apparent leader. All four members boasted strong singing voices, melding with impeccable harmonies. By successfully combining R&B and folk, The Searchers came up with the jangling harmonic, yet slightly edgy sound now taken for granted as folk rock.

Forming in 1960, guitar players Mike Pender (Pendergast) and John McNally, bass player Tony Jackson and drummer Chris Curtis (Chris Crummey), had all (with the exception of Jackson) been school friends in Liverpool, and had played in various local groups like The Wreckers and The Confederates before joining forces. Taking their name from the 1956 John Wayne western, The Searchers earliest days were spent backing another Liverpool singer, Johnny Sandon.

When this arrangement came to an end the group followed The Beatles to Hamburg in 1962. The Searchers big break was to become the resident band at Liverpool's Iron Door Club, situated at 13 Temple Street. It was here that the group recorded a demo tape of their stage act and sent it to Pye A&R boss Tony Hatch. Hatch signed them up, making The Searchers one of the few Liverpool outfits to slip through Brian Epstein's fingers, thus enabling them to avoid playing second fiddle to the Fab Four. Hatch provided them with some astute material unknown in England, like their first chart topper 'Sweets For My Sweet', originally performed by The Drifters.

Hatch also gave them a composition of his own, 'Sugar And Spice', written under the pseudonym Fred Nightingale. This peaked at number two, and was only kept off the top spot by Gerry & The Pacemakers. By 1963 The Searchers were widely regarded as the second best band, if not in Britain, then certainly in Liverpool. When their classy take on 'Needles And Pins' gave them their second number one it was official. The song had been written by Jack Nitzsche and Sonny Bono for Jackie De Shannon but The Searcher's unique harmonies and twin guitar approach improved on the original and made it their own. It also provided them with their first US Top 20 breakthrough. The band was definitely on a roll. Their next single, 'Don't Throw Your Love Away' (originally by girl group The Orlons), gave them a third number one in April 1964 and followed 'Needles And Pins' into the American Top 20.

Then, at the height of their powers, things started to unravel. Tony Jackson (known as 'Black Jake' due to his mercurial temper) sang lead on the majority of the group's output to 1964 but 'Needles And Pins' and 'Don't Throw Your Love Away' featured Pender's vocal. After various backstage manoeuvrings Jackson finally quit in May. He was replaced by Frank Allen from Cliff Bennett's Rebel Rousers and Pender took over the lead vocal role. After a slight hiccup with 'Someday We're Gonna Love Again', (number eleven, July 1964), the hits continued with 'When You Walk In The Room' – another Jackie de Shannon song which the group made their own with another distinctive 12-string Rickenbacker riff – (number three, September 1964), the folky 'What Have They Done To The Rain?' (number 13, December 1964) and 'Goodbye My Love' (four – March '65). The group were equally popular in America, and received an unexpected Top Five hit there, when 'Love Potion No 9' (recorded when Jackson was still a member) peaked at three in December.

The group tried their hand at writing original material for a tenth single with 'He's Got No Love', a wall of heavily compressed sound which still charted respectably at 12 in July. It would prove to be their last Top 20 placing, however. A cover of Bobby Darin's 'When I Get Home' fared miserably at 35 in October, while a last commendable stab at folk-rock with P.F Sloan's 'Take Me For What I'm Worth' only just made the lowest rung of the Top 20 in December. The fact was the beat boom was over, and to all intents and purposes, had been for some time. R&B and nascent psychedelia were the in-thing and despite still being relatively popular it seemed that The Searchers weren't symptomatic of the times.

Chris Curtis was the next to go after an Australasian tour with The Rolling Stones in March 1966 and was replaced by John Blunt for what was essentially the group's decline. The Stones gave The Searchers the forthcoming *Aftermath* track, 'Take It Or Leave It' but the public chose the latter; reaching 31 in April. A Clarke-Hicks-Nash song, 'Have You Ever Loved Somebody?', also recorded by Paul and Barry Ryan, marked the Searchers last chart entry (number 48 in October)

Pye dropped the band in 1967 after two straight flops, 'Popcorn Double Feature' (later covered in 1989 by The Fall and written by Scott 'Hi Ho Silver Lining' English) and 'Secondhand Dealer'. After a brief but fruitless flirtation with Liberty Records in '68 (including a single under the pseudonym Pasha) the group found themselves back on the club and cabaret circuit. One last line-up change occurred in 1969 when Billy Adamson replaced Johnny Blunt, after which, the group remained pretty much stable throughout the Seventies and Eighties.

Thanks to the Rickenbacker sound being revived, most notably by Tom Petty & The Heartbreakers, the group signed with the relatively hip Sire Records in 1979 and valiantly tried to re-establish themselves as a top name once again. They didn't manage it of course. Today there are two sets of Searchers still doing the rounds: Mike Pender's Searchers and The Searchers featuring John McNally and Frank Allen.

When Tony Jackson left in 1964 he put together a group called The Vibrations, and had a Top 40 single release with a cover of Mary Wells' ' Bye Bye Baby'. This was the first in a string of singles for Pye and CBS between 1964-66, while commercially unsuccessful, were actually strong versions of contemporary numbers. The Tony Jackson Group became popular on the Continent, resulting in a very rare EP release. The group's worthwhile legacy can be sampled on the compilation *Just Like Us* (Bam Caruso 1991). He was last heard of running a golf club in Essex. Chris Curtis released one Pye single, 'Aggravation', in 1966, that promptly sank without trace. The following year he formed Roundabout, featuring ex-Artwoods organist Jon Lord, ex-Outlaws guitarist Ritchie Blackmore, bassist Dave Curtis and ex-Maze and M.I.5 drummer Ian Paice (over his original choice of Bobby Clark). After a short stint in Germany they regrouped without Curtis renaming themselves Deep Purple. Curtis shrugged, and became a civil servant in his native Liverpool.

(see also The Artwoods, Cliff Bennett & The Rebel Rousers, The Flowerpot Men)

THE SENATE

Glasgow soul merchants who could show the Sassenachs a thing or two on how to play punchy R&B, The Senate (Sol Byron, Dave Agnew, Alex Ligerwood, Bob Mather and Tony Rutherford) made a name for themselves on the mid-Sixties club and college circuit backing visiting US artists like Ben E King, who wrote and produced the group's killer single 'Can't Stop'. The Senate also released a live album *The Senate Sock It To You One More Time* on United Artists in 1968, and provided the accompaniment for Garnett Mimms on his UK-recorded 1967 live album.

The Senate

The Sheffields

SHAPES AND SIZES

This five piece group, with a penchant for wearing matching patterned shirts, featured a male-female lead singing duo and an outlandish drummer. They released one poppy single on Decca in 1966, 'A Little Lovin' Something', which, needless to say, did a little lovin' nothing in Britain but saw some chart action in Germany.

Shapes & Sizes

SANDIE SHAW

Her name may have been a bit tongue in cheek but there can be no denying her appeal. Born Sandra Goodrich in Dagenham, Essex, she didn't wear shoes, had great hair and won the 1967 Eurovision Song Contest with 'Puppet On A String' – people have been remembered for a lot less!

Working as a secretary at the Ford car plant, at the age of 17 she bluffed her way backstage at an Adam Faith concert, and sang for him. Faith was impressed by her voice and recommended her to his matriarchal manager Eve Taylor. Signed by Pye Records Sandie's first single 'As Long As You're Happy, Baby' flopped, but the follow-up, a superior reading of Burt Bacharach and Hal David's '(There's) Always Something There To Remind Me', reached number one in October 1964.

With her trademark sultry looks, model height and 'barefoot' TV and concert appearances, she epitomised the style of the Sixties, regularly sporting the latest fashions. Teaming up with Faith's songwriter, fellow Essex native Chris Andrews, Sandie's hit run continued into 1966 with 'Girl Don't Come' (number three-

December 1964), 'I'll Stop At Nothing' (four – February 1965), 'Long Live Love' (her second number one in May '65), 'Message Understood' (six – September '65) and 'Tomorrow' (nine – February '66). Although 'Puppet On A String', her 1967 Eurovision Song Contest entry and her third number one, is arguably the song she will always be remembered for, in later years, Sandie resolutely refused to perform or talk about the song. Like rivals Dusty, Cilla and Lulu, the BBC presented her own series entitled *The Sandie Shaw Supplement* in 1968, but her last substantial hit was 'Monsieur Dupont' in February '69. Having married fashion designer Jeff Banks the year before, Sandie effectively retired from pop music, until 1982 when she recorded with Sheffield electronic merchant's Heaven 17 offshoots BEF. In 1984 Morrissey from The Smiths coaxed her out of retirement to record 'Hand In Glove', with The Smiths backing her, resulting in a memorable *Top Of The Pops* appearance of our Sandra writhing on the studio floor in a black leather miniskirt.

SHOTGUN EXPRESS

A short-lived revue formed in 1966 from the remnants of Steam Packet and The Peter B's. Vocalists Rod Stewart and Scouse warblette Beryl Marsden fronted the band which featured keyboardist Peter Bardens and drummer Mick Fleetwood. The outfit cut two unsuccessful, heavily orchestrated singles for Columbia: 'I Could Feel The Whole World Turn Round' (1966) and 'Funny Cos Neither Could I' (1967) before splitting. Marsden went solo, Stewart joined The Jeff Beck Group, Fleetwood joined John Mayall's Bluesbreakers, while Bardens eventually formed Village.

(see also Brian Auger Trinity, The Jeff Beck Group, The Bo Street Runners, The Cheynes, John Mayall's Bluesbreakers, The Peter B's, Rod Stewart, Steam Packet)

SKIP BIFFERTY

Formerly known as The Chosen Few this Newcastle band (Graham Bell – vocals, John Turnbull – guitar, Mickey Gallagher – keyboards, Colin Gibson – bass and Tommy Jackman – drums) changed their moniker to the odd Skip Bifferty in 1966. The following year they arrived in London, playing the Marquee and ended up signing a management deal with Don Arden.

They released three singles and a self-titled album, produced by future Jam producer Vic Coppersmith-Heaven, for RCA, none of which made any impression, despite being fine examples of the freakbeat-psych genre . 'On Love' was built around a repetitive grungy riff, while their equally powerful final single 'Man In Black', was produced and arranged by Small Faces' Steve Marriott and Ronnie Lane.

The group masqueraded for a while as Heavy Jelly in a vain attempt to get out of Arden's managerial grasp but gave up after one extra flop on Island. Bell, Gallagher, and Turnbull played together in Bell And Arc in the early Seventies. Gallagher also played with Loving Awareness in 1976 before becoming one of Ian Dury's Blockheads.

SMALL FACES

Often dubbed 'the most perfect English pop group', due to their uniformity of height and Mod attire as well as their musical catalogue, The Small Faces are arguably more popular today than in their original Sixties heyday. Their official catalogue, although not particularly huge, consists of three studio albums and 12 singles, and has been the subject of probably the most exhaustive (and exploitative) reissue programme of any band of their era.

Formed in May 1965 in the East End Of London with an original line-up of former child actors Steve Marriott (vocals and guitar) and Jimmy Winston (nee' Langwith) (organ), alongside drummer Kenny Jones and fledgling bass player Ronnie 'Plonk' Lane, whom Marriott met by chance thanks to his job at the J60 musical instrument shop in Manor Park. After only a month together The Small Faces (named by a girl fan because of their dimunitive stature and a Face being a top Mod) were signed by self-styled record biz mogul and wheeler dealer Don Arden to his Contemporary Records organisation. Four months later they had nationwide success with a début single 'What'cha Gonna Do About It' – songwriter Ian Samwell's thinly disguised rewrite of Solomon Burke's 'Everybody Needs Somebody To Love' – at number 14 in the British charts.

Winston's repeated two notes on the record betrayed his true capabilities. The fact that he was taller than the others didn't help his chances either. He was ousted in favour of ex- Muleskinners and Boz People organist, Ian 'Mac' McLagan. As well as being a better musician, more crucially imagewise, he was also the right height! The current single, 'I Got Mine', a hastily self-penned number by Marriott and Lane, interrupted the band's carefully plotted rise to fame by failing to chart. This prompted Arden to insist on outside professional help in the recording of an all-important third single, 'Sha-La-La-Lee', co-written by singer/songwriter Kenny Lynch (who contributed the high-pitched backing vocals) and Mort Shuman, which reached number three in March. Lynch foisted more material upon the reluctant Faces to record, some of which turned up on their self-titled, best selling début album – a hastily recorded but enthusiastic set that captured the excitement of their stage act – released in May. Disaster averted, Marriott and Lane delivered a second self-penned number, 'Hey Girl', that restored confidence by climbing to number 10 the same month.

Three fast months later, with a rabid and frenzied female following, The Small Faces were at number one, knocking no less than The Beatles from the top spot with 'All Or Nothing'. The group were riding high but were less than enthused when a rough mix of a

track 'My Mind's Eye' was released as a fait accompli by Arden – a blow not softened when it ascended to a creditable four on the charts. With 1966 turning into '67 and The Beatles leading the way with studio experimentation, the Faces yearned to get off the gruelling treadmill that was proving lucrative for all but themselves, and spend more time in the controlled setting of the recording studio.

The group ditched Arden and Decca, who responded by issuing an unauthorised single 'Patterns' and album *From The Beginning* – a collection of leftovers stretching back to Jimmy Winston's time with the group. The Small Faces felt compelled to take out music press ads stating 'There Are But Four Small Faces – and There Is Only One Small Faces Album And It's On Immediate Records'. Marriott had known Andrew Oldham since his early days fronting Steve Marriott's Moments. When Oldham, hearing of the Faces' disenchantment, dangled the carrot of creative freedom and unlimited studio time, they jumped at the chance. 'I Can't Make It', recorded for Immediate but issued on Decca as a contractual obligation was followed by classic single after classic single – 'Here Comes The Nice' (a blatant homage to a speed dealer – number 12 in June '67), 'Itchycoo Park' (based on a real life park in the East End – number three in August '67), 'Tin Soldier' (with Immediate songstress P.P Arnold on backing vocals – number nine – January '68), and 'Lazy Sunday' (two – May '68). This last was extracted (against the group's wishes) from the Faces' ground breaking *Ogden's Nut Gone Flake*. Housed in an award winning, innovative round sleeve, resembling a tobacco tin, the entirely self-composed album featured such strong originals like 'Afterglow Of Your Love' (later released as the group's posthumous single) and 'Song Of A Baker' on one side, while the second told the tale through words (courtesy of gobbledegook merchant, the late Stanley Unwin) and music of Happiness Stan. The album went to number one thus putting the band on an equal footing with the best of British, and all within three short years.

And suddenly it was gone. 'The Universal', a Marriott solo record in all but name, failed to rise no higher than sixteen, much to his chagrin. The group's ever restless leader was conscious of the Faces still being regarded as a teenybopper band and was looking to expand their horizons. A move to bring in ex-Herd guitarist Peter Frampton as auxiliary guitarist met with resistance from the other members. Finally, on December 31, 1968, Marriott stormed off stage at the band's New Year's Eve show at the Alexandra Palace and announced he was quitting. He went on to form Humble Pie with Frampton, ex-Spooky Tooth bassist Greg Ridley and Kenny Jones protegé, ex-Apostolic Intervention drummer Jerry Shirley.

The remaining trio toyed with a name change to Slim Chance with Lane as frontman before settling on a replacement for Marriott in the unlikely guise of ex-Jeff Beck bassist Ron Wood. The group expanded to a quintet with another ex-Beck man Rod Stewart on vocals, and after a brief detour as Art Wood's Quiet Melon (with Art

Wood and Kim Gardner), they restyled themselves as The Faces.

Marriott went on to enjoy considerable American success with Humble Pie in the Seventies. When that group disbanded in 1975, he continued with Steve Marriott's All-Stars and various solo projects before being distracted by a short-lived and ill-fated Small Faces reunion with Jones, McLagan and, initially, Lane who was replaced by Rick Wills. When this fell apart in 1978, Marriott returned to America, assembling a new version of Humble Pie. Returning down on his luck to Britain in the mid-Eighties Marriott formed various pub circuit bands, with ex-Fat Mattress bassist Jim Leverton in tow, and occasionally, Shirley on drums. He died tragically in a house fire at his cottage in Arkesden, Essex on April 20, 1991.

Upon leaving The Faces in 1973 Ronnie Lane pursued a nomadic gypsy lifestyle with his bands Slim Chance and Passing Show. He continued to write and record until the debilitating effects of multiple sclerosis brought these activities to a halt. Moving to Texas for treatment he sang with local musicians (including McLagan on occasion) before his battle against MS finally claimed him in Trinidad, Colorado on June 4, 1997.

After the demise of The Faces in 1975 McLagan moved to Los Angeles and the session scene there. He has recorded and toured with The Rolling Stones, Bonnie Raitt, and Bob Dylan amongst others, and is currently part of Billy Bragg's band, The Blokes. Jones replaced Keith Moon in a reconstituted Who in 1978 and played on several mega-grossing American tours. After his time with The Who, he played with ex-Free and Bad Company vocalist Paul Rodgers in The Law. In 1995, with The Small Faces legacy swelling, thanks to praise from the likes of Blur and Oasis, Jones instigated litigation against the various companies responsible for a litany of sub-standard Small Faces reissues from which the band received no profit. The following year, Castle Communications paid a six-figure sum to the ex-members, together with a future royalty agreement. For Marriott and Lane it was too little, too late. *(see also Apostolic Intervention, P.P Arnold, The Herd, Steve Marriott, Steve Marriott's Moments, The Muleskinners, Jimmy Winston's Reflections)*

Small Faces

WHISTLING JACK SMITH

More novelty nonsense, this time from the whistling wonder that was Whistling Jack Smith, aka Billy Moeller, the younger brother of Unit Four Plus Two singer Tommy Moeller. This Liverpudlian chancer had a number five hit in 1967 with an irritating tune that he whistled from start to finish, except he didn't actually whistle it. 'I Was Kaiser Bill's Batman' was in fact the work of a session whistler (!), and what's more it reached number twenty in the US. Smith had a further whistle through 'Havah Nagilah', and an album *Around The World With...* Thankfully none charted.

THE SMOKE

Formerly known as The Shots, The Smoke (Mick Rowley – vocals), Mal Luker and Phil Peacock (guitars), John 'Zeke' Lund (bass) and Geoff Gill – drums) were discovered by Northern millionaire businessman Alan Brush while supporting P J Proby in Yorkshire. The Shots had released one single, 'Keep A Hold Of What You've Got'/ 'She's A Liar' on the Columbia label in 1965, but this failed to impress the record buying public. Peacock dropped out and a name change to The Smoke, the cheerful northern terminology for London and a nudge-nudge nod to certain substances, saw the four-piece band remain with Columbia. Their first release was 'My Friend Jack', a coy reference to the voguish habit of putting drops of liquid LSD on sugar lumps. The distinctive whiplash guitar sound, achieved through optimum use of the tremelo knob, could only reach number 45 in March 1967 but the single was a huge hit in Germany (later being covered by Boney M of all people) where the band redirected their energies.

TV, radio, and press followed and the band embarked on successful tours of the Fatherland. Their German-only 1967 album release, *It's Smoke Time*, featured several tracks in a similar freakbeat vein, including 'I Want To Make It With You', and 'High In A Room' – another sly tale of swinging London, bust-fearing potsmokers.

The drugs weren't working because The Smoke's UK follow-up single to 'My Friend Jack' was the ghastly 'If The Weather's Sunny'. The Smoke's future looked cloudy when the single flopped and the group were dropped. Moving to Chris Blackwell's Island label in late '67 they released 'I'm Only Dreaming' under the pseudonym Chords Five. The band also underwent a complete image change from sharp Mod to far out psychedelia, a move that utterly confused what audience they had left. A swift name change back to, simply, Smoke, for 'It Could Be Wonderful' and a final unreleased single – a cover of Traffic's 'Utterly Simple' – were to no avail.

Lund, Luker and Gill fell back on session work for producer Monty Babson's Morgan Blue Town label, while several early Seventies singles credited to 'Smoke' appeared on various labels, with only a loose connection to the original line-up.

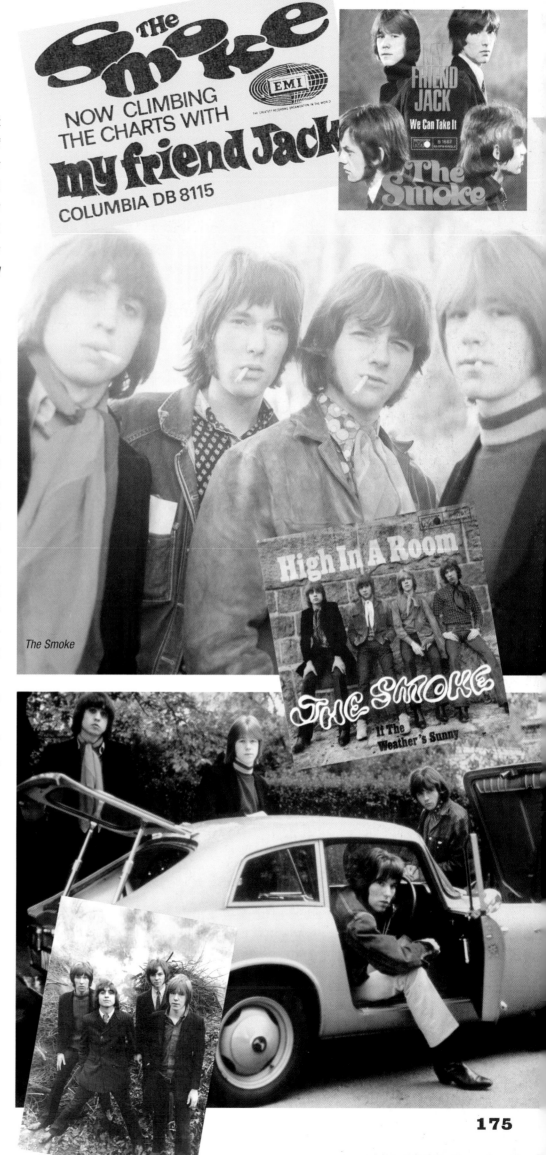

The Smoke

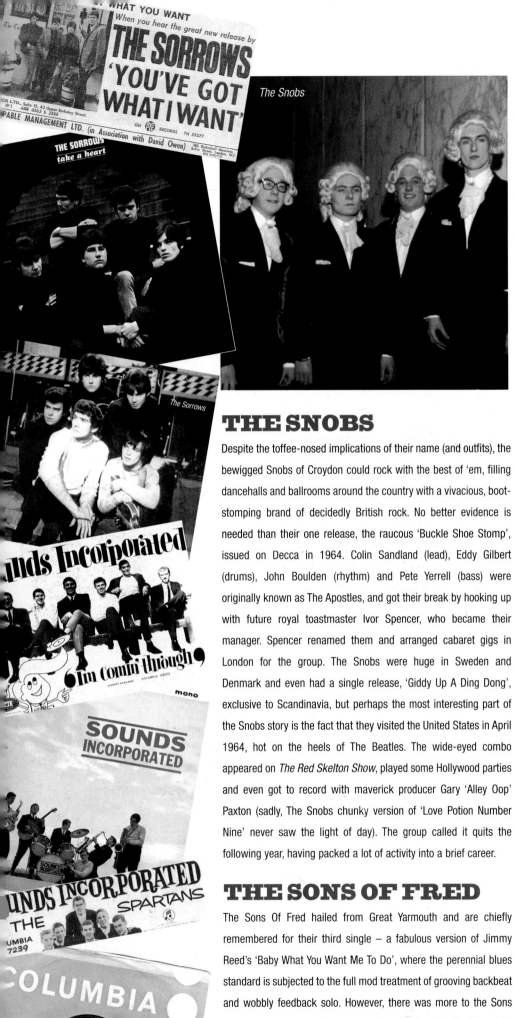

The Snobs

The Sorrows

THE SORROWS

Coventry's Sorrows were another in a long line of mid Sixties outfits who deserved more than the brief (and minor) success they achieved. Formed in 1963, the group (Don Maughn – vocals, Pip Whitcher and Wez Price - guitars, Philip Packham - bass and Bruce Finley – drums) were signed up in Pye's sweep of the country's budding beat groups. However it was this glut of signings that undermined the group's potential longevity.

The group were paired up with songwriter Miki Dallon, whose compositions 'I Don't Wanna Be Free' and 'Baby' (based on The Mojos 'Everythings Alright' staccato rhythm) were released as their first two unsuccessful Piccadilly singles. For their next two attempts The Sorrows transformed 'Take a Heart' and 'You Got What I Want' into 'freakbeat' classics. (Both had already been recorded in embryonic form by The Boys Blue as an HMV single released in May 1965). 'Take A Heart', with its unusual pulse-like beat and throbbing bass, reached number twenty one when released in September 1965. However the raging 'You Got What I Want' flopped completely, and like other Pye outfits such as The Primitives and The Riot Squad, The Sorrows failed to get their fair share of the label's attention. The Sorrows' only English album, inevitably named *Take A Heart*, is an excellent collection of tough-edged Mod pop but didn't sell well at the time and is now substantially rare.

Maughn left in 1967 after the Sorrows run of consistently high standard singles failed to achieve a foothold. Undaunted, the rest of the band carried on; recruiting organ player Chris Fryers and relocating to their most popular territory, Italy. Once there, it was a different story and the group scored several Italian only hits that saw them though to their split in 1970.

Under his alter-ego Don Fardon, Maughn saw chart action (number three) with a cover of John D. Loudermilk's 'Indian Reservation' in 1970 – also covered in the US by The Raiders (without Paul Revere).

THE SNOBS

Despite the toffee-nosed implications of their name (and outfits), the bewigged Snobs of Croydon could rock with the best of 'em, filling dancehalls and ballrooms around the country with a vivacious, boot-stomping brand of decidedly British rock. No better evidence is needed than their one release, the raucous 'Buckle Shoe Stomp', issued on Decca in 1964. Colin Sandland (lead), Eddy Gilbert (drums), John Boulden (rhythm) and Pete Yerrell (bass) were originally known as The Apostles, and got their break by hooking up with future royal toastmaster Ivor Spencer, who became their manager. Spencer renamed them and arranged cabaret gigs in London for the group. The Snobs were huge in Sweden and Denmark and even had a single release, 'Giddy Up A Ding Dong', exclusive to Scandinavia, but perhaps the most interesting part of the Snobs story is the fact that they visited the United States in April 1964, hot on the heels of The Beatles. The wide-eyed combo appeared on *The Red Skelton Show*, played some Hollywood parties and even got to record with maverick producer Gary 'Alley Oop' Paxton (sadly, The Snobs chunky version of 'Love Potion Number Nine' never saw the light of day). The group called it quits the following year, having packed a lot of activity into a brief career.

THE SONS OF FRED

The Sons Of Fred hailed from Great Yarmouth and are chiefly remembered for their third single – a fabulous version of Jimmy Reed's 'Baby What You Want Me To Do', where the perennial blues standard is subjected to the full mod treatment of grooving backbeat and wobbly feedback solo. However, there was more to the Sons than that; the group had an excellent earlier single for Columbia, 'Sweet Love'/'I'll Be There', and were a popular attraction on the south coast in the mid-Sixties. They changed their name to The Odyssey for a nondescript release on the Strike label in 1966, and later still evolved into the duo Tandem.

SOUNDS INCORPORATED

If this lot had been American they could have found fame as top-flight session musicians, in the same vein as the West Coast's fondly namechecked 'Wrecking Crew'. As it is they've ended up as a musical footnote primarily for their Beatles association.

A sad state of affairs because Sounds Incorporated were a prolific recording outfit in their own right, featuring guitarist John Gilliard, bassist Wes Hunt, and a brass section of Barrie Cameron, Alan Holmes and Griff West. Like the Mike Cotton Sound the sextet were a popular London-based showband and had also done the inevitable Hamburg stint, backing Gene Vincent, where they crossed paths with you know who. In 1963, they were signed to Brian Epstein's NEMS organisation to back such Epstein protégé's as Cilla Black and Tommy Quickly, and

were offered a recording contract in their own right with EMI Columbia. The group managed to hit the charts twice in 1964; number 30 with 'The Spartans' and 35 with 'Spanish Harlem'.

However it's the Fabs connection that interests most. They appeared together on a Jack Good-produced TV special *Around The Beatles* in May 1964, and a month later, undertook a world tour of Denmark, Holland, Hong Kong, Australia and New Zealand as the Fab Four's support act. Their exuberant supporting stage antics were immortalised in the film documenting the Beatles' historic concert at New York's Shea Stadium in August 1965. In 1967, the horn section were called in to Abbey Road to provide the beefy brass on John Lennon's blistering *Sgt Pepper* contribution 'Good Morning, Good Morning'.

But by then instrumental bands had become passé and the Incorporated's individual members went their own way. Newman achieved a higher profile later with his work drumming for Jeff Beck, David Bowie and Marc Bolan.

(see also Jeff Beck Group)

SPOOKY TOOTH

Spooky Tooth (singer-pianist Mike Harrison, Luther Grosvenor – guitar, Greg Ridley – bass and Mike Kellie – drums) evolved out of the ashes of Island group The V.I.P.'s who in turn became Art; the only non-original member being American keyboard player Gary Wright.

The group started off with the US West Coast psych-sounding 'Sunshine Help Me' (a favourite underground non-hit) and two critically acclaimed yet poor selling albums *Its All About A Roundabout* (1968) and *Spooky Two* (1969) before the first of numerous line up changes shook their stability.

First to depart was Greg Ridley (joining Humble Pie) in 1969 to be replaced by Andy Leigh, whose first contribution to the band was heard on the disastrous *Ceremony* album (1969). This was an experimental collaboration with French electronics boffin Pierre Henry that was considered so woeful the Tooth temporarily broke up. The group reformed shortly thereafter and continued to release several albums with a variety of line-ups, alongside concurrent solo activities, until finally calling it a day in 1974.

Grosvenor joined Stealers Wheel and then Mott the Hoople where he went under the zany appellation Ariel Bender. Wright enjoyed several years of solo success in the States. Kellie played in Frampton's Camel and The Only Ones, while Ridley remained with Humble Pie until they disintegrated in 1975.

(see also Art, The VIPs)

DUSTY SPRINGFIELD

Possibly the UK's finest white female soul singer, Dusty was born Mary Isabel Catherine Bernadette O'Brien in Hampstead, London. After singing with The Lana Sisters and her brother Tom's folk trio The Springfields, a visit to New York and exposure to The Exciters' classic 'Tell Him' made clear the solo direction she wanted to pursue. Her first hit, 'I Only Want To Be With You' reached number four at the end of 1963 and carved a path of eight further classic Top 10 hits between 1964 and 1969. These included 'I Just Don't Know What To Do With Myself', 'In The Middle Of Nowhere', 'Some Of Your Lovin'' and a number one million seller with 'You Don't Have To Say You Love Me' – an English translation of an Italian lyric – in April 1966.

Dusty became a Sixties icon with her familiar beehive blonde hairstyle and dark 'panda' eye mascara. She frequently won 'Top Female Singer' awards, outdistancing contemporaries like Cilla, Sandie and Lulu, while championing the cause of black American soul and R&B in Britain; hosting a special 'The Sound Of Motown' edition of *Ready, Steady, Go!* in 1965. In 1967 she moved unsteadily into the world of light entertainment with her own shows for the BBC and ITV.

In 1968, Dusty teamed up with Atlantic Records' production geniuses Tom Dowd, Jerry Wexler and Arif Mardin, to record the classic *Dusty In Memphis* album, which included 'Son Of A Preacher Man', later used to great effect in Quentin Tarantino's film noir *Pulp Fiction* in 1994. It was also Dusty's last Top 10 hit until her acclaimed collaboration with The Pet Shop Boys, 'What Have I Done To Deserve This', reached number two in 1987. Throughout the Seventies and Eighties, Dusty kept a low profile, relocating to Los Angeles for failed comebacks while battling with her personal demons. She returned to Britain in the Eighties and sporadically resumed her recording career, still boasting that fine voice, but her interesting but turbulent life was cut short with her tragic death from cancer on March 2, 1999.

STATUS QUO

The first (and best) Quo line-up featured Francis Rossi (guitar/vocals), Rick Parfitt (born Richard Harrison (guitar/vocals), Rob Lynes (organ), Alan Lancaster (bass) and John Coghlan (drums). The group made their live début at the Samuel Jones sports club in 1962 calling themselves The Spectres. They continued to play working men's clubs for two years until a gas fitter by the name of Pat Barlow offered to manage them and arranged a Monday night residency at the Cafe des Artists in London's Brompton Road, and a support gig with The Hollies. In 1965 the group accepted a four month contract at Butlins, and the following year they were introduced to Pye recording manager John Schroeder. The group signed to Pye subsidiary Piccadilly, and released their first single, 'I (Who Have Nothing)', which failed to chart.

The next two singles, 'Hurdy Gurdy Man' (no relation to the Donovan song of the same name) and 'We Ain't Got Nothin' Yet' (a note-for-note cover of the Blues Magoos' US hit) were both flops and in February of '67, the group changed their name to Traffic Jam, under which name they released the aptly-titled 'Almost But Not Quite There', which the BBC banned on suggestive grounds. Around the same time Steve Winwood left The Spencer Davis Group and

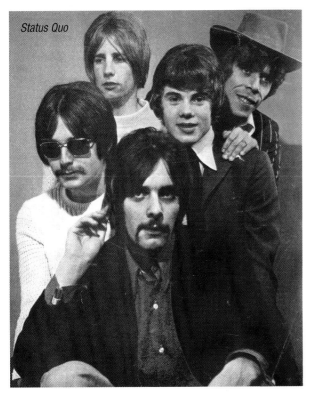

Status Quo

formed Traffic, so Barlow suggested another name change, this time to Status Quo.

After a stint working as Madeline Bell's backing group, the Quo's first Pye release was 'Pictures Of Matchstick Men' in January 1968. With its distinctive phased riff and catchy chorus the song caught on immediately and rose to number seven the following month. The South Londoners became a frequent sight on *Top Of The Pops* with their Mod coiffures and Carnaby Street clobber. On April 5, the band began a 28-date UK tour with Gene Pitney, Amen Corner, Don Partridge, and Simon Dupree & The Big Sound. A follow-up, 'Black Veils Of Melancholy' was too stylistically similar to 'Matchstick Men' and flopped completely; causing great alarm within the group. An outside source, Marty Wilde contributed the poppy 'Ice In the Sun' which restored them to the Top 10 in September but until an image makeover beckoned, the going would be rough. All five albums the group recorded for Pye – *Picturesque Matchstickable Messages*, *Spare Parts*, *Status Quotations*, *Ma Kelly's Greasy Spoon* and *Dog Of Two Heads* – failed to sell in great quantities, while 'Make Me Stay A Bit Longer', 'Are You Growing Tired Of My Love?', and a slowed-down heavy version of The Everly Brothers' 'The Price Of Love' fared equally dismally. Seeing the writing on the wall the group's sound became much heavier and their hair longer. Quo Mark II were launched with 'Down The Dustpipe', which restored their fortunes in 1970.

Today, they are still actively touring (15 years after their farewell shows!) but sadly, they no longer resemble the great act they once

were. Only Rossi and Parfitt remain from the original Sixties and Seventies line-up. In 1995, they returned to Butlins for a thirtieth anniversary concert. In truth, Butlins is now where they belong.

STEAM PACKET

This ambitious R&B package was like an early 'search for a star' road show. It lasted for less than a year, didn't release any records (although some studio demos & live material appeared in the Seventies) and yet it honed the careers of some of Britain's most distinguished musicians and performers. After their brief stints with the rolling revue all three vocalists resumed what until then had been flagging or non-existent solo careers, only to find they now had a solid audience and fan base on which to build. Long John Baldry went it alone, Julie Driscoll kept her solo option open but also teamed up with organist Brian Auger, in another version of his previous band The Trinity, while Rod Stewart, the most stage-nervous of the three, opted for another group set-up and joined Shotgun Express. Those who also served were Rick Brown, Micky Waller, and Vic Briggs.

(see also Brian Auger's Trinity, Long John Baldry, Eric Burdon & The New Animals, Jeff Beck Group, Cyril Davies R&B All-Stars, Julie Driscoll, Shotgun Express, Rod Stewart)

CAT STEVENS

Many years before Yusuf Islam began his teaching career at a North London Islamic school in 1979, he was known to millions as Cat Stevens, recording star. Stevens, a young Londoner born of Swedish/Greek extraction whose real name was Steven Georgiou, released his first Top 30 45, 'I Love My Dog' in October 1966 for Decca's new avant-garde label Deram. He followed this with two further, self-composed Top 10 hits 'Matthew And Son' (number two), and 'I'm Gonna Get Me A Gun' (number six) but his good luck chart streak ended when the ambitious 'A Bad Night' stuttered to 20, while 'Kitty' only just scraped into the Top 50. Three final flops for Deram followed, before serious health problems forced his withdrawal from public view in 1969.

He would re-emerge a year later with 'Lady D'Arbanville' as Cat Stevens Mk II, a sensitive troubadour much admired by women of all ages, and embark on an equally successful run of albums and singles throughout the Seventies. He then found the Muslim faith and became Yusuf Islam, denounced his musical roots, grew a long beard and turned over his royalties to Islamic education.

Recorded by STATUS QUO on Cadet Records

Ice In The Sun
Words and Music by MARTY WILDE and RONNIE SCOTT

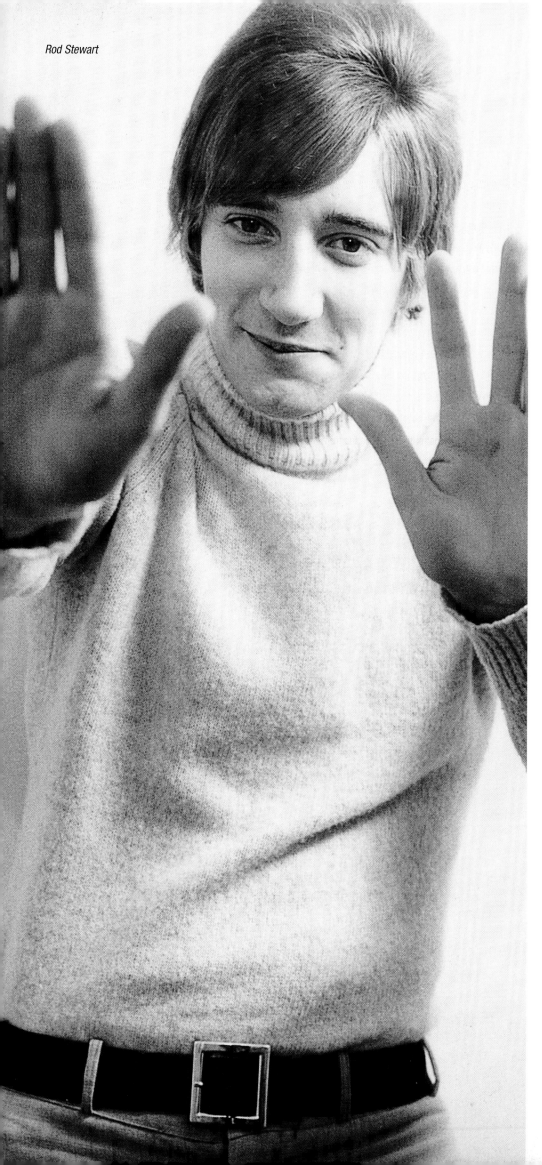

Rod Stewart

THE PAUL STEWART MOVEMENT

Formerly singer with London soul combo Hamilton's Movement (aka Hamilton & The Hamilton Movement), Stewart branched out on his own with a single, 'Queen Boadicea' on Philips (1966) and 'Too Too Good' – his only Decca release in 1967.

ROD STEWART

Roderick David Stewart was born in London of Scottish parents and from 1964 to 1969 he served his musical apprenticeship in The Hoochie Coochie Men (with Long John Baldry), Steam Packet (alongside Baldry, Julie Driscoll and Brian Auger), and Shotgun Express (with Beryl Marsden) and the Jeff Beck Group (with Beck and Ron Wood). In 1964, Rod The Mod's début solo single – a jazzy, Georgie Fame take on 'Good Morning Little Schoolgirl' was released; recorded contemporaneously in a more bluesy fashion by The Yardbirds. Decca dropped the spiky haired one and an equally unsuccessful stint at Columbia produced the Spectoresque pop of 'The Day Will Come' (1965) and a cover of his idol Sam Cooke – 'Shake' (1966). He was highly regarded within the music industry and the distinctive rasp of his voice had him regularly featured as a session singer for Immediate Records.

In 1967, Stewart covered a Mike d'Abo composition, 'Little Miss Understood' but the single got lost amongst Immediate's erratic output (Stewart also went on to record d'Abo's 'Handbags And Gladrags'; made successful in 2001 by The Stereophonics). Rod's biggest break came when he joined The Jeff Beck Group as their lead singer. During May and June of 1968, the group toured America for six weeks, including concerts at New York's Fillmore East, San Francisco's Fillmore West, Detroit's Grande Ballroom and Los Angeles' Shrine Auditorium. Rod received standing ovations at each. Executives from Mercury Records were so impressed with Rod's vocals that in 1969 they signed him as a solo artist, with Lou Reizner producing.

In June of that year, Stewart teamed up with Ian McLagan, Ronnie Lane and Kenny Jones, of The Small Faces, and former Bird Ronnie Wood. Shortening their name to The Faces, they signed to Warner Brothers and made their concert début at Cambridge University as Art Wood's Quiet Melon, supplemented by Ronnie's elder brother Art, and another ex-Bird Kim Gardner. The Faces would go on to great success in the Seventies, though the increasing popularity of Rod's solo work eventually estranged him from the rest of the group. *(see also Long John Baldry, Jeff Beck Group, Shotgun Express, Steampacket)*

THE SWINGING BLUE JEANS

Formed from the ashes of various Merseyside skiffle groups The Swinging Blue Jeans' key members, singer guitarist Ray Ennis, second guitar Ralph Ellis, bass player Les Braid, and drummer Norman Kuhlke got together as early as 1959.

They had already held residencies as The Bluegenes, in Liverpool's Cavern Club and Hamburg's Star Club before changing their name to The Swinging Blue Jeans in 1963.

The advent of the Beatles and the Merseybeat boom that followed them was undoubtedly significant at the time. It may also have been a contributing factor in the group's subsequent singing to EMI's HMV label but it didn't guarantee success. The SBJ's début single 'It's To Late Now' only just made it into the Top 30, and their second, 'Do You Know?' ominously missed the charts altogether.

Luckily fate dealt the group a couple of lucky breaks. Firstly Levi's jeans sponsored the group's own weekly radio show 'Swingtime' on Radio Luxembourg. Secondly the group appeared in a cameo role in the Xmas Day 1963 edition of the top rated TV show *Z Cars*. Naturally such heightened exposure took the group's third single, a cover of Chan Romero's 'Hippy Hippy Shake' straight to the number two spot in January '64. Accusations of fluke or bandwagon jumping safely averted the group attempted to repeat the process by covering Little Richard's 'Good Golly Miss Molly' as a follow up. This nonetheless worked to a certain degree making number 11 in the UK and in the US at 24 in March.

A touch of restraint came into play next with a cover of Betty Everett's 'You're No Good' which did better by reaching number

three in July '64. A string of less successful singles followed before Ellis ruined the group's identity by unexpectedly quitting in 1965, being replaced by by ex-Escorts member Terry Sylvester in January '66. A decent cover of the Dionne Warwick hit 'Don't Make Me Over' almost made the Top 30 that year but was their last chart contender. Bands like The Swinging Blue Jeans and their ilk had quite simply failed to keep abreast of the times. Even the group's name sounded antiquated. They did try a name change in 1967 to Music Motor but this only hastened their journey to obscurity.

A compromise resulted in the frankly desperate sounding Ray Ennis & The Blue Jeans, who released one dreadful single 'What Have They Done To Hazel?', but this did nothing to stop the inevitable. In January 1969 Sylvester took the career lifeline of replacing Graham Nash in The Hollies and effectively the band were finished. As Blue Jeans the Columbia single 'Hey Mrs Housewife' was basically a last wash cycle for what had been The Swinging Blue Jeans.

Ennis and Kuhlke formed a new Swinging Blue Jeans line up in 1973 and like most of the fallen bands from that era created a new career as a cabaret attraction. Sylvester stayed with The Hollies until 1981 when he began a solo career, achieving some success in Germany. He had already released an album *I Believe* in 1974. Ennis still fronts a version of the band today. *(see also The Escorts)*

The Swinging Blue Jeans

181

Studio Six

St. Louis Union

The Syndicats

St. Valentine's Day Massacre

THE SYN

Formed in North London in 1965, The Syn (originally The Selfs) featured Steve Nardelli (vocals), Andrew Jackman (keyboards), Chris Squire (bass). Peter Banks (guitar), and Ray Steele (drums). The group were signed to Decca's progressive subsidiary and released two 1967 singles: 'Created By Clive' which was easily outshone, by it's moody, Who-like B-side 'Grounded' and 'Flowerman'/'14 Hour Technicolour Dream' – an unashamed cash-in all things flowery at the start of the Summer of Love. The Syn were one of the many bands to appear at the legendary event immortalised on the B-side and became a popular club attraction at the Marquee and the UFO. When the group broke up that year, Squire and eventually Banks hooked up with Jon Anderson (ex-Warriors) to form Yes in 1968.

The Syn

THE SYNDICATS

The Syndicats (Tom Ladd – vocals, Steve Howe – guitar, Kevin Driscoll – bass, and Johnny Melton – drums) from London were formed in 1963. Their first single, a cover of Chuck Berry's 'Maybelline', issued in March 1964, was the first of three Columbia singles produced by Joe Meek. Their second single, the raw R&B of 'Howlin' For My Baby' was promoted with an appearance on BBC-2's *The Beat Room* in October '64 but got lost in the deluge of maracca-shakin' R&B hairies. When their third single, a cover of Little Willie John's 'Leave My Kitten alone' was rejected by EMI in mid-65, Ladd was replaced by Johnny Lamb while Howe quit to join The In Crowd and was replaced by Ray Fenwick. It is Fenwick's storming, abrasive, metallic lead runs that stamp all over 'Crawdaddy Simone' – the B-side of a cover of Ben E. King's 'On The Horizon', the third and final Syndicats single, released in September '65. 'Crawdaddy Simone' will ensure The Syndicats cherished place in the affections of freakbeat conneisseurs.

(see also The Four Plus One, The In Crowd, Tomorrow)

Tales Of Justine

Ten Feet

at your record counter today

TEN FEET
Got everything
but love
RCA 1544

**KATE
SMITH**
What kind of fool
am I?
RCA 1546

RCA VICTOR

**THE
GO LUCKY
FOUR**
Off to Dublin in
the green
MD 1058

emerald
45 rpm records

The Decca Record Company Ltd. Decca
House Albert Embankment London S E 1

TALES OF JUSTINE

Tales of Justine were reputedly among the earliest British groups to espouse a self-consciously psychedelic style. The Hertfordshire combo recorded one pleasant if unremarkable Donovan-esque single 'Albert' on HMV in 1967, produced by then-EMI staffer and future Knight Tim Rice but tended to perform meatier fare at the underground haunts of London. Rice was impressed enough by singer David Daltrey to later include him in the rock opera he was producing with associate Andrew Lloyd Webber – *Joseph & His Amazing Technicolour Dreamcoat*.

TEN FEET

An obscure five piece that recorded a pair ofbeat 45s 'Got Everything But Love' (RCA 1966) and 'Shot On Sight' for CBS (1967).

TEN FOOT FIVE

A five piece from Andover, Hampshire, The Ten Feet Five (Dave Smith –vocals, Chris Penfound and Chris Britton – guitars, Pete Staples – bass, and John Hayward – drums) who recorded a solitary single, 'Baby's Back In Town', for Fontana in 1965. Guitarist Britton and bassist Staples were poached by rival Andover band The Troggs.

(see also The Troggs)

THEE

Legend has it that this Hampstead group were discovered by the late Reg King, notorious hardman chauffeur to Rolling Stones' maven Andrew Loog Oldham. Certainly King is credited on the label to the group's sole 1965 Decca release, a dramatic Jagger/Richard composition 'Each And Every Day' (the Jagger-sung demo of which appeared on the Stones' 1975 *Metamorphosis* collection). Group member Andy Mitchell penned the flipside 'There You Go'; unremarkable except for a marvellously inept guitar break.

The T-Bones

Thee

Ten Years After

Them

THEM

One theory behind the naming of Belfast's favourite sons Them, is that Van Morrison changed the line up so often he never bothered to get to know anybody. Well that's my belief anyway. Perhaps a more plausible explanation can be attributed to the Fifties sci-fi horror flick *Them*.

Blues and jazz purist Morrison (vocals/harmonica/sax) had sung in Germany with an R&B group The Monarchs in 1963. Returning to Belfast, he hooked up with like-minded souls Billy Harrison (guitar), Alan Henderson (bass), and Ronnie Mellings (drums) to form the first of many line-ups of Them.

The group started a lauded residency at the Maritime Hotel, converting the regulars to the likes of Ray Charles, Bobby Bland, Sonny Boy Williamson, Jimmy Reed and John Lee Hooker. Eric Wrixen was added on keyboards and Them's Maritime marathons became big news around town, reaching the unlikely ears of The Bachelors' manager Phil Solomon. Solomon recommended the group to infamous Decca A&R man Dick ('don't mention The Beatles…') Rowe, who liked what he saw and heard and arranged a recording audition in London on July 5, 1964.

They recorded seven demos in a bid to find a début single and released the most un-commercial, a cover of Slim Harpo's 'Don't Start Crying Now' and a Morrison original 'One Two Brown Eyes' on the flip. Released in September, the single flopped totally on the mainland but predictably went down well in loyal Belfast. Rowe sidelined the surly band members after this session and brought in players like Jimmy Page to back Morrison on the follow up; a cover of Big Joe Williams' 'Baby Please Don't Go' which reached number ten in January '65. The B-side, 'Gloria', recorded at the July session, was a stomping simplistic three-chord anthem.

Along with 'Louie Louie' and 'Twist And Shout' it became an American garage rock staple, providing a hit for Chicago's The Shadows Of Knight in 1966, who toned down the lewd lyrics for radio play. New-found pop success sat uneasily on the group's shoulders, and journalists came to rue interviewing the broody Belfast bunch. The pressures of playing one-nighters resulted in the first upheaval when Wrixen and Mellings were respectively replaced by brothers Jackie and Patrick McAuley.

An EP consisting of both sides of their first 45 along with 'Baby Please Don't Go' and 'Philosophy' bridged the gap between releases, in February. The American producer Bert Burns who listed among his numerous credits 'Hang On Sloopy' by The McCoys, 'Under The Boardwalk' by The Drifters and co-writing 'Twist And Shout' was brought in next. The result was Berns own 'Here Comes The Night' (previously recorded by Lulu & The Luvvers), a number two smash hit classic in April 1965. Berns hung around long enough to produce an unsuccessful single '(It Won't Hurt) Half As Much' and 'Little Girl' included on the group's self-titled début album; a raw document unhampered by Decca's sterile production, released in June. That same month, the follow-up to 'Here Comes The Night', the soulful,

passionate 'One More Time' failed to chart, causing panic among the Decca top brass and more line-up chaos within the truculent team. Peter Bardens (ex-Cheynes) replaced Jackie McAuley in April for a six-month stint before leaving to form The Peter B's; his place being taken by Belfast native Ray Elliott. Patrick McAuley was sent packing in July to make way for Terry Noon. (The McAuley brothers then formed The Belfast Gypsies). The normally steadfast Billy Harrison was replaced by Jerry Boni before Morrison and Henderson went the whole hog and sacked the whole band in September '65.

While Morrison and Henderson retreated back to Belfast to consider their next move, Decca released 'Mystic Eyes' – the wild, powerful bluesy instrumental with an impromptu rap from Van towards the song's fade that opened the group's début album – as a single in November 1965; a move that incensed Morrison. Morrison and Henderson returned to London with a new Them line-up of Jim Armstrong (guitar), Ray Elliott (keyboards), and John Wilson (drums). This line up – apart from Wilson who was replaced by David Harvey – appeared on the sleeve of *Them Again*, the group's second album, released in January, 1966 and widely acknowledged to be once again the work of session men. Producer Tommy Scott had cobbled the album together from various sessions, which reflected a more stylistic diversity than the group's raw, untamed début. Although punkers like 'I Can Only Give You Eveything' and conventional R&B covers were included, more reflective material like 'Hey Girl' and Could You, Would You' indicated Morrison's future direction. Four solo solo tracks, including the equally distinctive 'Friday's Child' later dribbled out on various B-sides and a Dutch only EP.

By early '66 Them's situation reached farcical levels when a bogus Them, consisting of ousted ex-members, were competing for bookings. The real Them's manager, Phil Solomon, slapped a lawsuit on Reg Calvert and Terry King, the pair behind these shenanigans. In a tit for tat situation, when Calvert registered the name Them Ltd., Solomon took the names of Calvert's prize acts The Fortunes and Pinkerton's Assorted Colours, and furthermore, demanded Decca pay him their due royalties! Decca directly intervened, forcing Calvert to back down.

The original Them imploded after two last gasp singles – 'Call My Name' (released March '66) and a cover of Paul Simon's 'Richard Cory' (May '66), plus a disastrous US tour, which started in New York in April and ended up on the West Coast a month later, playing a residency at the Whiskey-A Go-Go, on the same bill as Captain Beefheart and The Doors. Eyewitness accounts testify to a unique 20 minute rendition of 'Gloria' with the two Morrison's trading verses.

On returning to England to find 'Richard Cory' had been released as an A-side, instead of his choice of 'Mighty Like A Rose', it was the last straw for Morrison who quit and returned to Ireland. Them regrouped in Los Angeles without Morrison. Henderson, who had done well to last the distance, was now at the helm and Belfast

singer Ken McDowell (from Them's Maritime Hotel support The Madlads) was brought in to replace Morrison. The new-look Them recorded two albums for the US Tower label *Now And Them* (1968) and *Time Out, Time In For Them* (1968), the second without Ray Elliott who kept the spirit of Them alive by quitting and returning to Ireland. Eventually the group disintegrated with only Henderson stubbornly clinging on to the Them mantle, making two more albums for the Happy Tiger label, *Them* (1970) and *In Reality* (1971), featuring hired LA session men like Jerry Cole, Ry Cooder and Jack Nitzsche. *(see also The Belfast Gypsies, The Wheels)*

subsequently become a firm favourite on the Mod/soul club scene). Three more Deram singles, including the languid psych B-side 'Gone Is The Sad Man' all flopped and in 1969, the members regrouped (without Holmes) as progressive rockers Patto.

When Patto split after three albums in 1973 Mike Patto spent time with Spooky Tooth, and made the occasional appearance with Tim Hinkley and John Halsey in Hinkley's Heroes before lymphatic leukaemia claimed him in 1979.

Halsall continued to be an in-demand guitarist, playing in Tempest and Boxer, where he was reunited with Patto, alongside ex-Sounds Incorporated and Jeff Beck Group drummer Tony Newman. Halsall formed a partnership with Kevin Ayers, and worked with John Halsey on *The Rutles* soundtrack in 1977 (the latter played drummer Barry Wom in the film), before a life of hard living finally caught up with him in 1992. Bad luck continued to curse the ex-members. Halsey and Griffiths were involved in a serious road accident in 1983, resulting in the latter's semi-paralysis and memory loss. A recuperated Halsey runs a pub in Suffolk.

Tintern Abbey

Timebox

TIMEBOX

Timebox were formed at Southport Art College in 1966 by bass player Clive Griffiths, Albino pianist Chris Holmes, and guitarist Peter 'Ollie' Halsall. Moving to London, they encountered ex-Bo Street Runner and Chicago Line Band singer Michael Patrick 'Patto' McCarthy. Joining in the venture were ex-Felder's Orioles drummer John Halsey.

Originally signed to the Piccadilly label for two unsuccessful singles, 'I'll Always Love You' and a cover of Cal Tjader's 'Soul Sauce' they switched to Deram in 1967. Their first release for the label, a cover of Tim Hardin's 'Don't Make Promises' (featuring Halsall on sitar) was another flop but 'Beggin' (a cover of The Four Seasons' US hit) clocked up a minor hit at number 38 in July 1968. (It has

TINTERN ABBEY

A short-lived psychedelic outfit (singer David MacTavish, Dan Smith –guitar, Stuart MacKay – bass, and John Dalton – drums) that survived less than a year but managed a one off highly collectable 1967 Deram single – the psychedelic 'Beeside', and its tough Who-like B-side 'Vacuum Cleaner'. Smith was replaced by Paul Brett and the group were due to issue a second Deram single 'How Do I Feel Today'. Brett went on to form The Paul Brett sage with members of Fire. *(see also Fire)*

Tomorrow

TOMORROW

Tomorrow were one of the leading psychedelic creations of 1967. Their roots lay in a host of mid-Sixties R&B groups: The Syndicats (featuring Steve Howe), The In Crowd (previously known as Four + One, with Keith West and bassist John 'Junior' Wood) and The Fairies (with drummer John 'Twink' Alder). In 1966, The In Crowd, now featuring Howe and Alder, dropped their repertoire of soul covers and changed their name to Tomorrow.

After failing to get the gig as the walk-on band in Antonioni's swinging Sixties thriller, *Blow Up*, despite demoing two songs for the film, the group became popular on London's nascent underground scene, playing at the launch party for the underground newspaper *International Times* in October 1966.

This in turn led to a regular residency at the UFO Club on Tottenham Court Road – the focal point for hippie happenings in the capital in 1967. The group also secured an EMI deal with Mark Wirtz, through West's association with the German producer. Wirtz was planning an ambitious project entitled 'A Teenage Opera', that was to involve a film and a double album, and west was brought in to assist. The enterprise was to have repercussions on Tomorrow's longevity.

In May, Tomorrow's début single, 'My White Bicycle' was released but failed to chart despite being one of the most evocative psychedelic releases from that halcyon year. The song was inspired by the owner-less bicycles distributed around liberal Amsterdam as an environmental/anti-automobile statement by the Provo political organisation. The record was completely overshadowed by 'Excerpt From A Teenage Opera' – produced by Wirtz and written and sung by West with a children's choir. The record reached number two in August.

Tomorrow's next studio venture was 'Revolution', a song written in response to the events surrounding the Rolling Stones' recent drug trials, and released as a single in September. Once again it failed to chart. Despite playing tours with Pink Floyd and Jimi Hendrix, and the Christmas On Earth Revisited event at the Olympia, Kensington in December, the group failed to gain a higher profile. This state of affairs was compounded by the group's hastily-recorded, self-titled début album being released about six months too late in February 1968. By then the group had splinted off to do various solo recordings; Alder and Wood recorded '10,000 Words In A Cardboard Box' as Aquarian Age. Howe recorded an unissued instrumental single 'So Bad', while West was hatching solo plans, having terminated his association with Wirtz, after 'Sam' – the follow-up to 'A Teenage Opera' – anti-climatically fizzled at number 38. By April, Tomorrow were yesterday's men.

Howe assisted West with his third solo single, 'On A Saturday' and formed Bodast, whose demos were produced by West. He eventually joined progressive rockers Yes and AOR merchants Asia. West joined MGM as a producer, released two singles on the Deram label in 1973 and 1974 and formed Moonrider, with ex-New Animals and Family guitarist, John Weider, and Bruce Thomas (ex-Bodast, Quiver, and future Attractions bassist). West now works in production and writes music for the advertising industry. *(see also The Fairies, Four Plus One, The In Crowd, The Pretty Things, Tomorrow)*

TRAFFIC

Traffic were the pioneers of the "getting it together in the country" ethic that was seized upon by scores of hugely advanced and stoned hippie heroes that basically didn't have a song ready between them. Traffic got their particular act together in April 1967 after retreating hermit-like to a farmhouse in Aston Tirrold, Berkshire. The four-piece consisted of guitarist-keyboardist-singer Steve Winwood, fresh from The Spencer Davis Group, ex-Hellions guitarist and drummer Dave Mason and Jim Capaldi (who ironically had provided percussion on the last few Spencer Davis singles) and SDG roadie Chris Wood (sax/flute). The fruits of their personal hibernation was début single 'Paper Sun', a hazy hallucinogenic recording of a hazy hallucinogenic afternoon, featuring Mason on sitar which went to number five in June. The follow up, arguably the worst example of a 'supposedly' psychedelic 45 in a year when musical liberties were being taken, was all Mason's. 'Hole In My Shoe' featured sitar, childish (rather than childlike) lyrics and a candyfloss arrangement. It reached number two in October but created a division in the group and by the end of the year, Mason had left (not for the first time).

Mason's tweeness was all over *Mr Fantasy*, the group's début album released in December, in songs like 'Berkshire Poppies', 'House For Everyone', and 'Utterly Simple', although he did redeem himself slightly with the blistering solo on 'Dear Mr. Fantasy', which he repeated the following year on The Rolling Stones' 'Sympathy For The Devil'. Elsewhere Winwood excelled on 'Heaven Is In Your Mind', 'No Face, No Name, No Number' and 'Coloured Rain'. Recorded at Olympic Studios with producer Jimmy Miller the album reached number eight.

Traffic

As well as 'Hole In My Shoe' the group had another unexpected pop hit with the theme to 'Here We Go Round The Mulberry Bush', a number eight in December (the soundtrack album also coincidentally featured Winwood's old band the Spencer Davis Group). Mason rejoined the group in May '68 in time to record their second album *Traffic* which was much less of a psychedelic period piece and boasted some of the group's strongest songs in 'Feelin' Alright', 'Pearly Queen', and '40,000 Headmen' while Mason's light touch prevailed on 'You Can All Join In' and 'Vagabond Virgin'. Further enhanced by Miller's inspired production the album was released in October '68 and reached number nine. Mason quit again in October and Traffic temporarily split. Island swiftly issued a last-rites album of leftovers *Last Exit* and a *Best Of Traffic*.

Winwood joined Blind Faith (with Eric Clapton, Ginger Baker and Rick Grech), while Mason, Capaldi, Wood and keyboard player Wynder K Frog (aka organist Mick Weaver) basically reformed Traffic under the banner Mason, Wood, Capaldi and Frog. After the demise of the doomed Blind Faith Winwood left for the equally fated Ginger Baker's Airforce which crashed in 1970. Winwood then recruited Capaldi and Wood to help record *John Barleycorn Must Die*, which ended up being credited to Traffic.

The group continued into the Seventies to record various albums with various expanded line-ups including *Welcome To The Canteen*, *The Low Spark Of High-Heeled Boys*, and *Shoot Out At The Fantasy Factory*, that sold better in America where the group constantly toured, before splitting for good in 1974.

Winwood pursued a solo career while arguably keeping the lowest profile of any top-flight Sixties musician. Capaldi had success in 1974 with an update of the Everly Brothers 'Love Hurts' and continued to develop his abilities as a songwriter and is now based in Brazil. His *Living On The Outside* album (released in 2001) featured Traffic acolyte Paul Weller and one of the last performances from close friend George Harrison. Mason's solo career included a collaboration with the late Mama Cass and a stint in the Nineties version of Fleetwood Mac. Wood died on July 12, 1983 from liver disease. Winwood and Capaldi resuscitated Traffic in 1994; touring the States with an accompanying album *Far From Home*. *(see also Cream, The Spencer Davis Group)*

THE TREMELOES

A case of the backing band outshining the main man The Tremeloes flourished chartwise between 1967 – 1970 while Brian Poole was consigned to obscurity as an Essex butcher.

The original line-up featured singer-guitarists Alan Blakely and Rick West, drummer Dave Munden, and bassist Alan Howard who was replaced in May 1966 by Mick Clark. Later that year the Dagenham connection was tempered with Clark's replacement, Len 'Chip' Hawkes from Shepherd's Bush, who added a third vocal to the line up.

The Trems' début single, a Paul Simon composition, 'Blessed', flopped and ended their relationship with Decca in 1966. A move to CBS brought another failure with a cover of 'Good Day Sunshine' before the band found their stride with a Latin carousing sing-a-long

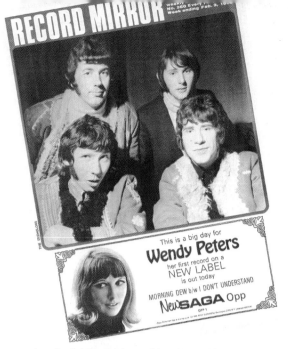

version of a Cat Stevens' song 'Here Comes My Baby' that gave the group a number four single in the UK and a number 13 in the US. The follow up cover of The Four Seasons B-side 'Silence Is Golden' – a masterstroke of a ballad – shot to number one for three weeks at home and became a US million seller. The Trems' became chart regulars, making unashamed good-time party pop records that endeared them to the teeny market. The group had a number four with 'Even The Bad Times Are Good' (September '67), and number six with 'Suddenly You Love Me' (February 1968). Throughout 1968 they continued to have hits with the Dave Dee-alike 'Helule Helule' (14 – June), 'My Little Lady' (number six – October) and a string-laden version of Bob Dylan's 'I Shall Be Released' which just cracked the Top 30 at the end of the year.

Despite being an unashamed pop group the group started to experiment more with their singles such as 'Call Me Number One' – a number two hit in November '69 and 'Me And My Life' (number four – October 1970). That same year, they decided to change musical direction completely by becoming a 'heavy' band and made an excruciatingly bad and misguided album *Master* and declared all their material up to that point was rubbish, describing their fans as morons for buying it. This brilliant PR masterstroke resulted in the group being shunned like the plague and a last-gasp single, 'Hello Buddy', limped to number 32 in July 1971. Hawkes left and the others were forced on to the cabaret circuit where the serious rock aspirations were conveniently forgotten.

Hawkes unsuccessfully tried his hand at a career in country music and moved to Nashville in 1974. West and new boys Aaron Woolley, and Bob Benham still play the odd gig as The Tremeloes while Alan Blakely died from cancer in 1996.

(see also Brian Poole & The Tremeloes)

THE TROGGS

The Troggs were formed in Andover in 1964, originally featuring singer/guitarist Dave Wright, Howard 'Ginger' Mansfield, lead guitar, drummer Ronnie Bullis (aka Ronnie Bond) and bass player Reg Ball. When Wright and Mansfield departed The Troggs, Staples and Britton joined from the defunct Ten Foot Five, with Reg taking over the lead vocalist role.

In early 1966, ex-Kinks manager Larry Page agreed to become their manager, while *NME* journalist Keith Altham suggested to the incredulous singer the new surname of 'Presley'. Despite already having all the Troggs ingedients – thudding drums, moronic riffs, and Reg's West Country burr – their February 1966 début single on CBS, 'Lost Girl' was an instant miss. Page got the band a two-single deal with Fontana and, in a stroke of fortune, he picked up on a demo written by American songwriter Chip Taylor for an obscure band called The Wild Ones.

The Troggs took 'Wild Thing' and turned it into their very own, a brash and raw performance and the only number two to feature an ocarina solo! Reg quit his job bricklaying as it roared up the charts and encouraged by Page, found time to knock out a follow up – the group's third single, 'With A Girl Like You'. Much publicity was made of the fact that the group came from yokel Hampshire and shunned the London scene. The group also made it plain that they were a no-nonsense, pragmatic group who had little time for the pomp and graces of pop stardom. It also didn't hurt that Reg also specialised in a nice line of suggestive songwriting.

In July, The Troggs were at number one simultaneously in both the US and UK with 'Wild Thing' and 'With A Girl Like You' respectively. Page set up his own record label Page One and its flagship release was The Troggs fourth single. 'I Can't Control Myself' was threatened with a BBC radio ban due to the raunchy line "Your slacks are low and your hips are showing" which meant the record received very little airplay, being banned outright in Australia. It still got to number two regardless. As Hollie Graham Nash commented on their primitive earthiness, "The Troggs are so behind, they're ahead!"

The band's two 1966 albums – *From Nowhere* and *Trogglodynamite* – both successfully made the Top 10. The hit singles continued throughout '66 and '67 and the group even toyed with psychedelia on 'Night Of The Long Grass', accompanied by a typically surreal promo clip from Peter Goldmann (who directed The Beatles 'Strawberry Fields Forever' and 'Penny Lane' clips). The plaintive and beautiful 'Love Is All Around' reached five in the UK and number seven in the US the following March but then all of sudden The Troggs hit run stopped. Their last chart placing was 'Little Girl' which just made the Top 40. Staples was ignominiously sacked to be replaced by Tony Newman, from Plastic Penny. A handful of lacklustre singles came and went unnoticed and albums from the period included *Cellophane* and *Mixed Bag* – the title of the latter an apt summation of their quality.

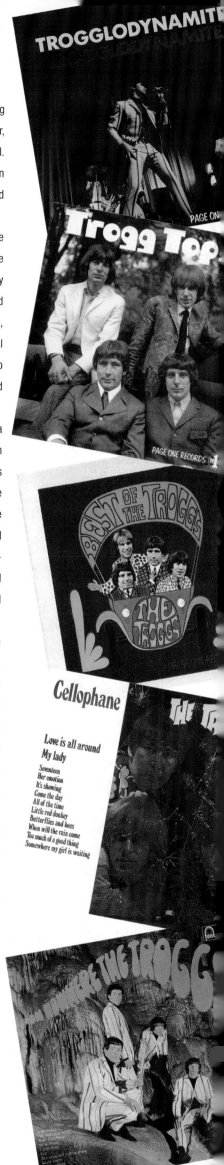

The Troogs

In 1969, The Troggs split with Presley, Bond and Britton all releasing solo material on Page's label. Inevitably, they came back again when Presley, Bond, and Murray reformed the band in 1972 with Colin Frechter.

The group's cult status was assured in the mid-Seventies with the discovery of the infamous 'Troggs Tapes'. Unaware they were being recorded, a studio tape left running captures the band constantly arguing, swearing and failing miserably (and hilariously) to come up with the right arrangement to a song they were working on, ironically named 'Tranquility'!

While this riotous recording continued to provoke mirth within the music business, The Troggs credibility rating was given a further boost in 1992 with the release of *Athens Andover* made with one half (Peter Buck and Mike Mills) of R.E.M.

Wet Wet Wet also swelled Presley's coffers when the Scottish quartet took their version of 'Love Is All Around' to the top spot for a record-breaking three months. Presley and Britton still perform as

The Troggs and to their credit have largely managed to avoid the cabaret trap that ensnared so many of their contemporaries. Pete Staples runs an electrical business in Basingstoke. Sadly, original drummer Ronnie Bond died in 1992. *(see also Ten Foot Five)*

The Troggs

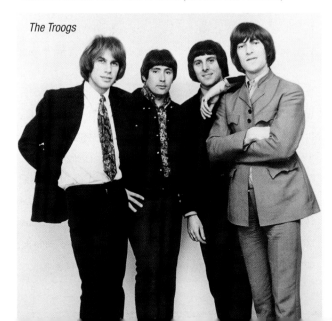

23rd TURNOFF

This Liverpool band were famously named for the exit that leads off the M6 towards Liverpool, and had previously been known as The Kirkbys. Their sole recorded legacy was a dreamy psychedelic number 'Michael Angelo', a high point among the Deram catalogue, released in 1967. *(see also The Kirkbys)*

TWICE AS MUCH

Following in the footsteps of Peter & Gordon, Chad & Jeremy, and David & Jonathan, Twice As Much were a pair of public school boys who fancied themselves as pop stars.

Andrew Rose and David Skinner had a handful of songs that they took to Andrew Loog Oldham in 1966 in the hope of a deal with Immediate Records. Oldham gave them the Jagger-Richards' *Aftermath* offcut 'Sittin' On A Fence', above their own efforts, and the song became a minor hit at number 25.

The duo's own compositions with 1966-67 singles such as 'Step Out Of Line', 'True Story' and 'Crystal Ball' were less successful as were two Immediate albums *Own Up* (1966) and *That's All* (1969), that featured typically grandiose Andrew Loog Oldham Orchestra arrangements, including a bizarrely slowed-down version of 'Sha-La-La-Lee' and a duet with label songstress Vashti on 'The Coldest Night Of The Year'. Skinner popped up again in 1979 as part of a reformed Roxy Music.

THE TWILIGHTS

Formed in 1964, The Twilights were perfect pop practitioners, often labelled as Australia's Hollies due to their magic vocal blend. Natives of Adelaide (though some of the group were English migrants), the group (including Glenn Shorrock – vocals, Paddy McCartney-vocals, Terry Britten – guitar) moved to Melbourne in 1965 and became popular nationwide with several number one hit singles 'down under' including covers of The Hollies 'Yes I Will,' The Beatles version of Larry Williams' 'Bad Boy,' (unreleased in Oz at the time) and The Velvelettes' 'Needle In A Haystack'.

In 1966 the group won the prestigous Hoadley's National Battle Of The Sounds, and as their countrymen The Easybeats had done before them, the six-man team made the long trip to Blighty. They were to return home in frustration a mere six months later, though not before having undertaken a recording session at Abbey Road in December that resulted in the superlative singles 'What's Wrong With The Way I Live?' (a Hollies cover), its fab flip, '9.50' and the harmony-perfect 'Young Girl'. With their overseas experience under their belts and with Britten wielding a sitar, The Twilights wowed Australian audiences with note-perfect live renditions of *Sgt. Pepper*, and went on to make a much-regarded 1968 concept album, *Once Upon A Twilight*. Shorrock and Britten went on to become successful songwriters; Shorrock with The Little River Band, Britten penning songs for Cliff Richard and Tina Turner.

TWINKLE

Twinkle was born Lyn Ripley in 1947. At 17, after a brief spell at the Guildhall School of Music, she became Twinkle and recorded the controversial teenage anthem 'Terry', a 'death disc' about a teenage motorbiker who responds to a lover's tiff by roaring into the night to his death. It reached number four in December 1964, and caused such a stir at the time that it was even banned on *Ready, Steady, Go!*

Eminent writer Ted Wills called it 'dangerous drivel!' and when Twinkle attempted to visit America with the song in 1965, she had her work permit refused. "Oh well," she sighed, "I shall have to stay at home working on my novel about the ups and downs of adolescence." But all was not lost; the pirate stations played it repeatedly and, appearing before The Beatles and The Rolling Stones, she performed the song at the 1965 *NME* Poll Winners Poll Concert at the Empire Pool, Wembley. Thankfully, she was also coaxed out to accompany Decca labelmates The Bachelors on a tour of Australasia in September '65. That February, her follow-up, and only other chart success, 'Golden Lights', entered the charts, reaching number 21, and was covered as a B-side in 1986 by The Smiths, thanks to girl singer acolyte Morrissey. In recent years, Twinkle was part of the 'Solid Sixties' golden oldie hit tours, where she was seen again performing well.

23rd Turn Off

Twinkle

THE TWILIGHT

The Twilights

Twinkle

THE UGLYS

Originally The Dominettes, the prettily-named Uglys – Steve Gibbons – (guitar/vocals), Bob Burnett (guitar), John Gordon (keyboards), John Hustwayte (bass) and Jim Holden (drums) – were formed in Birmingham in 1962 and signed to Pye three years later. Their first single, the quirky 'Wake Up My Mind' flopped in the UK but was an unexpected hit in Australasia. Gordon was replaced by Jim O'Neill (from The Walker Brothers touring band) and the group released three more singles for Pye, including a cover of The Kinks' 'End Of The Season'. A switch to CBS and further personnel changes did zilch to help their commercial prospects and after one last single – a blistering tour de force 'I See The Light' on MGM – The Uglys were no more. Gibbons and Tandy formed Balls with ex-Move man Trevor Burton, ex-Lemon Tree drummer Keith Smart and bassist Dave Morgan. A stint with the remains of The Idle Race led to the formation of The Steve Gibbons Band.

(see also The Idle Race, Denny Laine, The Move)

THE UNDERTAKERS

The Undertakers who formed in Wallasey, Liverpool in 1961 consisted of singer Jim McManus, guitarists Geoff Nugent and Chris Huston, Brian Jones (sax), Dave (Mushy) Cooper (bass), and Bob Evans (drums). Originally known as The Vegas Five the quartet changed their name after being wrongly billed as The Undertakers. In 1961, Evans was replaced by Bugs Pemberton and in January '62 Cooper was replaced by Jackie Lomax. The group started turning up at gigs in a hearse, dressing the part in top hats and frock coats. In 1962, McManus left to join The Renegades so The Undertakers continued as a five-piece.

They released four singles for the Pye label – of which 'Just A Little Bit' was a minor hit (number 49) in 1964. Their last, a cover of The Drifters' 'If You Don't Come Back' was credited simply to The 'Takers. After the group split Lomax formed The Lomax Alliance, recording for CBS, before old pal George Harrison signed him as one of the début acts for the Apple label in 1968, producing his single 'Sour Milk Sea' and 1969 début album *Is This What You Want?* among others. In the Seventies Lomax emigrated to America's West Coast.

UNIT FOUR PLUS TWO

Unit Four Plus Two were formed in Hertfordshire by singer-songwriter Brian Parker in 1962 as vocal outfit Unit Four (Parker, Peter Moules, Tommy Moeller and David 'Buster' Meikle) who accompanied themselves with acoustic guitars. Unfortunately ill health forced Parker into a behind the scenes role as the band's lyricist. Howard Lubin stepped up to the mike to replace him in '63 and the band added a rhythm section (bassist Rod Garwood and drummer Hugh Halliday) to boost their sound. They amended their name accordingly to Unit Four Plus Two and signed to Decca in 1964.

The Untamed

The band's début single 'The Green Fields' reached the Top 50 but the follow up 'Sorrow And Pain' went wide off the mark. It was third time lucky when Parker and Moeller came up with one of the catchiest songs of the decade. The pair adapted an old American gospel song 'Concrete And Clay' into a worldwide hit, which reached the top spot in April '65. Things weren't so lucky for new boys Garwood and Halliday, who had been replaced by ex-Roulettes members Russ Ballard and Bob Henrit. '(You've) Never Been In Love Like This Before' was an anti-climax – peaking at 14 in June and five successive flops followed. Meikle left in 1967 and the group carried on as a confusing five piece on Fontana until their demise in 1969. Ballard and Henrit joined Argent, while other members showed up in Capability Brown.

(see also The Roulettes)

THE UNTAMED

The Untamed were formed in Worthing, Sussex in 1964 by leader – guitarist Lindsay Muir, with an original line-up of Tony Everett (guitar), Ray Jarvis (organ), Jez Loveland (bass), and Terry Slade (drums). Originally known as The Untamed Four, the group played a stylish mix of R&B, jazz and soul in southern England's clubs. Produced by Kinks-Who man Shel Talmy, two Untamed singles on Decca – ('So Long' 1964) and Parlophone ('Once Upon A Time') – went nowhere. A near-miss occurred with a version of James Brown's 'I'll Go Crazy' on Stateside before the line-up splintered in mid-65.

Muir returned to Worthing to build a new Untamed featuring Brian Breeze (guitar), Wes (bass), Keith Hodge (drums) and Alan Moss (organ). Talmy selected 'It's Not True' from The Who's first album *My Generation* that he had recently produced and released it on his newly-minted Planet label in December '65. To compensate for its lack of success the group played a four-month residency at the London Hilton. However continual arguments resulted in a third Untamed line-up featuring Muir, Moss, Brian Hire (drums) and Andrew Dickson (bass). A fifth single, 'Daddy Long Legs' (featuring Jimmy Page, credited to Lindsay Muir's Untamed) was released in May but Muir hated it and Moss quit to be replaced by Pete Kelly. This final line-up became popular on the Continent, particularly in Germany. Muir struggled on for a few more years with a three-piece version of The Untamed before calling it a day at the end of the decade.

THE V.I.Ps

A Carlisle group that provided future members of The Nice, Mott The Hoople, Humble Pie and The Only Ones, amongst others. The V.I.Ps (Mike Harrison – vocals, James Henshaw and Frank Kenyon – guitars, Greg Ridley – bass, and Walter Johnstone – drums) leaned towards the R&B side of the fence and issued some sought-after freakbeat-style records, including a one-off single for RCA, 'Don't Keep Shouting At Me' (1964), 'Wintertime' (as The Vipps) for CBS (1966) and two for Island – 'I Wanna Be Free' (1966) and 'Straight Down To The Bottom' (1967). Keith Emerson (ex-Gary Farr & The T-Bones) joined as organist for a spell before leaving to form The Nice. The V.I.Ps also made a handful of recordings that only ever surfaced on the continent, where the group spent a good deal of their later career. In 1967, while still the V.I.Ps, the group recorded a full album for Island *Supernatural Fairy Tales* under the name Art, before changing their name to Spooky Tooth.

(see also Art, Gary Farr & The T-Bones, The Nice, Spooky Tooth)

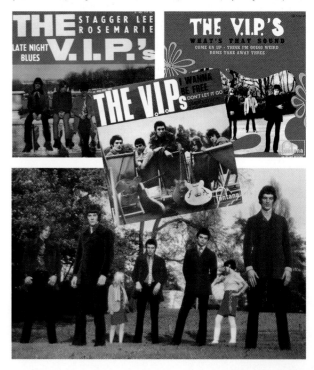

The Warriors

THE WALKER BROTHERS

Although American, the moody good looks of this Californian trio were an instant success upon their British chart breakthrough in 1965. Scott (Scott Engel), John (John Maus) and Gary (Gary Walker) had played in various West Coast surf and instrumental outfits and Scott and Gary had recorded together and even appeared with dyed bleach-blonde hair as The Walker Brothers doing 'The Jerk' in a forgettable beach flick *Beach Ball*. Leeds had drummed with The Standells and in Jet Powers band. When Powers (now PJ Proby) achieved success in Blighty in 1964, Leeds persuaded Scott and John to make the trip over the Atlantic.

Signed to Philips, their first release, 'Love Her' only managed to enter the Top 20 but it set the pattern of the group's singles; heavy doomy arrangements with a Spectoresque production. The next release catapulted them to stardom when Jerry Butler's 'Make It Easy On Yourself' got to number one in September while 'My Ship Is Coming In' reached three in December.

The moody trio (particularly vulnerable frontman Scott) endeared themselves to the nation's hysterical teens whose walls were adorned with pin-ups of these hunky Yanks. In April '66 the group achieved their second number one with 'The Sun Ain't Gonna Shine Anymore' (originally recorded unsuccessfully in the US by Frankie Valli). It was downhill from there as pressures of success and personality differences were played out in the pages of the musical and national press. After further minor hits, the Brothers split in May 1967.

John had an unsuccessful solo career, Gary formed Gary Walker & The Rain, while Scott pursued his own idiosyncratic path with a series of solo albums, while keeping one foot in the mainstream with his own BBC TV series *Scott*. In 1974, the trio reformed for an unsuccessful album *No Regrets* and a Top 10 hit single with the title track in 1976. John now resides back in his native California, Gary was last heard of as an Essex courier, while Scott remains in Garbo-esque seclusion.

(see also Gary Walker & The Rain)

GARY WALKER & THE RAIN

It's a tremendous irony that at the height of The Walker Brothers mid-Sixties UK chart storm, due to peculiar contractual reasons, drummer Gary Leeds didn't actually perform on any of the transplanted American group's records. However the toothy Leeds – an early member of The Standells and associate of P.J Proby – did sing on a couple of cash-in solo singles released on CBS, 'Twinkie Lee' and 'You Don't Love Me'. It's what Leeds did after The Walker Brothers' 1967 break-up that has gained him retrospective notoriety.

The short-lived Gary Walker & The Rain was assembled to fulfill Leeds' contractual obligations with the Philips label with an eye on capitalising upon continued interest in The Walkers in Japan. Joining the drummer were Merseyside musicians and accomplished singers/writers all; ex-Fruit Eating Bears and Masterminds guitarist Joey Molland, ex-Universals bassist John Lawson and ex-Cryin' Shames Paul Crane on guitar. On the flip of an Easybeats cover, 'Come In You'll Get Pneumonia', 'Francis' is a particular pop-psych gem as are the contents of a super rare 1968 Japan-only LP, *Album No. 1*, both now amongst the most coveted psychedelic artefacts of the era. Lawson joined Pete Dello in Lace while Molland went on to join Badfinger.

(See also The Cryin' Shames, The Honeybus, The Walker Brothers)

THE WARRIORS

Accrington's only contribution to rock's vibrant tapestry (that I know of) were Jon Anderson's early beat merchants The Warriors. Formed in 1962, the group consisted of Anderson and his brother Tony on vocals, Rod Hill and Mike Brereton (guitars), David Foster (bass), and Derek Thornhill (drums).

In 1964, the Lancashire group reached the finals of an *NME* sponsored competition in London and were offered a contract with Decca.

The Warriors lone 1964 single, 'Don't Make Me Blue' led to their appearance in the low-budget film musical *Just For You*, with the likes of The Orchids and Peter & Gordon. Despite an extra plug on *Thank Your Lucky Stars* the record did nothing. Hill and Thornhill left and the group remained a five piece with the addition of drummer Ian Wallace before Brereton and Tony Anderson threw in the towel. Rod Hill rejoined, and with Brian Chatton on keyboards, The Warriors became a popular attraction in Germany.

The group split in 67, and Anderson under the patronage of Marquee owner Jack Barrie, released two flop singles on Parlophone in 1968 as Hans Christian Anderson. After a fleeting acquaintance with the Gurvitz Brothers in Gun, Barrie introduced Anderson to Chris Squire, and the seeds of Yes were sown.

(see also The Syn)

The Who

The Wheels

THE WHEELS

Punkified rhythm n' blues from Belfast, The Wheels dwelt in the shadow cast by their more successful contemporaries Them, whose 'Gloria' and 'Don't You Know' was covered as their first single. However The Wheels had a certain fire of their own as their striking recorded legacy demonstrates. The group, who at one time featured ex-Them organist Eric Wrixen, featured Herbie Armstrong, Victor Catling, Tito Tinsley, barbaric-looking, shaven-headed organist Brian Rossi and singer-guitarist Rod Demick. The Wheels evolved from Rossi's Golden Eagles, the house band at Belfast's Plaza Ballroom, though the group actually made their name playing clubs in the north of England, before signing to Columbia in 1965 and making their three much sought-after singles. The menacing second single featured 'Road Block' and 'Bad Little Woman' (covered in America by Chicago garage legends The Shadows Of Knight), while the third was a cover of Paul Revere & The Raiders' '66 US hit 'Kicks', with another tune from Morrison's men, 'Call My Name' on the flip. Demick went on to Seventies pub rockers Bees Make Honey while Armstrong came full circle by working with Van Morrison.

(see also Them)

THE WHO

Part of the Holy Trinity (with The Beatles and The Rolling Stones) to emerge from the Sixties, The Who combined the creativity of guitarist Pete Townshend's songwriting with an exciting stage act; both feeding off a dynamic running on the friction generated from four very diverse personalities.

The group began life in West London as The Detours, formed and led by Roger Daltrey. John Entwistle joined on bass and trumpet, and six months later, his school friend Peter Townshend joined as guitarist replacement. For two years from 1962 The Detours slogged around the West London pub and club circuit learning their trade with an ever-changing line-up featuring original drummer Doug Sandom. It was Townshend's art school friend, Richard Barnes, who suggested changing their name to The Who.

At this time – early 1964 – the group gained a manager, Helmet Gorden, a publicist, Peter Meaden and the last piece of the jigsaw in Keith Moon, who memorably auditioned by sitting in at one of The Who's regular local gigs at the Oldfield Hotel and smashing part of their stand-in drummer's kit. Meaden was part of the burgeoning Mod culture in London, and persuaded the group to change their image and name to The High Numbers.

However the makeover wasn't entirely successful and one single for Fontana 'I'm The Face' flopped disastrously. Gorden and Meaden were replaced at the helm by two assistant film directors Kit Lambert and Chris Stamp (brother of actor Terence) who were on the look out for a group to feature in a proposed documentary film about pop. After seeing The High Numbers in action at the Railway Tavern, Harrow, the film idea was forgotten and the pair became the group's managers, changing their name back to The Who again.

With Lambert's flair for promotion and Stamp's street suss, a visually striking white on black poster (with Townshend in mid-power chord) promising 'Maximum R & B', was designed and flyposted all over London. The band made a devastating impact on Tuesday night audiences at the Marquee Club, with Townshend's

THE WHO I'M A BOY

SMASH into the charts !! on reaction 591004

Managed & distributed by Polydor Records for the Robert Stigwood Organisation Ltd.

'Birdman' windmilling chords and feedback solos, Keith Moon's demented thrashing on the kit, singer Roger Daltrey screaming himself hoarse, while John Entwistle anchored the mayhem down with dive-bombing bass runs. This Tuesday night residency laid the foundations for The Who's transition from London club obscurity to world domination.

Lambert and Stamp secured a deal with American expat producer Shel Talmy and a contract with American Decca, that although successful in chart terms was to prove disastrous financially. The Who's first single, 'I Can't Explain' was released in January, 1965. After a start-stop chart run, it finally reached number eight. But after the expenses were deducted, thanks to Decca's penny-pinching royalty rate, both band and management came away with virtually nothing.

The follow-up 'Anyway Anyhow Anywhere' (May 1965) was less commercial (number 10) but accurately encapsulated The Who's stage sound onto vinyl. The group started to wear flamboyant Pop Art clothing, including target T-shirts and Union Jack jackets. By now, The Who were notorious for the visual (and expensive) spectacle of demolishing their equipment on stage; a demonstration tailor-made for their third single, the classic anthem 'My Generation' (October 1965) which closed their shows amid smashed guitars, broken drums and speared amplifiers.

The single rose to number two, being kept off deserved number one honours by The Seekers' 'The Carnival Is Over'. 'My Generation' arrived at a time when The Who came very close to breaking up. It was an open secret that the group didn't get on and after a hostile incident between Daltrey and Moon on tour in Denmark, Daltrey was fired. Lambert and Stamp became his unexpected allies; persuading the others to reinstate him after promises of good behaviour.

The Who's début album, *My Generation*, followed in December, and was a mixture of stage cover versions and fine Pete Townshend originals in 'The Kids Are Alright', 'The Good's Gone', 'It's Not True' and 'A Legal Matter'. The group were unhappy with their failure to break through in America and their relationship with Talmy and Decca, and, due to release 'Circles' as their fourth single, they jumped ship to Robert Stigwood's Reaction label and released the song as the B-side to a new Townshend composition, 'Substitute', in March 1966. Talmy reacted predictably by taking his case to the High Court, having the record withdrawn on the grounds that he had sole rights to The Who's recording contract.

'Substitute' was hastily repressed with a new B-side, 'Waltz For a Pig' – an instrumental performed by The Graham Bond Organisation as Talmy's injunction prevented The Who from recording. The single eventually reached number five, while Decca pulled 'A Legal Matter' off *My Generation* for competing sales (it reached no higher than 32).

With a recording embargo hanging over them, The Who consolidated their position as the most exciting group on stage in Britain and Europe. The situation was finally settled in Talmy's favour who continued to receive a five per cent override on all Who recordings for the next five years. On the encouragement of Kit Lambert Townshend continued to experiment with his songwriting. A song he'd written for an unrealised project called Quads – where parents can order the sex of their children – was hived off to become The Who's fifth single, 'I'm A Boy'.

Their most ambitious and complex single yet, 'I'm A Boy', featuring glorious Beach Boy harmonies, ringing chords and thundering drums, rewarded The Who with another number two in September 1966. 'Happy Jack' and the group's second album *A Quick One* followed in December. The single reached number three while the album got to number four. *A Quick One* was something of a democratic work, thanks to Chris Stamp securing the group a publishing deal. Unfortunately it was a case of being too democratic for its own good as the quality of songwriting demonstrated. Entwistle's 'Boris The Spider' became something of a Who favourite while 'So Sad About Us' had previously been given away to The Merseys. 'A Quick One (While He's Away)' – the 'mini-opera'- was written in response to Lambert challenging Townshend to write a lengthy piece that incorporated six different themes. The seed for *Tommy* was hatched.

In 1967, The Who diverted their attention to cracking America where 'Happy Jack' had made inroads into the American charts by reaching No. 24. The Who first toured there in March, playing five shows a day on a multi-artist bill in New York, emcee by DJ and self-styled 'Fifth Beatle', Murray the K. In June, The Who returned to America to play the prestigous Monterey International Pop Festival in California where their autodestructive act was an undoubted showstopper, despite Jimi Hendrix's upstaging antics.

Meanwhile, the group continued to release top-class singles in 'Pictures Of Lily' – the first release on Lambert and Stamp's newly formed Track Records label and a number four in April – and 'I Can See For Miles' in October. The latter was written as The Who's 'ace in the hole' should they require a readymade single, and deserved to do better than its number nine placing. For many it remains The Who's finest moment.

The song also featured on their third album *The Who Sell Out* (December 1967); parts of which were linked by crass American radio jingles in memory of pirate radio which had been outlawed by the British government in August 1967. (Pirate radio had played a great part in breaking new acts like The Who.) The album also contained a waft of great Townshend songs, including 'Our Love Was', 'I Can't Reach You', 'Relax' and the ambitious follow-up to 'A Quick One', 'Rael' (Part 1 & 2)'.

In 1968, the group spent most of their time on the road while considering their next move. 'Call Me Lightning', one of Pete's earliest compositions and something of a throwaway was released as an American single in March. In Britain, it became the B-side to 'Dogs', a comical ditty about greyhound racing, that limped to number 25 in June. 'Magic Bus', another early composition that had been recorded the year before by the group The Pudding, was released in the US in July and Britain in October but stalled at number 26. With the group away for long periods, their following in Britain was fast depleting. By now, Pete Townshend was hard at work on composing an ambitious story – a 'rock opera' – based around a deaf, dumb and blind boy named Tommy. When the double album was released in May 1969, it reversed The Who's fortunes almost overnight. The group suddenly became one of the highest concert draws in America while re-establishing their reputation as one of rock's finest live acts. The success of *Tommy* and albums like *Who's Next* and *Quadrophenia* sustained The Who thoughout the Seventies, until the sudden death of Keith Moon (ironically at a time when he was slowing down from a life of excess) in 1978 put a question mark over their future.

The band elected to continue, adding ex-Small Faces and Faces drummer, Kenney Jones and Free, Crawler keyboardist John 'Rabbit' Bundrick. Pete Townshend, who nearly echoed his own wish for a premature demise in 1981 after a drug overdose, brought The Who to a halt in 1983. Since then, there have been sporadic reunions, including a shambolic appearance at Live Aid in 1985 and a money-milking American 25th Anniversary tour in 1989. With the addition of Zak Starkey (Ringo Starr's son) on drums, and with Bundrick on keyboards, The Who have entered the 21st century as a stripped down, powerful unit that continues to tour sporadically. The sudden death of John Enwistle in June 2002, just as the 21st Century Who were gearing up for another American tour, puts their future in further doubt, though this didn't stop them from fulfilling this latest round of lucrative concerts.

(see also The High Numbers)

The Winston G. Set

Jimmy Winston's Reflections

WORLD OF OZ

out of the frying pan

WYNDER K. FROG

WIMPLE WINCH

Hailing from Merseyside, Wimple Winch (Demetrius Christopholus – guitar/vocals, John Kelman – guitar, Barry Ashell – bass, and Lawrence Arendes – drums) released three fantastic freakbeat singles for the Fontana label. The first 'What's Been Done', released in April '66 features punchy Who-type powerchords to a vaguely Merseybeat commercial chorus. However the real stunner followed in June: 'Save My Soul' was a vicious 'fuck you' to a former lover with peaks and troughs driven along by a thunderous fuzz bass riff and clattering drums. (The son has been covered by legions of garage bands, most notably The Lime Spiders). In January '67, the group's third and final single 'Rumble On Mersey Square' – an atmospheric *West Side Story* yarn about brawling scousers – was released and a fourth planned release 'Atmospheres' actually snuck out as a B-side on some pressings.

THE WINSTON G. SET

This mid-Sixties outfit starred the mysterious Mr. G, whose 1965 Parlophone début 'Please Don't Say' featured Ginger Baker in the drummer's seat. Subsequent singles were credited to Winston G & The Wicked, or simply Winston G. Sadly, for such a coolly named character, they are mostly weak soul-flavoured efforts.

(see also Cream)

JIMMY WINSTON'S REFLECTIONS

Like The Beatles' Pete Best, Jimmy Winston (nee James Langwith) was unceremoniously dumped by his bandmates on the eve of stardom. In his case it was The Small Faces who deemed they no longer needed his van driving capabilities, let alone his ivory tinkling skills. Unbelievably Winston only learned of his fate when he turned up at a Lyceum Ballroom gig in November 1965 to find his piano stool already occupied by his successor, Ian McLagan.

Decca Records showed Winston a modicum of loyalty by retaining the deposed keyboard player at the label. Winston formed another group, Jimmy Winston & His Reflections.

In one of rock's more bizarre twists, their first single 'Sorry She's Mine', a Kenny Lynch composition, was also recorded by Winston's estranged Faces at the same time and released on their 1966 début album. (Lynch had co-penned 'Sha-La-La-Lee'.) The single failed to chart and Decca moved Winston to RCA in 1967.

He renamed the band Winston's Fumbs for their one and only single, 'Real Crazy Apartment'. With Winston now on guitar The Fumbs featured future Yes keyboardist Tony Kaye, Alex Paris (bass) and ex-Shevelles drummer, Ray Stock. As its title suggests, 'Real Crazy Apartment' was of the manic variety, featuring wild Hammond organ fills and Small Faces-style high backing vocals. It was the last Winston waxing, whereupon he faded into obscurity, only to reappear in the stage show *Hair*, and minor acting roles, including

the sci-fi series *Dr. Who*. Winston now runs a successful recording studio in London's East End. Incidentally, his parents' pub, the Ruskin Arms, where he grew up in Manor Park, is now the home of an annual Small Faces Convention.

(see also Steve Marriott's Moments, The Small Faces)

WORLD OF OZ

Afforded the luxury of a self-tiled album – unusual, considering their non-hit status – World Of Oz, as the name suggests, were typical of the childlike whimsy frequently found in the Deram acts of the period. With a lead vocalist by the name of Christopher Robin and material, based on nursery rhymes, like their début 'The Muffin Man', this Birmingham quartet's records have not dated well. It's highly likely that Christopher Robin wasn't the singer's real name but those whose names were probably their own were Geoff Nicholls, Rob Moore, and Tony Clarkson.

The Writ

THE WRIT

A fairly anonymous band who released a Lovin' Spoonful cover 'Did You Ever Have To Make Up Your Mind?' on Decca in 1966, produced by Jonathan King who also wrote the flip side 'Solid Gold Teardrops'.

WYNDER K. FROG

Hard to tell if these fellows were ever a 'real' band. Mr. Frog himself was actually session organist/organist Mick Weaver, who made two Island albums *Sunshine Superfrog* (1967) and *Out Of The Frying Pan* (1968) plus one for United Artists, *Into The Fire* (1970).

Assorted 1966-68 singles are filled with groovy instrumental soul/R&B workouts like 'Green Door', 'I'm A Man' and an in-demand reworking of The Rolling Stones' 'Jumping Jack Flash'. Weaver and most of his sidemen, including Neil Hubbard (guitar), Chris Mercer (sax), Bruce Rowland (drums), and Alan Spenner (bass), went on to form the Keef Hartley Band, Fair Weather and The Grease Band.

(see also Joe Cocker, Traffic)

The Yardbirds

THE YARDBIRDS

Hailing from Surrey, The Yardbirds were among the most prominent of the many English R&B bands emerging in the wake of The Rolling Stones. While lacking a distinctive vocalist or songwriter, what set them apart from other innovators was a triumvirate of guitar heroes who emerged from the group with their reputations fully established as rock icons. The Yardbirds started life as The Metropolis Blues Quartet, featuring Keith Relf (vocals), Anthony 'Top' Topham (guitar), Chris Dreja (rhythm guitar), Paul Samwell-Smith (bass), and Jim McCarty (drums). When Topham left the group to continue his studies, his replacement was 18-year-old guitarist Eric Clapton. Clapton (born Eric Clapp, March 30, 1945, in Ripley, Surrey) had undertaken brief stints with The Roosters and Casey Jones & The Engineers and despite his introverted demeanour, had actually sung blues favourites at the legendary Ealing Club alongside the likes of Mick Jagger. It was a punishing period of reclusive behaviour, learning to play the demanding licks on authentic Chicago rhythm and blues records, that put Clapton ahead of the pack.

The Yardbirds were managed by Giorgio Gomelsky and, thanks to this connection, the group took over The Rolling Stones' residency at the legendary Crawdaddy Club, Richmond in 1963. The band played their sets to wild, enthusiastic audiences and backed visiting bluesmen, most notably Sonny Boy Williamson (a recording of which was first released by Fontana in 1966). With R&B being the new thing Columbia signed the Yardbirds up in 1964. Their first single, a cover of Billy Boy Arnold's 'I Wish You Would' failed to chart while the follow-up, 'Good Morning Little Schoolgirl' peaked at 44 in November. The best place to experience The Yardbirds was in a live setting where numbers like Howlin' Wolf's 'Smokestack Lightning' and Bo Diddley's 'I'm A Man' were often launching pads for instrumental improvisations, or 'rave-ups' as they came to be known in Yardbird terminology. The group secured a Friday night residency at the Marquee at its new base of 90 Wardour Street, Soho and an album (*Five Live Yardbirds*), recorded at the club and released in December, perfectly encapsulated the excitement of those shows. Clapton was the band's most fashion conscious member, with close-cropped hair, turned-up Levis and desert boots, that inspired many emulators. However he was dissatisfied with the band's continuing commercial direction, including a tour with Billy J. Kramer and a season supporting The Beatles during their Xmas shows at the Hammersmith Odeon. The last straw came when the band recorded a Graham Gouldman composition 'For Your Love' as their next single. Despite contributing the song's rhythm part in the bridge, Clapton

was appalled and quit in March 1965, as the song ascended to number three. His replacement was another Surrey guitar whizz-kid, Jeff Beck (b June 24, 1944, Walton-on-Thames, Surrey).

The band achieved their greatest success with this line-up, releasing a succession of classic singles starting with 'Heart Full Of Soul' which reached number two in June. The song was to originally have featured a sitar player contributing the distinctive riff until Beck replicated his part on fuzz guitar. The self-composed double A-side, 'Evil Hearted You'/'Still I'm Sad' (number three in October) featured a Shadows-like solo on the former while the latter employed a gimmicky Gregorian chant. Perhaps their finest moment, 'Shapes Of Things' with it's social commentary lyrics and feedback invested, rave-up in the solo, was a revolutionary record, presaging psychedelia and rewarding the group with another third chart placing in March 1966. The B-side, 'Mr. You're A Better Man Than I', penned by Manfred Mann's Mike Hugg, was an equally solid slice of contemporary commentary, with a Beck solo to die for. Having parted company with Gomelsky to be managed by Simon Napier-Bell, The Yardbirds finally delivered their first studio album, simply entitled *Yardbirds*, but often referred to as 'Roger The Engineer', from Chris Dreja's sleeve cartoon drawing. The album was a mixed bag but featured more works of improvisatory genius, most notably 'Rackin' My Mind' and 'Lost Women', featuring Samwell-Smith's hypnotic bass riff and Relf's wailing harp and Beck's feedback duel in the solo. The album also contained their next single, 'Over Under Sideways Down', based around the rhythm of Bill Haley's 'Rock Around The Clock'. It gave the Yardbirds their last Top 10 hit.

Another crucial personnel change occurred when Samwell-Smith decided to quit after a drunken Oxford May Ball appearance

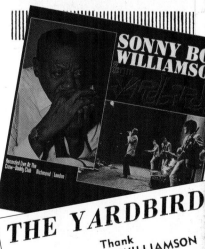

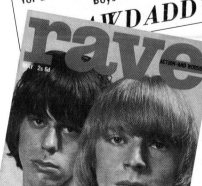

The Yardbirds

with The Hollies in June 1966. It was Beck's idea to introduce his friend, Jimmy Page, into the fold. Ironically, Page (born January 9, 1944) had initially been approached to replace Clapton, but declined due to his lucrative employment as a session musician. Page initially started off playing bass, but when Chris Dreja moved over to the instrument, the unique but ultimately short-lived Beck-Page twin-guitar axis came into being. The line-up played support on a Rolling Stones/Ike & Tina Turner swing around Britain in September and recorded one absolutely awesome single 'Happenings Ten Years Time Ago'/'Psycho Daisies'. Unfortunately, it went way above the heads of the general pop populace and could only stagger to number 43 in October. The song was instrumental in consolidating The Yardbirds as sonic pioneers where their following threatened to overtake their British popularity. Many of the new San Franciscan bands were taking The Yardbirds' extended improvisatory 'rave-up' formula and running with it. The Beck-Page partnership was captured to great effect in Michelangelo Antonioni's Mod 'Swinging London' film, *Blow Up* (filmed 1966 and released a year later). Having been unsuccessful in securing The Who's services Antonioni required The Yardbirds to provide a guitar-smashing facsimile, for which they rewrote a live favourite, Johnny Burnette's 'Train Kept A-Rollin'' as 'Stroll On'.

Beck dramatically walked out of a Dick Clark 'Caravan Of Stars' package tour and was officially declared an ex-Yardbird in December. Throughout 1967 until their demise in July, 1968, The Yardbirds soldiered on as a four-piece; concentrating on the American market, while changing managers from Napier-Bell to Peter Grant and having pop producer Mickie Most choose their material. This resulted in a string of unrepresentative singles, 'Little Games', 'Ha! Ha! Said The Clown', 'Ten Little Indians' and 'Goodnight Sweet Josephine', that went nowhere in Britain and fared only modestly in the States. After one final gig at Luton Technical College The Yardbirds called it a day. Page picked up the pieces to form a new 'supergroup', Led Zeppelin, but that's another story...

(see also Jeff Beck Group, Cream, John Mayall's Bluesbreakers, Jimmy Page)

The Zombies

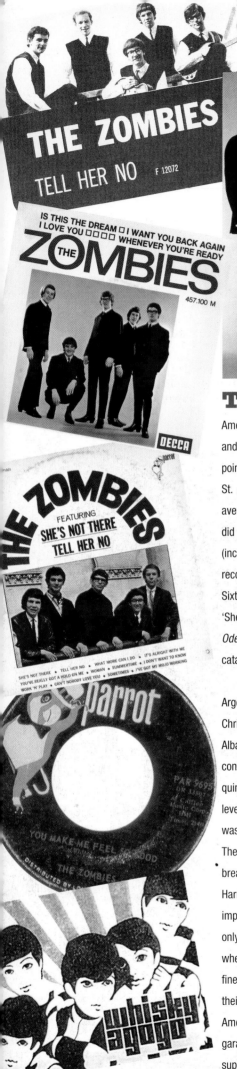

THE ZOMBIES

America often has a more objective view of British Sixties heritage and their deep and ongoing affection for The Zombies is a case in point. With just one brief Top 20 entry in 1964, the fab five from St. Albans are regarded in their homeland as merely an above-average beat group. But in the United States and elsewhere, not only did the group have extensive record success during their lifetime (including a Stateside chart-topper) but The Zombies are widely recognized as one of the best groups this country produced in the Sixties. It's an undeniable truth that, from their astounding début 'She's Not There', to the group's 1967 swansong masterpiece *Odessey & Oracle*, The Zombies' small but perfectly formed catalogue is among the most underrated in the annals of British pop.

Formed in 1963, The Zombies (Colin Blunstone – vocals, Rod Argent – keyboards, Paul Atkinson- guitar, Paul Arnold, replaced by Chris White – bass, and Hugh Grundy – drums) hailed from the St. Albans area of Hertfordshire. In winning a local Herts Beat talent contest, the prize was a contract with Decca. Much was made of the quintet's 'brainy' image with the group sharing copious 'O' and 'A' levels between them. The Zombies début single' 'She's Not There' was one of the most startling in a year (1964) of landmark releases. The song's delicate arrangement was enhanced by Blunstone's breathy, unique vocal and Argent's jazzy solo. Beatle George Harrison voted it a hit on *Juke Box Jury* in July but despite such an important endorsement and the song's undeniable quality, the song only reached twelve in September. It was a different story in America where it climbed all the way to number one in November. The equally fine follow-up, 'Tell Her No' reached six in January but only 42 in their homeland. The group responded by looking toward the American market where their sound influenced a host of wannabe garage bands. Over the next two years, the group released seven superb singles, an EP and a début album *Begin Here* that failed to cause any ripples chartwise despite The Zombies reputation as a group's group.

In April '65, the group filmed an appearance in the Otto Preminger mystery *Bunny Lake Is Missing* while the year was spent consolidating their success in America. Singles like 'Indication' (1966) were experimental within a three minute format without losing their commerciality. In '67 the group switched to CBS to have one-last shot at reversing their fortunes. Recording at Abbey Road the group laid down tracks like 'Friends Of Mine' and 'Care Of Cell 44', which were released as singles in a vain interest-maintaining mission. The resultant album *Odessey And Oracle* – with deliberate spelling mistake – was the group's consummate masterpiece and one of the finest albums of the late-Sixties. Each exquisite track was crafted with care despite the tight budget mean't that studio time was thin on the ground. 'Care Of Cell 44' was a breathtakingly-harmonised ode to a homecoming female jailbird, 'Beechwood Park' evoked a picturesque English summer, the joyful optimistism of 'This Will Be Our Year' and 'I Want Her, She Wants Me', and the powerfully graphic antiwar 'Butcher's Song'. Unfortunately, despite polite reviews upon its release in England in 1968, the album got lost in the shuffle and The Zombies folded by common consent to uncertain futures.

There the story would end but for a bizarre and ironic footnote. *Odessey And Oracle* continued to be raved about by those in the know, and a copy found its way to fellow CBS artist Al Kooper who pressured label subsidiary Date into releasing the album in America on the strength of one track alone, 'Time Of The Season'. The song was extracted as a single (as it had been in England) and radio stations across the country picked up on the record. Suddenly here was a hot-selling record but the band who'd recorded it had split up for the best part of a year. With the single reaching number three in February '69 tenth rate acts started trading themselves off as 'The Zombies', without the slightest trace of guilt, until, eventually several touring English musicians blew the whistle on these charlatans.

Argent, Grundy, ex-Mike Cotton Sound bassist Jim Rodford and Rick Birkett (guitar) polished off some left-over tunes like 'Imagine The Swan' as the last gasp of The Zombies; effectively acting as a dry-run for Argent. Grundy was soon replaced by ex-Roulettes/Unit Four Plus Two drummer Bob Henrit. Blunstone pursued an on/off solo career, scoring a Top 40 entry in early-'69 with a radical update of 'She's Not There' under the name Neil MacArthur and a Top 20 hit (under his own name) in 1972 with a fine version of Denny Laine's 'Say You Don't Mind'. Atkinson went on to work in the business as A&R man for Columbia and Capitol in America. Grundy runs a public house in Hertfordshire and Argent opened a successful Denmark Street musical instrument shop as well as continuing in session and film scoring work. In December 1997, to launch the release of a box-set anthology *Zombie Heaven*, all five original members played together again for the first time in 30 years at London's Jazz Café.

Eric Burdon & Alec Palao

Acknowledgements

I would like this book to be a reminder of two great individuals.
One was a personal friend, Kim Gardner, and the other an inspiration, George Harrison.
Gawd bless em!

First up in the acknowledgements roster is my San Francisco 'oppo' in all things beaty, psychedelic
and wonderfully obscure, Alec Palao. His exhaustive information research and contribution was invaluable
and deserves a special mention.

Secondly is the most reliable man in the design business, Paul McEvoy
and his crew at Bold Graphic Design - Julien Potter, Kerry Oldham and James Barnes.

Those up for commendations are Keith 'Beatle' Badman (look no further for Fab facts – he knows it all),
Omnibus editor Chris Charlesworth for never losing his love of music, Reg Pippett for yet again tireless help,
and Andy Neill for straightening out my text.

Thanks must also go to the following: Diane Daley; Phil Smee at Strange Things; Mike Chapman for your patience;
Sean at Helter Skelter likewise; and Steve Diggle for the same reason; also Jim McDonald and Jim Guynan,
Steve Speirs, Glen Colson, Little Steven and Holly at Renegade Nation (here's some groovy beat facts for you Steve),
Stephanie Bennett, Don Paulsen and Peter Wilde, Psychedelic Kev who moved away and was never seen again.
Lesley Benson and my girls Molly, Nancy and Geraldine.

Oh, one other thing before we go - I would like to point out to the more astute of you that I am well aware that
some entries included stretch the limits of what could be legitimately be termed 'British Beat'. And yes, I know
there are also some glaring omissions. This was due to the power of committee, and therefore out of my control.
My apologies go to those who fell foul of the editor's knife.

Jimmy Winston's Reflections

Dedicated to the memory of George Harrison